"Throughout the ages, when explorers have returned home they have written of their travels to guide those who follow. If you are holding this book, you are thinking of taking a journey. Here is your guide. Get going."

  —Thomas J. Burke, *deputy director, medical development,*
   Medical Advanced Development Agency

"A comprehensive learning center with the most forward thinking leadership theories, and a laboratory for personal growth, *The Leadership Odyssey* provides learners with the context for personal insight and professional enrichment.

  —Patricia Walls, *manager, human resources development,*
   Okidata Corporation

"Like an odyssey, this book has a kinesthetic feel, guiding leaders at all levels on a journey of self-discovery, complete with a new leadership model, an easy-to-use assessment tool, and practical strategies to chart a new course for personal and professional success."

  —Marilyn C. Vernon, *chief, management programs,*
   The Federal Judicial Center, Washington, D. C.

"Gets to the real issues challenging managers in turbulent times—and provides practical help in addressing them. For managers in a shifting-sand environment, this book offers some bedrock and practical help to move toward it. The insights and guides work in government as well as business organizations."

  —Fern Piret, *planning director, The Maryland-National Capital Park*
   and Planning Commission

"For managers, this book is about getting a life, a life that's got more spirit, meaning, and fun than most of us have been used to in the past. *The Leadership Odyssey* is not a quick trip but a journey—one worth taking personally and professionally."

  —Robert W. Stieg, Jr., *headmaster, Grafton School*

THE LEADERSHIP ODYSSEY

THE LEADERSHIP ODYSSEY

A Self-Development Guide to New Skills for New Times

Carole S. Napolitano
Lida J. Henderson

Foreword by Barry Z. Posner

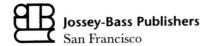

Jossey-Bass Publishers
San Francisco

Library of Congress Cataloging-in-Publication Data

Napolitano, Carole S., date.
The leadership odyssey : a self-development guide to new skills for new times / Carole S. Napolitano, Lida J. Henderson.
p. cm.
Includes bibliographical references.
ISBN 0-7879-1011-2
1. Leadership. I. Henderson, Lida J., date. II. Title.
HD57.7.N37 1997
658.4'092—dc21   97-17810

FIRST EDITION
PB Printing   10 9 8 7 6 5 4 3 2 1

THE JOSSEY-BASS

BUSINESS & MANAGEMENT SERIES

CONTENTS

To our families and friends, who believed in us
and in the worthiness of this effort
and
To our longstanding friendship, which not only survived
this project but, indeed, flourished as a result of it

FOREWORD

Barry Z. Posner

Once upon a time, and not all that long ago, there were scholars and practitioners who claimed that managers and leaders were not the same, that they were different types of people. The truth of the matter in their discussions often was obscured by semantics and stereotypes. The distinctions became even more clouded when qualifiers like "good" and "bad" were introduced. While an interesting conversation—often heated, sometimes stimulating and thought-provoking—the debate needs to be put to rest. Leadership is not merely an option in today's organizations. Effective managers must be leaders (although leaders do not have to be managers). Leadership is not a position or a place in an organization. It is an attitude and a responsibility that belongs to everyone. Organizational vitality requires that leadership be everyone's business.

Another of these endless leadership debates has formed around the question, Are leaders born or are leaders made? In all my years of leadership research and executive development efforts, curiously enough, no one has ever raised the question of whether managers are born or made. Really, this is just another version of the debate about whether leaders and managers are different. Leadership is a set of skills, and while we've yet to be able to explain completely all the component parts, we know a great deal.

Carole Napolitano and Lida Henderson have brought a considerable portion of that knowledge about leadership together in this book. And they've provided resources for building, enhancing, and sustaining our capabilities as leaders.

I feel the most pernicious myth of all has been that leadership cannot be learned. If you believe this, then this book offers little value or hope for you. But if you believe, like I do, and like Napolitano and Henderson do, that each of us is capable of leading, of making a difference, then this book provides hundreds of ideas, pathways, techniques, and strategies for liberating the leader within each of us.

The Leadership Odyssey starts with an exploration of the inner territory: Who am I? What do I care about? How do I feel about people? These are among the questions that leaders wrestle with from the beginning and will return to again for reflection in difficult and challenging times. Leadership has to do mostly with who the leader *is,* not just what leaders *do.* Since most innovations are failures in the middle, a key requirement for leaders is their ability to persist and to find within themselves the answers to such age-old questions as: Why should I care? Why should I work so hard? What keeps me going? How can I be sure?

Jim Kouzes and I began asking people to tell us about their personal-best leadership experiences nearly two decades ago. Hundreds upon thousands of stories later, stories spanning the globe, across myriad industries, functions, levels, and the like, we've yet to find a story of leadership that tells of doing it alone. Leadership is always a relationship, between those who lead and those who would be led. And, in truth, the essence of transformational leadership is just that—leaders transform their followers into leaders. Anything less is not just less effective, it borders on exploitive and unethical. Hence, the second stage of *The Leadership Odyssey,* appropriately enough, addresses the skills required for people leadership.

Change is what leaders eat for breakfast. Leaders are those people who take us to places we've never been before, yet how can we expect to get there by simply following the status quo? How can we expect that doing the same thing over and over again will eventually produce different results? An important contribution from Napolitano and Henderson is their recognition of the systemic aspects of leadership. In the third phase of *The Leadership Odyssey* they turn our attention to organizational leadership, which creates an environment where change is embraced and where people are connected with each other in communities, so that when opportunity comes around they are willing to open their doors and consider the possibilities.

And then there's that question about whether leadership is an art or a science. The answer is "yes." Napolitano and Henderson have integrated much of the science, stripped of its jargon and qualifying phrases ("like," "it all depends," "under some circumstances," and so on) and preserved its artistry. As every great painter knows deeply the science of colors, of brushes, of strokes, of light and shadows and perspectives, so do great leaders learn to appreciate certain facts about people, about settings, about structures, about systems and their subtleties. No two leaders are identical, nor are two situations entirely alike. Leaders are artists who express themselves in real-time circumstances that are continuously changing, often tumultuously. When we can appreciate how a butterfly flapping its wings in Tokyo can create a tornado in Texas, Napolitano and Henderson suggest, then we'll understand the false dichotomy between the science and art of leadership.

The authors suggest that we'll all have to live with more ambiguity (permanent white water) in the future than in previous times. What they've given us in their book are ideas about what to take on the journey, and, for once we've left the safety of the harbor, more ideas about how to make the most from the storms and the lulls between them. They've even suggested that our destinations most likely will change once we depart, and that's the good news. Having an internal compass is critical, a capable crew essential, and a spirit of adventure the only thing that makes living worthwhile.

You should enjoy and prosper from this book. I did.

August 1997   BARRY Z. POSNER
Dean, Leavey School of Business and Administration
Santa Clara University (Santa Clara, California)
Coauthor of *The Leadership Challenge* and *Credibility*

A TRIP DOWN THE RIVER

CHARTING YOUR OWN COURSE TO PERSONAL AND PROFESSIONAL SUCCESS

It was the best of times. It was the worst of times.
—CHARLES DICKENS, *A TALE OF TWO CITIES*

If you're a manager—or think you might be headed in that direction—and find yourself less and less able to shut down for the day or too "wired" or anxious to sleep at night, it's no wonder. Gone are the days when managers could rest easy, secure in the knowledge that as long as they kept things under control in their unit, got the budget in on time, and did a decent job of meeting their objectives, their bonuses and promotions—or jobs, for that matter—were virtually guaranteed. Those were the days of what some have called "mere" managers who took comfort in the knowledge that it was up to someone else to deal with the bigger, thornier issues of where we should be heading and how, in God's name, we would get there. In a former time, if you *were* that executive charged with setting direction, at least you had sufficient information and time to make sound strategic decisions.

All that has changed, quickly and dramatically. Today's managers, at every level, are faced not only with a new order of responsibilities but also with several overwhelming and potentially unnerving dilemmas, including how to chart their own course for long-term personal and professional success.

Underlying these dilemmas is the phenomenon of unprecedented change. In recent years the metaphor of permanent white water has become popular as a way of describing a business environment that is increasingly volatile and tumultuous. The image of surging rapids without a break is particularly compelling, because it taps into a physical experience that graphically represents both the exhilaration and the terror of coping with today's business realities. The scenario goes something like this: imagine yourself (a manager) in a boat or raft (the organization). A global marketplace, intensified competition, rapidly changing technology, a "new age" workforce, and a "new deal" with respect to employment are just part of the chaotic, roiling tumult that rages around the craft. Like rapids, these forces pose dangers—pitching the craft this way and that, obscuring rocks and sudden dropoffs, defying the most skilled navigator to stay the course. In this scenario the manager cannot afford to stand by waiting for someone at the helm to take the lead or hoping for calm waters ahead, but instead must play an active role in setting direction and responding to changing conditions. Today's managers must also be leaders.

The notion of combining managing and leading raises one of the most vexing challenges for today's organizations, the empowerment proposition—a notion as fuzzy as it is fearsome, which strikes terror in the heart of many managers with the prospect it raises of chaos, anarchy, and loss of control—where everyone is suddenly entitled to do his or her own thing, never mind the risks to the organization. We are told by the theorists and even some experienced practitioners that empowerment *is* the answer, that the trick is to do it right. But we know that "doing it right" takes time—time we don't have, given the pressure for short-term results. We know too that the obstacles of transforming an organizational culture at times seem insurmountable. And quite frankly we don't know just what, exactly, we're supposed to do differently or how this is going to affect our position. Most sobering, we suspect that what it's really all about is our taking on the responsibility for a completely different level of relationship with others at work that could be like opening Pandora's box—and we're right.

Equally unsettling is the deep, nagging anxiety about whether or not we have the right stuff to meet the challenges of a world turned upside down. In the scenario just described, the white water is an external force—those elements outside ourselves with which we must contend. But external forces are only part of the story. There is the turmoil within each of us as we grapple with the demands of family, work, and community, and our own very personal and, at times, unpredictable life odysseys. And as the pressure grows to succeed in every arena—to stay fit, to raise successful children, to discover and develop our latent talents, to serve our communities, *and* to produce ever more extraordinary results at work—we are struck with the harsh realization that what we thought we knew may not count any longer. For the obvious corollary of rapid, discontinuous change is the need to learn, and learn continuously, not only new knowledge and technical skills but also—and this is the hard part—new ways of looking at and thinking about the world. Furthermore, the terms of employment have changed:

no longer will the company act as caretaker of our security and our career advancement; if we can't adapt to changing skill requirements, take the initiative in preparing for opportunities, or find ways to continuously add value to the organization, we may find ourselves going nowhere or, worse, looking for work.

The simple fact of the matter is that we are all faced with what Joel Barker (1992, p. 140) calls "going back to zero": the need to literally start over as a result of the shift to a fundamentally different model of the relationships among people, work, and organizations. However successful we may have been when our world was a more solid, more certain place, where change was gradual and the clarity of a hierarchical structure provided us with highly defined roles and rules, those successes guarantee us nothing for the future. In fact, clinging to what we think we know may represent our greatest liability if we fail to *un*learn what will no longer work. So questions plague our waking (and sometimes sleeping) hours: Where to next? How to proceed? What risks should I be willing to take, and will I survive? What sacrifices will be necessary, and what can I expect in return? How can I continue to add value to the company in a way that is recognized? Should I keep my resume updated?

No question about it: the future for managers is daunting. As human resource professionals, we have witnessed the toll such unrelenting pressure can take: the stress, the burnout, the cynicism; the estranged or broken relationships; the irreversible health problems; the lost dreams. Yet it seems reasonable to expect that if the challenges of the future are unprecedented, so too are the opportunities— opportunities for more creative and satisfying work, more productive organizations, more synergistic relationships, greater self-direction, and more balanced and integrated lives. The task, then, is to make ourselves ready so that we can avail ourselves of those opportunities.

The Leadership Odyssey is intended for manager-leaders in organizations of all types. Our hope is that it will speak with as much value to those in the not-for-profit and public sectors as to those in the private sector. *The Leadership Odyssey* is written to assist managers at all levels, as well as those who aspire to these ranks, in making what may be a difficult passage to a new place. It is a practical book— a "how-to," if you will, that is designed to be used in a variety of ways: by individuals as a self-paced tool for development, or by entire populations of managers within organizations as a supplement to existing training and development programs; by internal human resource professionals and external consultants as a compendium of ideas for addressing the needs of specific work units or clients. It is an attempt to bridge the existing gap between theory and application; for although many have spoken eloquently about what the manager of the future must *be* and *do*, few have addressed the equally urgent question of *how to acquire* the requisite skills.

Our vision in writing *The Leadership Odyssey* was to lay out a process for accomplishing this feat first by identifying and describing what we believe are the skills most critical to managing and leading successfully in the future, and then by providing a variety of tools for personal assessment and self-development. An obvious challenge in trying to identify the critical attributes and skills for a construct as broad-based as leadership is not to lose focus in the attempt to address every aspect. With that in mind we have focused on (1) personal, interpersonal, and organizational leadership attributes and skills rather than on technical proficiencies; and (2) attributes and skills that we believe are newly emerging (such as systems thinking), shifting in terms of approach (such as employing a dynamic planning process), or assuming renewed importance (such as integrity). We have not addressed attributes or skills that are highly generic (such as sense of humor or active listening).

The result is a constellation of thirty-seven attributes and skills in three domains—self-leadership, people leadership, and organizational leadership. Why these thirty-seven? Any attempt to reduce leadership to a list—and a short one at that—poses the obvious risk of oversimplification. On the other hand, to understand a concept as abstract as leadership we need some way of breaking it down into more specific, manageable parts. Think of this group of attributes and skills, then, not as a list and certainly not as a comprehensive analysis but rather as a distillation of those attributes and skills we believe provide a profile for effective management-leadership as we approach the twenty-first century. Based on our reading, observation, and experience we have defined, described, and developed these attributes and skills as the basis for a three-part assessment tool and a selection of self-directed developmental activities.

The Leadership Odyssey is a kind of guidebook that, unlike most management and leadership texts, is designed to be *used* as well as read. It is not a scholarly work, nor does it rely on original research as its basis. Rather we have worked to synthesize and build on what we consider some of the best thinking in the field of management and leadership as well as in the larger arena of human experience. Organized around a new model of managerial leadership (see "Spheres of Influence" in the Introduction), *The Leadership Odyssey* is composed of three major parts.

Part One

The first part of the book contains narrative chapters that examine specific attributes or skills in the areas of Self-Leadership, People Leadership, and Organizational Leadership.

Self-Leadership: Exploring Values and Perspectives

The two chapters in this section focus on the personal formation of the leader—those qualities of mind critical for effective leadership today and for the future. They engage the reader in assessing those aspects of self that comprise the foundation of management—leadership, as that role is evolving.

Chapter One. "Values: Qualities of Being" looks at work as an extension of self and describes some starting points for the personal formation of today's manager-leader. Ten essential values or combinations of values—vision, integrity, passion and courage, optimism and self-confidence, focus and discipline, flexibility, tenacity and resourcefulness, humanity, self-renewal, and balance—are discussed in terms of what each involves and why it is important.

Chapter Two. "Perspectives: Habits of Mind" serves as the complement to Chapter One in examining the kinds of thinking that best serve today's manager-leader in coming to terms with complexity and change. We need new perspectives—on how to learn, where to focus, how to think, what to change, and how to work together in ways that transcend the competitiveness and parochialism we have accommodated in the past. This chapter explores the behaviors involved in embracing change, testing assumptions, shifting paradigms, thinking holistically, tolerating ambiguity and paradox, trusting intuition, taking risks, seeking synergies, and modeling values.

People Leadership: Fostering Empowerment

This section addresses the primary concern of the manager: working with others on the job, including direct reports and work teams within his or her work unit as well as colleagues throughout the organization. These two chapters look at the many ways manager-leaders can influence positive outcomes at a very personal level, day-to-day, through the way they engage in and manage collegial relationships, create an empowering work environment, facilitate employee development, and deal with performance issues.

Chapter Three. "Enabling Individuals and Teams to Perform" considers the shift in the role of the manager from that of directing and controlling direct reports to one of supporting and guiding the development of each individual's or team's unique capabilities to contribute to our organization. Topics discussed in this chapter include setting parameters, re-presenting the organization, creating access to information and new knowledge, cultivating diverse resources, promoting continuous learning, facilitating contribution, and advocating feedback and recognition.

Chapter Four. "Managing Across Boundaries" addresses the need for today's manager-leader to create alliances throughout the organization as a way of responding to the demand for more flexible, responsive, customer-focused approaches to providing products and services. Building collaborative relationships, engaging in dialogue, and achieving integrative agreements are the topics discussed in this chapter.

Organizational Leadership: Shaping the Enterprise

This section of the book acknowledges the responsibility of manager-leaders to extend their influence beyond the boundaries of a single work unit, division, or department to the organization as a whole, particularly with respect to change initiatives. The chapters in this section address the need for managers at every level to help shape a system that is responsive to changing forces and conditions in both the external and internal environment as well as to the interests of diverse stakeholders.

Chapter Five. "Creating a Culture" examines the role of the manager-leader in shaping a culture in which people are encouraged to do the right things. This endeavor involves stretching both organizational and interpersonal boundaries to build a stronger sense of community across functions, to act with a sense of social responsibility, and to recognize the interconnectedness of elements within the organization and in its operating environment, all in the interest of enhancing the long-term as well as short-term value of the enterprise. Attributes discussed in this chapter include developing core values, taking a systems approach, and building community.

Chapter Six. "Anticipating the Future" prepares the manager-leader to guide the organization in meeting the challenges that lie ahead with spirit and confidence and in a way that allows the organization to work with changing circumstances to create a future of its choosing. Topics in this chapter include staying current with emerging trends, thinking strategically, inspiring pursuit of a shared vision, employing dynamic planning, and enlarging the organization's capacity for change.

Part Two

The second part of the book contains a three-part assessment kit for you, the reader, to use as a means of gathering personal feedback from others who have observed your performance relative to the attributes and skills discussed in Part One. The assessment kit contains a form to use in rating yourself and to distribute to selected respondents, as well as an analysis guide to assist you in summarizing and interpreting the feedback.

Part Three

The third part of the book contains developmental exercises to use in addressing skill deficits or enhancing existing strengths identified through the assessment process. It also provides an in-depth discussion on self-directed learning, a reflective learning model, and guidelines for maximizing the learning value of the exercises.

◆ ◆ ◆

The Leadership Odyssey is a book about steering a course and learning to ride the waves. It is based on some bedrock assumptions:

- That managing and leading are not mutually exclusive but, rather, complementary. Today's realities require that the manager's ability to implement plans and accomplish results be integrated with the leader's ability to set direction and inspire and engage others.
- That the *primary* role of the manager-leader is to influence others' performance by helping to shape an organization in which people can realize and express their capabilities and, in so doing, contribute more fully.
- That new problems and uncharted territory, such as those we are facing now, demand new skills and new patterns of behavior—and that these can be learned.
- That leadership, by its very nature, implies a degree of risk and anxiety that no amount of preparation or development can ever finally eliminate.
- That when operating in highly ambiguous situations, sometimes living with the right questions is more important than insisting on immediate answers.
- That the manager-leaders who are most effective over time are those who strive, regardless of how intense the pressures become, to integrate the important areas of their lives—personal, family, community, and work—with some degree of balance. Effective manager-leaders are whole people.
- That managing is an art, and as such has much to learn from a variety of other disciplines, such as psychology, physics, history, sports, literature, and the arts.

We hope that this book will speak to you in many ways. You will find that we have drawn on many voices—poetic, historic, scientific, academic; from the worlds of sports, entertainment, and the arts, as well as from the world of business—to shape this conversation. Many of these voices are famous—you will know them right away; a few you will no doubt encounter for the first time.

You will find, as well, that the developmental experiences we recommend are not limited to professional activities but include family, personal, and community activities as a way of encouraging the kind of balance and integration that we feel will best serve the manager-leader over the long term. Most important, you will find that this is a book about values as well as techniques and, as such, represents a unique tool for personal and professional development.

White water is a terrible and a wonderful thing. If you can manage its perils, you will have the ride of a lifetime! The Introduction, which follows, presents the Spheres of Influence model of managerial leadership, the centerpiece around which *The Leadership Odyssey* is organized.

Acknowledgments

In the sense that this book has been in some process of gestation throughout our lives, the influences to whom we owe a debt run both broad and deep—too numerous to list and in some cases too subtle or profound to fully recognize. Family members, friends, colleagues, clients, mentors, and teachers of all types—both contemporary and ancient, remote and near at hand—all have played a part. We thank them, and we thank those who have personally supported us—as sounding boards, as hand holders, as encouragers—nudging us to keep moving and, finally, to "get the darned thing done!"

Special thanks go to Margaret Wheatley and Peter Senge, whose breakthrough ideas and deep faith in the unfolding possibilities of our organizational universes have provided the philosophical underpinnings for much of this effort. To the staff at Jossey-Bass and especially our editors: Bill Hicks, who saw value in our ideas; Cedric Crocker, who guided, most patiently, the long "birthing" process; Michele Jones, whose keen eye, attentive ear, and discerning mind helped shape and polish our prose; and David Horne, whose production skills transformed the manuscript into a book. To those who reviewed drafts of the manuscript and provided their critiques and their endorsements. And to Barry Posner, who took on the task of writing the Foreword despite other pressing commitments.

Our most heartfelt appreciation goes to Pat Gaines, who lovingly provided the requisite "clean, well-lighted place"; to Dr. Patrick Connor, who offered counsel, shared sources, and put in a good word in a high place when it really counted; and to Suzanne Wilcox, who brought diligence and delight to the endless details of research and retrieval.

September 1997

Carole S. Napolitano
Round Hill, Virginia

Lida J. Henderson
Leesburg, Virginia

ABOUT THE AUTHORS

Carole S. Napolitano holds a master's degree in English from the University of North Carolina at Chapel Hill and has pursued advanced studies in public and organizational communication at the University of Maryland at College Park.

In addition to teaching in the honors program at the University of Maryland at College Park, Napolitano has provided communication consulting and management training for a variety of public and private sector organizations including the Department of Health and Human Services, the Department of Agriculture, the Department of Defense, NASA, the Federal Judicial Center, Bureau of the Census, Marriott, Glaxo, Upjohn, Okidata, Freddie Mac, the Optical Society of America, and the Maryland National Capital Park and Planing Commission. In addition, she has maintained a long-standing relationship with the Xerox Corporation, where she functioned as a key developer for the middle management school on leading change and coauthored a number of management programs, including the Human Resources Management Inventory for first-line managers, the Xerox Experiential Development System (a self-paced learning tool for middle and upper-level managers), and Destinations (a self-directed career development handbook for managers and employees).

Napolitano has been affiliated with the Center for Creative Leadership and is an instructor for several management programs offered through the University of Maryland National Leadership Institute and the Office of Executive Programs.

She currently serves as the educational consultant for the Seaboard Region of State Farm Insurance Companies.

Lida J. Henderson holds a bachelor's degree in psychology and a master's degree in counseling. She has built a twenty-four year career with the Xerox Corporation, primarily in the area of management development. She currently holds a program management position with the corporate education and development group.

Henderson has been closely involved in developing and implementing leading-edge management and personal development training for employees at all levels of the corporation. Key efforts include introducing alternatives to classroom training through innovative technology, initiating self-managed development and continuous learning programs, and working with senior management to integrate a systems approach to prioritizing and managing business issues.

Other responsibilities Henderson has assumed at Xerox include managing the corporate first-level management program, facilitating middle-level management training, managing personal development training, and instructing potential sales and service trainers. Prior to joining Xerox, she gained experience in the areas of academic and personal counseling, civil service test development, and contract negotiations.

THE LEADERSHIP ODYSSEY

INTRODUCTION

The Three Spheres of Leadership

I find the great thing in this world is not so much where we stand,
as in what direction we are moving.
— OLIVER WENDELL HOLMES, *THE AUTOCRAT OF THE BREAKFAST TABLE*

If you pay attention to language you are likely to have noticed a very telling phenomenon occurring in the way organizations and organizational leadership are being talked about these days. Start with the term *leadership*. We used to know, pretty clearly, what leaders were supposed to be, how they were supposed to act, and what distinguished them from their followers. We described leaders in clear, straightforward terms that we all understood. Leaders were in charge. They were heroes. They were the generals who took the hill; the answer providers and order givers; the problem solvers; the power wielders and brokers. Today leaders are described in terms that may seem strange to our ears and somewhat foreign to our understanding: we speak of leaders as listeners, learners, and teachers; as stewards and meaning makers (Morgan, 1986); leaders are encouraged to develop "skills of incompetence" (Vaill, 1996) and to take on "beginners' minds" (Kim, 1993, p. 32); such terms as *servant leadership* (Greenleaf, 1977) and *post-heroic leadership* (Huey, 1994, p. 42) are gaining ascendance.

The language used to talk about organizations has a similarly alien quality. Instead of defining organizations in terms of pyramids and hierarchies and organizational charts we are now conceiving of organizations as communities, as "practice fields" (Senge, 1990b, p. 21), as self-organizing systems, as collective intelligences, as webs or nests (Wheatley, 1996). Instead of structure and order we now talk of messiness, "organized abandonment," (Morris, 1995, p. 39) the "edge of chaos" (Wheatley, 1994) and "chaords" (Hock, 1995, p. 6). Business

1

communication, formerly all about contracts, agendas, memos, meetings, and reports, has evolved in the direction of dialogue, conversation, feedback, and stories. This new language that is transforming the way we talk about and think about organizations and organizational leadership mirrors the transformation in the way we must learn to *be* in organizations as we enter the twenty-first century.

In considering the many ways in which the role of the manager is evolving in response to what can only be described as a brave new world of business, we sought to design a model reflective of the new work of the manager-leader. The pages that follow describe Figure I.1, which serves as the centerpiece around which this book is organized.

FIGURE I.1. SPHERES OF INFLUENCE: MANAGER AS LEADER.

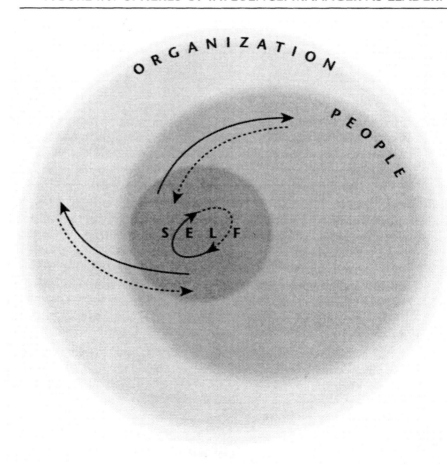

The first thing you may notice about the Spheres of Influence model is its circular shape, a radical departure from the pyramid traditionally used to symbolize organizational structure. The pyramid connotes strength and solidity. It visually expresses hierarchy. Its boundaries are well defined, suggesting that each span of control is self-contained. At a time when tasks were more discrete, when change was gradual, and when we believed that a highly structured organization was the best guarantee of efficiency and control, the pyramid model seemed useful. Today, however, what were once the virtues of a pyramid are often its most profound liabilities. Ricardo Semler (1989, p. 78), CEO of Semco, a family-owned Brazilian manufacturing firm, believes that pyramids are "the cause of much corporate evil" because "[they] emphasize power, promote insecurity, distort communication, hobble interaction, and make it very difficult for the people who plan and the people who execute to move in the same direction."

Today's demand for a high degree of coordination and responsiveness requires a different approach. The model presented here consists of concentric circles representing a less hierarchical, more interactive model of managerial leadership. In this model, the boundaries are not rigid; instead they are intentionally permeable to suggest the importance of making a critical shift—from a *span of control* limited to a single department, division, or work unit, to *spheres of influence* that start with self but extend outward to direct reports and colleagues, to the organization as a whole, and, ultimately, to the operating environment.

In the new world of organizations, managers must also be leaders who not only get day-to-day results in their units but also play a role in shaping an enterprise that aligns personal and organizational values, that contributes to the larger community of which it is a part, and that sustains personal and professional growth as well as profitability.

The Self-Leadership Sphere

Of the many books on leadership that have flooded the market in recent years, surely one of the stand-outs is *Leaders: The Strategies for Taking Charge,* by Warren Bennis and Burt Nanus (1985). Based on a two-year study of ninety successful public and private sector leaders, the authors painstakingly winnowed out of a wealth of data what they consider to be the "kernels of truth" about leadership. They are otherwise known as the four strategies: (1) attention through vision, (2) meaning through communication, (3) trust through positioning, and (4) the deployment of self. It is particularly instructive to note that the core of each of these "strategies" has as much to do with what the leader *is* as with what the leader *does.* Instructive because it gets at something we have not always recognized or appreciated: that what we can do is inextricably tied to who we are. At a time when organizations are struggling to find new and better ways of managing the chaos of the times, the implications of this kind of thinking are significant.

It was not so long ago, after all, that efficiency experts did almost anything they could think of to minimize the personal, human component in enterprise. What organizations wanted from people was predictable performance, so they took pains to codify what they could expect. By conducting time and motion studies, researchers gauged how much people could produce and how fast; then they routinized the process by creating assembly-line operations. That was at the worker bee level. For managers they identified "competencies," attempting to reduce a complex, dynamic process to a list of "things" that could be packaged as training modules and systematically delivered to managers who would then be "certified" as having the "right stuff." The argument here is not with competencies but rather with the failure to recognize that effective management is not a matter of superimposing aggregates of skills or techniques in the absence of an examined self. As Max De Pree (1989, p. 55), CEO of Herman Miller and author of *Leadership Is an Art,* has observed, "Managers who have no beliefs but only understand methodology and quantification are modern-day eunuchs. They can never engender competence or confidence."

Self-leadership is the central sphere of our model; it is, we believe, the core of leadership and the starting point for our odyssey.

The People Leadership Sphere

Ask people to close their eyes and picture a leader in action, and you're quite likely to get scenarios that include the following elements: the leader is highly visible— out in front of a crowd or standing above them on a balcony or platform; the leader has a title and is dressed in clothing indicative of special status—a decorated uniform or ceremonial garb; the leader is prevailing over the crowd—making a speech, leading the pack, or in some other way setting direction.

It is easy to explain where these images come from and to understand how deeply they are imbedded in our collective consciousness. Nurtured on the idea of rugged individualism and on the cherished myths of the old West, industrial barony, and military prowess, we conjure up leaders with heroic proportions: the cowboy who faces off against the bad guy at high noon in Dodge City; the general who masterminds the war effort on the Pacific front. We expect a leader to be singular and charismatic—to stand apart, to be confident and sure in the face of uncertainty and risk, to act on our behalf and protect us. We like our leaders to take charge—to make the future knowable and safe. And we need our leaders to be larger than life.

As useful and appropriate as this model of leadership can be in some instances (Dodge City, for one), it is less and less suited to the "quantum" world of today's organizations. It is simply unreasonable and unrealistic to expect that any one individual can bear the burden of leadership in every situation. We are faced with too much information, too many changing variables, too many demands and opportunities, and too little time.

Hence the need for a new model of leadership in which the leader supports and facilitates the contributions of others rather than prevailing over them or for them, a model in which the leader develops relationships as a means of producing synergies rather than acting as a Lone Ranger.

The idea of participatory management has been around since the early sixties, when Douglas McGregor (1960) challenged prevailing notions about absolute authority as the basis of managerial control. McGregor's famous Theory Y—the belief that humans are not only capable of exercising a high degree of creativity in carrying out organizational objectives but also that, under the right conditions, employees will actually *seek* responsibility for no other incentive than ego satisfaction—ushered in experiments in a more democratic form of management. A theoretical belief in the value of more fully tapping the resources of employees at all levels of the organization has persisted since that time. Evidence of this belief can be seen in the proliferation of mechanisms aimed at increasing employee involvement—quality circles and TQM teams; decision-making models that feature consensus and delegation; an emphasis on open, two-way communication; and widespread efforts at "empowerment." Despite how difficult it has been for managers brought up in a hierarchical, individualistic culture to give up control, we have nonetheless observed a perceptible shift toward a more participatory approach. Yes, managers are seeking more employee input. Unfortunately, when this endeavor occurs within the context of organizational structures that continue to honor hierarchy and reinforce paternalism, employees often remain dependent on management to fix problems and assume responsibility for dealing with hard issues.

The People Leadership sphere of the model represents a new relationship with employees in which the manager-leader works to build a true partnership by clearly communicating the larger purposes; facilitating access; providing support; creating opportunities; and engendering a sense of shared responsibility for the success of the enterprise.

Although these kinds of activities speak fairly directly to the manager's role in relation to his or her employees, the People Leadership sphere also addresses the role of managers in relation to their peers and to other stakeholders both inside and outside the organization. People leadership is about building relationships, crossing boundaries, finding common ground, and building community across the organization. Whereas yesterday's managers focused largely on their limited span of control, today's manager-leaders are called on to broaden the scope of their influence. Today's manager-leaders act not so much as directors but rather as catalysts, and seek to enhance not only individual and team performance within their unit but also to discover opportunities for synergies throughout the system.

The Organizational Leadership Sphere

In his seminal book, *The Fifth Discipline,* Peter Senge (1990a) poses the following question: Of the many roles involved in operating a large ship—captain, navigator, helmsperson, ship designer, steward, officer of the day, social director, engineer, and so on—which best speaks to the *new* work of the manager-leader? Although it's possible to make a case for any of the roles, Senge's unequivocal answer is the ship designer. His reasoning is as follows: regardless of what other skills or capabilities the other roles afford, if the rudder of the ship needs to turn thirty degrees starboard and it is designed only to turn port, or it takes several hours to execute a starboard turn, then the ship can't do what it needs to do.

Modeled on concepts that have outlived their usefulness, most existing organizations are not designed to ride the waves of high-velocity change they suddenly find themselves having to navigate. Encumbered with old structures and with bureaucratic policies, procedures, and rules, they have built in consistency and conformity at the expense of agility and creativity. They have divided up the enterprise into functions and roles for the sake of efficiency—resulting in the isolation and parochialism of "stovepipes" and the proverbial "it's not my job" syndrome. Ironically, individuals come to feel powerless in the face of "the system," which takes on a life of its own. The very structures people set in place to facilitate their endeavors can begin to constrain them as those structures become entrenched and inflexible. At best, they inhibit creativity; at worst, they breed frustration and engender personal compromise, game playing, lack of trust, and other forms of dysfunctional behavior. Ultimately, they can undermine the organization's ability to thrive in a changing operating environment.

Organizational leadership today requires that managers become designers in a very real sense. No longer can they blindly accept existing organizational structures as givens and wait for new direction to be handed down from above. Nor can they concern themselves with only their limited span of control. Instead they must take an active role in recognizing the larger system the organization represents and of which it is a part. They must stay alert to changes and trends that could—directly or indirectly—affect their business. They must seek to remove barriers to effectiveness, teamwork, creativity, and momentum. They must help to transform not only their own units but the organization as a whole in ways that will allow it to become increasingly responsive to current and future demands.

Managers may fear that when employees take on the organizational problems that had formerly been the province of managers, then managers would be left without a clear role. But this is hardly the case. Although as organizations become leaner and flatter there will no doubt be fewer managers and levels of management, the manager role is not going away. It is, on the contrary, changing substantially in terms of scope, perspective, attitude, and approach. As employees participate at a higher level, managers can—and must—focus their attention on the larger issues that affect the destiny of the organization.

The shift in the role of the manager to that of manager-leader is no small thing. As recently as the mid-seventies, Abraham Zaleznik (1977) in his article "Managers and Leaders: Are They Different?" concluded unequivocally that indeed they are psychologically different types and that the conditions that foster the development of one are antithetical to the development of the other. More recently Zaleznik (1992) has called for organizations to seek out leaders instead of perpetuating the practice of promoting managers who have bought into a prevailing "mystique" of dedication to form—processes, structures, roles, power, and indirect communication—at the expense of substance—ideas, people, emotions, and straight talk.

We concur with Zaleznik's call for true leadership in organizations, and we believe that it is possible for individuals to become both managers and leaders. In fact, we believe that effecting a shift to a new form of managerial leadership—the manager *as* leader—is at the heart of shaping today's organizations for success in the twenty-first century.

PART ONE

THE NEW LEADERSHIP ATTRIBUTES AND SKILLS

SELF-LEADERSHIP

EXPLORING VALUES AND PERSPECTIVES

Increasingly . . . I am convinced that changes in the world around us
must be preceded by changes in the world within us as individuals—
in our internal landscapes.

—JUDY SORUM BROWN, *DIMENSIONS OF DIALOGUE,* P. 14

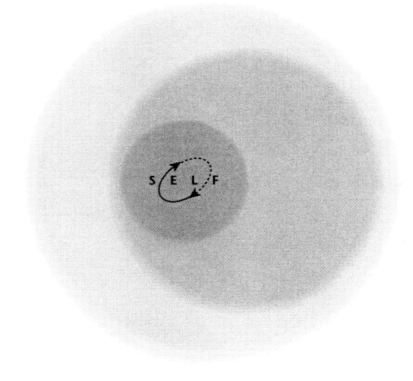

CHAPTER ONE

VALUES

Qualities of Being

*What lies behind us and what lies before us are tiny matters
compared to what lies within us.*
—OLIVER WENDELL HOLMES, *THE AUTOCRAT OF THE BREAKFAST TABLE*

The Leadership Odyssey begins with the Self-Leadership sphere and an exploration of the core values we believe are most critical to becoming an effective manager-leader. We start with values because it is through understanding and cultivating these qualities of being that we tap a powerful wellspring and source of energy for our choices and behavior. For we are motivated to possess, preserve, and carry out that which we most highly value, and, as Max De Pree (1992, p. 13) reminds us, "so much of leadership is music from the heart."

This chapter discusses the values of vision, integrity, passion and courage, optimism and confidence, focus and discipline, flexibility, tenacity and resourcefulness, humanity, self-renewal, and balance, which we believe best capture the heart and soul of managing-leading for the future. They are the cornerstones of self-leadership and, by extension, of people and organizational leadership as well. Some of these values, such as vision and courage and integrity, have long been associated with leadership but have taken on new significance in light of recent organizational challenges. Others of these values, such as self-renewal and balance, speak to a dawning recognition of those attributes that support and sustain the effective leader over time.

Vision

Possesses a vivid, compelling view of the future or is capable of imagining what the future could be; subscribes to the belief that one can influence the future by pursuing a desired end.

It is no failure to fall short of realizing all that we might dream. The failure is to fall short of dreaming all that we might realize.
—DEE HOCK, CEO EMERITUS, VISA INTERNATIONAL, "THE CHAORDIC ORGANIZATION: OUT OF CONTROL AND INTO ORDER," *WORLD BUSINESS ACADEMY PERSPECTIVES*

That vision has in some quarters taken on the onerous properties of a buzzword should not discredit its validity or its power. Despite the elusiveness of leadership as a construct, those who have studied leadership are in clear agreement that vision is at its core. This is significant but not surprising, if leaders are, as some have observed, people who take the rest of us where we otherwise might not have gone: their sense of another, better place must be keen. In an article on visionaries in *Esquire* magazine, contributing editor Lee Eisenberg (1983, p. 305) observed: "While their contemporaries groped at the present to feel a pulse, or considered the past to discern the course that led to the moment, these nine squinted through the veil of the future. Not that they were mystics. They were much more worldly than that. For most of them, reality was pure and simple; what set them apart was the conviction that a greater reality lay a number of years down the pike."

Vision is what allows us to lift ourselves out of the present moment and be transported in our mind's eye to what we dream about—and to see our dream as possible. This is not a mystical process, as some suspect. In fact, creating a vision has much in common with daydreaming and fantasizing—processes we engage in quite naturally, often in spite of ourselves. Nor should the process of creating a vision be viewed as a luxury to be indulged only when times are good. To the contrary. It is in times of difficulty—when the economy is depressed, when resources are shrinking, when the demands are intensifying—that we are most in need of something to inspire us, focus us, and impel us forward. An editorial in the *Washington Post* some time ago hypothesized that the real problem for people who abuse welfare is not dependency, as is commonly believed, but hopelessness—the lack of a vision of moving toward something better. Visions are about hope, about purpose, and about creating a future *of our choosing.*

A particularly graphic portrayal of the power of vision is described by Victor Frankl (1984) in his memoirs of the Holocaust. Limping in pain from the sores on his feet through bitter cold winds, he was obsessed with the endless problems of subsistence in the concentration camp—and disgusted with his unrelenting attention to such trivial concerns as where he could get a fragment of wire to serve as a shoelace or whether he should trade a hoarded cigarette for a bowl of soup: "Suddenly I saw myself standing on the platform of a well-lit, warm and pleasant lecture room. In front of me sat an attentive audience on comfortable upholstered seats. I was giving a lecture on the psychology of the concentration camp! All that oppressed me at that moment became objective, seen and described from the remote viewpoint of science. By this method I succeeded somehow in rising above the situation, above the sufferings of the moment, and I observed them as if they were already of the past" (pp. 94–95).

For the manager-leader, vision is what lends meaning and direction, at a personal level, to day-to-day activity. In Chapter Six we will be talking about creating a shared vision—a consensual *process* involving others; here our focus is on vision as a personal value that informs the manager-leader's approach. When we as individuals develop and pursue a vision for ourselves, our family life, and our work, we are acknowledging the need for aspiration, and we are claiming our ability to influence the future—to make the kinds of conscious choices in the here and now that take us in a particular direction. We intentionally move toward a desired state rather than finding that we have ended up somewhere by default. Vision represents a commitment to influence the future, to achieve or become something that adds value, to make a difference, to contribute to something that transcends pure self-interest. Vision is a means of rising above the fray, of seeing the big picture, of maintaining perspective in mediating short-term pressures with long-term aspirations.

What does it take to become visionary? First, we must be willing to understand the present. To create a viable dream, we need to come to terms with the environment in which we are operating and the particular shape of our current reality as a basis for determining what is possible. Second, we must be capable of imagining the desired future. Visions are, by definition, visual—the images and pictures in our mind's eye that translate the dream into concrete operational or personal terms and thus provide clues about how to make the dream happen. Third, we must be committed to making the kinds of choices, consistently, that begin to close the gap between what is and what could be.

Integrity

Adheres to high ethical standards; has internalized a system of values and beliefs; exemplifies moral soundness.

This above all to thine own self be true
And it shall follow like the night the day,
Thou canst not then be false to any man.

—WILLIAM SHAKESPEARE, *HAMLET*

As we seek new, more productive ways of working together these days, we hear the word *trust* being bandied about a lot. We endorse trust as an alternative to the hidden agendas, game playing, and other self-protective strategies that limit and at times undermine organizational effectiveness. We recognize trust as the basis of more open, honest relationships and the foundation of more collaborative, synergistic endeavors. What we may not be so clear about is where trust begins and what it involves at a very personal level. Trust is not something that is "out there" somewhere if only we could just put our hands on it, nor is it something that the CEO can accomplish by fiat merely because it suddenly makes strategic sense. Trust is not something an organization can appropriate apart from its individual members.

So where does trust come from, and how does the manager-leader foster it in the organization? Trust grows out a kind of constancy in others that gives us confidence that they mean what they say; that they will act in accordance with their words, stand behind their commitments, and keep their promises despite whatever winds of political expediency swirl about them; that their words and actions can be counted on over time to display coherence and predictability. In other words, we know that they will act with integrity.

The word *integrity* shares its etymological roots with words like *integrate* and *integer*—from the Latin *in* ("not") and *teg* ("to touch"). Integrity applies, then, to something untouched, whole, unblemished—something that can be trusted on the basis of its purity and its constancy.

A relative of one of the authors, known for his unnerving habit of stopping social conversations cold with an incisive question, posed the following to each guest at an intimate dinner party: "What issue do you feel strongly enough about to be willing to protest for?" His question was an integrity test. For unless we commit to beliefs we are willing to stand up for, we become, in Peter Block's word, "fencesitters" who honor caution and safety above all else, who shift with the political winds, who cannot be trusted (1987). Ultimately we risk the loss of our very identity. Willy Loman, the protagonist of Arthur Miller's classic play *Death of a Salesman* (1980), finds himself in such a predicament as he comes to terms with the fact that he has never cultivated or nurtured anything of lasting value. Having been seduced by the false value of outward appearances at the expense of being true to self, Willy undermines his own ability to achieve self-worth and his sons' ability to lead grounded, satisfying lives. In the end Willy becomes so desperate and confused that he commits the final violation of self in the act of suicide. The external pressures Willy surrendered himself to are just as real, if somewhat different in kind, for today's managers. Of course managers will, at times, have to support decisions or directions with which they don't fully agree, make trade-offs in reckoning with complex issues, or placate an unreasonable boss, employee, or customer. They will no doubt face situations in which judgment dictates that they "pick their battles." And as emerging markets expand the global arena, managers will inevitably find themselves operating in cultures whose practices and standards are at variance with their own. So the challenge for manager-leaders is to determine in each case what is a legitimate accommodation to the organization or to a cultural context, as opposed to what constitutes "selling out."

Acting with integrity also means not operating with a double standard. On a January morning in 1997, officer Steven Rogers of the Nutley, New Jersey, Police Department was on routine patrol in downtown Nutley, a town of twenty-seven thousand, when he spied an elderly woman struggling to cross the street. He pulled his squad car into the nearest available parking space and went to assist her. Once she was safely delivered, he stopped for a cup of coffee at the diner in front of which his car was parked. Moments later he received a page requesting that he investigate the report of a police car illegally parked on a downtown street. Sure enough, it was his car; he had never noticed the posted notice restricting parking in that spot.

How did he handle the situation? We all know that on the basis of his badge alone and certainly in light of the circumstances that had led him to park there in the first place, he could have justified his action and simply moved the car. But instead Rogers wrote himself a ticket and dutifully paid the full fine. Why? When interviewed (*Today Show*, Feb. 7, 1997), Rogers, who heads up the Nutley police department's community relations program, said that he believed it was important for him to live up to the same standards others in the community are held to (although when asked if he would have ticketed someone else in that situation, he indicated a preference for leniency).

Integrity is something we begin to develop at a very early age as our values are formed; however, our integrity can become compromised as we face the often conflicting norms and pressures of those around us in our society and in the organizations in which we work. Maintaining our integrity requires that we ask hard questions of ourselves about what we believe in and are willing to commit to; about how we have honored or failed those values in the past; and about what we are willing to do in the future. We must also come to terms with the honest answers to those questions. If we find ourselves lacking we can begin to restore integrity in small ways: by creating some personal litmus tests by which to judge our choices and decisions; by heeding our qualms when we find ourselves involved in something that is less than forthright; by monitoring the degree to which we succumb to external pressures and influences.

According to Warren Bennis (1989, p. 45), managers "do things right," whereas leaders "do the right things." His differentiation is pointed: if "mere" managers are to become leaders they must bring more than competency and efficiency to their role: they must also bring integrity.

By way of concluding this narrative on integrity, here is a simple footnote: Tom's of Maine, purveyors of unsweetened toothpaste and other natural products, grew from a modest mom-and-pop operation to $1.5 million in sales in just ten years. In 1982, as the company anticipated moving from health food stores into mainstream grocery and drugstore chains, cofounder and CEO Tom Chappell found himself under intense pressure from his management team and the board of directors to "get beyond that flavor problem" by doing what all other toothpaste manufacturers do—adding saccharin. But Chappell held firm—against artificial sweeteners and against the presumption that "Americans can't apply brush to teeth without something sweet in between." In the succeeding four years Tom's of Maine jumped to $5 million in sales. Chappell (1993, pp. 3–4) comments: "In elite business schools and large corporations, one idea is hammered into professional managers: Know thy market. But Kate [Tom's wife and the cofounder of Tom's of Maine] and I had built our little company on the basis of a much older imperative: Know thyself."

Passion and Courage

Is compelled by what he or she deems important; is willing to accept the personal consequences of difficult choices and decisions; can be relied on to stand up for what's right.

Blaze with the fire that is never extinguished.
—LUISA SIGEA, *DIALOGUE OF BLESILLA AND FLAMINIA 1522–1560*

Courage is the act of choosing to do the right thing when doing the right thing is not easy or convenient, comfortable, or safe. Courage is not foolhardiness or bravado or fearlessness. As a school teacher once explained to her class, "Having courage doesn't mean you're not scared. The difference between courage and foolhardiness is that the person with courage recognizes the danger but goes ahead in spite of it, knowing that that's the right thing to do." The courage of the manager-leader is seldom the dramatic variety of "courage" we associate with feats of daring but, rather, is the day-to-day choices and actions that inform his or her approach. The expressions *stepping up to* or *standing up and being counted* aptly describe the forward motion—deliberate, intentional, and risky—that courage implies. "Going public" with a personal vision to ask for support is an act of courage. Taking the initiative to repair a damaged relationship with a peer, assuming responsibility for a tough decision, or admitting that you have screwed up or that you don't know the answer are all acts of courage—and acts of leadership.

Opportunities to act with courage are not always dramatic. Despite the tendency of our culture to link courage with action heroes, courage as a leadership attribute does not always come down to a bold stand or a "career decision." Often courage is quiet and subtle. In the classic film *12 Angry Men* (1957), Henry Fonda's character stands up to the opposition of eleven other jurors who want to quickly render a guilty verdict in the case of a ghetto youth accused of killing his father so they can get on with their business. Some of the jurors are tacitly disapproving or visibly aggravated by Fonda's singular "not guilty" vote in the initial polling; some become openly hostile and aggressive. All except Fonda just want to get it over with: the room is stifling, they have better things to do, and they believe it's an open-and-shut case. Despite the pressure to back down, Fonda remains true to his belief that the young defendant whose life hangs in balance deserves the jury's thoughtful deliberation of the case. So Fonda quietly but firmly works to influence his fellow jurors. He asks searching questions and raises possibilities they have not considered. Like a skilled detective he examines seemingly irrelevant details for their implications and re-creates events to expose unchallenged assumptions. By the end of the film, all of the jurors have been brought to the point of reversing their verdict to "not guilty" based on reasonable doubt, and all have been brought to a greater awareness of self and a higher respect for the process of rendering a verdict.

We may shy away from courage because we sense potential danger, and fear what we might stand to lose—acceptance, a job, our well-being, our very lives. Yet in playing it safe we stand to lose something much more essential—our hearts and souls, and the chance to make a lasting difference.

Recognizing this simple truth is both sobering and liberating—an impetus for the many acts of courage the role of the manager as leader requires.

Optimism and Self-Confidence

Maintains a positive outlook based on a belief in his or her capabilities and the essential goodness of things; sees the glass as half-full rather than half-empty; views challenges as opportunities.

I think I can—I think I can—I think I can—I think I can. . . .
—WATTY PIPER, *THE LITTLE ENGINE THAT COULD*

These are sobering times for manager-leaders. Resources are diminishing as competition is intensifying. Organizations require more but promise less in return. And managers have not been spared when it comes to downsizing and layoffs—the human toll exacted by the harsh realities of today's marketplace.

Yet, by definition, leaders are people who instead of becoming cynical or defeated in the face of such conditions, muster a kind of spirit and determination that amounts to an act of faith—faith in the possibilities of the future and in the capabilities of themselves and others to create a future of their choosing. Warren Bennis calls it "self-deployment" and ranks it as one of the four essential strategies of leadership (Bennis and Nanus, 1985, p. 26). It has also been dubbed the "Galatea Effect" after the idealized statue carved by Pygmalion in Greek mythology. Whereas the Pygmalion Effect describes the self-fulfilling prophecy of one's expectations for *others*, the Galatea Effect is about generating—and fulfilling—prophecies for *ourselves;* bringing into being, as it were, the full realization of our potential.

Some might say that one's capacity for optimism is largely a matter of temperament—that whether we see the glass as half-empty or half-full is a function of propensities we are born with. Perhaps. On the other hand, the human species' ability to adapt is one of its most distinguishing features. We can allow ourselves to become overwhelmed by circumstances that may seem beyond our control, or we can act with the kind of spirit and purpose that actually seem to make things happen. Any number of maxims attest to the validity of the latter approach. We acknowledge, for example, that "God helps those who help themselves" and that success is "10 percent inspiration and 90 percent perspiration." Goethe, regarding what he deems "the elementary truth" about all acts of initiative, emphatically states: "the moment one definitely commits oneself, then Providence moves too." He advises that "whatever you think you can do or believe you can do, begin it. Action has magic, grace, and power in it" (cited in Cameron, 1992, p. 21).

The feature film *Rudy* (1993) illustrates the way that providence moves to support one who truly believes. Based on a true story, *Rudy* depicts the life of a young man from the Midwest who cherishes the dream of playing football for Notre Dame. On the face of it, Rudy has little reason for optimism: his family discourages him, he is too small to play high-powered college football, and he is not smart enough to get accepted to Notre Dame the first five times he applies. Yet driven by a dream too strong to die, he somehow manages to get into the university, practice with the varsity squad, and make the final play of the final game of his senior year, for which he is accorded the singular honor of being carried off the field by his teammates.

Manager-leaders are distinguished by a similar unwillingness to allow internal or external constraints to unduly limit their endeavors—or to be defeated by circumstances over which they have no control. Because they believe in themselves and in others and in the possibilities of the future, they inspire confidence and communicate a sense of power that derives not from title or position but rather from self-efficacy.

Focus and Discipline

Sets appropriate priorities in the face of multiple, competing demands; sticks with the task at hand in spite of difficulties or distractions.

Keep your eye on the ball.

—COACHES EVERYWHERE

When Morgan McCall and Robert Kaplan from the Center for Creative Leadership (1989) set out to study managerial decision making, their hope was to discover a prescriptive model. By the time they had concluded their field research, however, they were awash in data suggesting that managerial decision making was not an easily documentable, linear process but instead might best be described as a "twisted, unshapely halting flow" (Gore, 1964, p. 21) that "stretches back into a murky past and forward into a murkier future" (Burns, 1978, p. 379). These findings are consistent with what Mintzberg (1976) had found in his earlier study of managerial activity: that it is accomplished in fits and starts, that it is plagued with loose ends and interruptions, and that it requires managers to divide their attention among many different types of activities—from the short-term, mundane tasks of budgeting funds and coordinating day-to-day activity to the far-reaching pursuits of setting direction and developing strategic plans, all the while maintaining an awareness of how the short-term and long-term relate.

In short, one might argue that the primary occupational hazard for the manager is the fragmentation inherent to the job. Hence the need for focus, the ability to determine what should be attended to out of the welter of competing demands, and discipline, the ability to stick to the task at hand through the inevitable ebbs and flows of energy, through the tedium and the hassles and the countless interruptions, to successful completion.

Occasionally we achieve focus and discipline by dint of a critical deadline or cataclysmic event that focuses our attention. No doubt all of us have experienced a "flow state" in which all our energies become highly concentrated in the pursuit of a goal or the accomplishment of a task. We are able to work for hours on end, into and through the night, well beyond our usual tolerance.

The bombing of the Alfred P. Murrah Federal Building in Oklahoma City provided an example of this phenomenon on a larger scale. James Lee Witt, director of the Federal Emergency Management Agency, commented in an interview on the *Today Show* (April 26, 1995) that he had never seen such a united effort, referring to the way rescue workers from all over the country had dealt with what must have seemed an impossible task. Even a week after the bombing, when the effort had become incredibly tedious and laborious, when the rot of decomposing bodies amplified the horror of the original blast, and when there was little chance of recovering other survivors, team member Skip Fernandez reported that rescue workers' spirits remained high and that workers were having to be chased out after twelve-to fifteen-hour shifts because the next shift was so eager to begin.

In the workplace, high-visibility projects or tight deadlines can serve to bring focus and discipline to our efforts; more typically, however, our attention must be divided among many things, some of which are not necessarily urgent or compelling but nonetheless have to be done.

In light of the proliferation of information we must process, the increasing complexity and breadth of work issues we must deal with, and the intensifying demand to produce extraordinary results on a daily basis, we are vulnerable to debilitating stress and loss of performance. We can feel chronically overwhelmed, and we are easily distracted by the details closest at hand or by the brushfires flaring up all around us. Worse yet, we may fall into the trap of making irrevocably bad decisions.

An added complication for today's manager is the need, as organizations become leaner, to take on more of their unit's work production responsibilities, leaving them with little, if any, time in which to manage. Then too, new technologies impose their own burdens. The fax machine creates the expectation of an instant response, and the advent of electronic communication has brought about the need to receive and respond to countless voice and e-mail messages on a daily basis.

Under these circumstances, if we are able to achieve focus at all it is likely to be only for short periods and maybe only for those things closest at hand: we may latch on to the tasks most "doable" and most easily checked off the list but sometimes most incidental in terms of the overall scheme. So we lose precious hours doing what one friend calls "washing the cat"—sorting and answering electronic messages, returning phone calls, or completing paperwork, tasks that are more manageable but infinitely less important than tackling a breakdown in trust, working to develop a vision, setting strategic direction, or mapping out a strategy for improving customer service.

Somehow we need to find a way to prioritize the many things vying for our attention, in order to prevent our energies' becoming so fragmented or consumed by short-term demands or peripheral distractions that we are unable to focus on what is essential or of long-term importance. In the popular novel *The Brothers K,* by David James Duncan (1993), the oldest of the Chance brothers, Peter, tells the story of an East Indian elder, Drona, teaching a family of brothers the art of archery. After instructing the first brother to aim at a straw and cloth bird target, he asked the young man to describe *exactly* what he saw. "I see the tree, . . . and the bird, and my arm and bow and arrow. And you" (p. 164). Drona told him to stand aside, not even allowing him to shoot, and called forward the second, third, and fourth brothers in turn, giving each the same instructions. When asked what, exactly, they saw, each brother described the scene in increasing detail. Finally Drona called for Arjuna, the fifth brother, who strung his arrow and drew his bow back until it was so taut it formed a half circle.

"What do you see?" Drona asked Arjuna.

"A bird," he answered.

"Describe it."

"I cannot," Arjuna said.

"Why?" his teacher asked.

"I see only the neck."

"Release the arrow!" Drona said, and when the bowstring sang the arrow flew so fast that the brothers couldn't follow it. All they saw was the target bird's head, drifting like a leaf to earth [Duncan, 1992, p. 165].

Focus and discipline allow the manager to reconcile the immediacy of today's pressures and the importance of investing in tomorrow's opportunities, to know when unflagging attention to detail or to a preferred course of action is warranted and when "satisficing" (March and Simon, 1958) will do. (*Satisficing* is a term for proceeding in a way that is acceptable as opposed to optimal, that satisfies and suffices.) Stephen Covey (1989) suggests that we consider two factors when thinking about how best to focus our efforts: urgency and importance. Some activities, for example, are neither urgent nor important. These would include trivial or frivolous pursuits such as playing video games or working on a suntan. A ringing phone, on the other hand, is urgent—that is, it insists on action—but may be unimportant in terms of outcome. A crisis or a deadline on a critical project is both urgent and important. Then there are those things that are not urgent but are ultimately very important—such as self-renewal, maintaining health and overall fitness, building relationships, or anticipating future opportunities. Ironically, because these activities and goals are neither "in our face," so to speak, nor easy to accomplish, they are the areas we are most likely to neglect. Getting clear about what is truly important to us both personally and professionally is a necessary step in achieving the focus and discipline that will allow us not just to cope with multiple demands but to make choices about how best to discharge them.

Flexibility

Is able to adapt to different people, situations, and approaches; revises plans and objectives as circumstances warrant.

You've seen trees by a raging winter torrent,
how many sway with the flood and salvage every twig,
but not the stubborn—they're ripped out, roots and all.
Bend or break.

—SOPHOCLES, *ANTIGONE*

If you compare the metaphors currently in use for describing organizations with those traditionally used, you get some sense of just how important flexibility is in today's environment. It is surely no accident that water images prevail. Today we talk of "shooting the rapids," "reading the surface of the water," "sailing the craft," and "riding the waves." Yesterday's organization was based on a military model. We talked of "chains of command," "strategies," "campaigns," "recruits," "deployment," and "being in the trenches"—terms that reinforced the rigidity and regimentation of tall, vertical, highly segmented structures. Conversely, the ideal organization of today and tomorrow is not only flatter but more cross-functional, more collaborative, more responsive, more creative, and more empowered—in short, more *fluid* or flexible!

If "permanent white water" is the right metaphor for current and future conditions, then the need for flexibility is self-evident. To navigate rapids we must be able to respond in the moment as the surface of the water changes, adapting our maneuvers and our course to forces we cannot fully control. Without flexibility we become like a stick caught against a rock in a turbulent stream; defenseless against the force of the raging water, the stick is battered relentlessly. A stick that floats free, on the other hand, moves *with* the water rather than against it and is carried along unencumbered; thus the force of the water actually expedites the stick's progress along its way.

Derived from the Latin *flectere,* the word *flexibility* means to bend. Flexibility implies a kind of "give" that is responsive but at the same time strong. We know, for example, that if we increase the flexibility of our muscles through physical exercise, we can do more things. In the same way, when we develop the value of flexibility we enlarge our capacity to respond in a variety of situations *without losing sight of the goal.* For being flexible does not mean being undirected or capricious. Flexibility does not involve flitting in desperation from one panacea to another. Flexibility turns, instead, on the recognition that there can be many routes to the same destination.

The importance of flexibility as a fundamental value for today's manager can hardly be overstated. Obviously, rapid change necessitates making frequent course corrections and strategy revisions. Stephen and Shannon Wall report that in a worldwide survey of twelve hundred executives conducted by the International Consortium for Executive Development Research, "being flexible to meet new competitive conditions" was identified by respondents as one of the top five developmental needs (Wall and Wall, 1995, p. 12).

And if we are serious about empowerment, we are going to have to give others the room to meet objectives in ways that may not be exactly as we would have met them. These tasks may involve something simple, such as how a document is formatted, or something more complex, such as arranging for telecommuting to accommodate an employee's family situation.

Flexibility is also imperative if we are to truly value diversity. Unless we can adapt to and appreciate an increasingly varied mix of styles, perceptions, and approaches, we are unlikely to derive the potential benefits of a multicultural (in the broadest sense) workplace.

To the extent that it means giving over the need for ultimate control, there is something quite liberating about flexibility. When we embrace flexibility we permit ourselves to act *with* (rather than in spite of) our environment so that we are able to adapt while maintaining our core identity.

Like a stream that answers to the call of the ocean, finding its way around rocks in its path, like a sailboat that tacks on its way to port—flexibility becomes the means by which we manage chaotic processes to arrive at a desired outcome.

Tenacity and Resourcefulness

Persists in pursuing desired outcomes; "makes do" when situations are less than ideal; is creative in overcoming obstacles.

We will either find a way or we will make one.

—HANNIBAL

The expression "do more with less, faster" has by now become commonplace and speaks to the reality of fewer tangible resources and the need for greater resourcefulness. Resourcefulness is an attribute that embodies a number of traits. For example, it is persistent in finding ways of accomplishing things or overcoming obstacles when the obvious means are not available, when the path is not clear, or when one can't simply have one's way; people who are resourceful don't give up easily. It means being inventive and experimental; people who are resourceful think outside the box, make new connections, and try things. Thomas Edison is a good example of resourcefulness. When his discouraged assistant complained about "not getting anywhere" after weeks of false starts on a particularly vexing problem, Edison is said to have responded to the effect that they had, in fact, learned a lot: they now knew a thousand things that don't work!

I. M. Pei also provides a compelling example of resourcefulness in the way he dealt with the formidable challenge of designing a new wing for the National

Gallery of Art that would both complement the style of the existing museum and fit on a relatively small, highly irregular plot of land circumscribed by the acute angles characteristic of Washington, D.C.'s intersecting streets and avenues. To accomplish his task, Pei was forced to find new ways of thinking about structures and space. His solution was unusually creative: he used the acute angles as the organizing principle, divided the plot into two triangles, and designed companion triangular buildings. The resulting structure is considered to be one of his greatest achievements.

And finally there's Rudy, the Notre Dame hopeful we described earlier in this chapter (see "Optimism and Self-Confidence"). Despite the fact that his first several applications were rejected, he set about finding ways of getting closer to his goal: he moved to South Bend and attended a community college to improve his academics; he hung out on the Notre Dame campus and tried to join an extracurricular club so that he could pass for a Notre Dame student. So determined was Rudy to find a way to make his dream come true, he even managed to live for a time in the Notre Dame football locker room! And eventually, he achieved what most would have considered utterly impossible.

One obstacle to resourcefulness that can limit our resourcefulness is a syndrome called "functional fixation"—the failure to see beyond the designated purpose of an object, role, title, and so on. Most people when asked the purpose of a coat hanger acknowledge that it is for hanging up clothes *and* for opening a car when the keys are locked inside. It's a little more of a reach for people to see a coat hanger as a cooking implement (skewer, pasta-drying rack, grill) or as an instrument for producing sound (antenna, drumstick, banjo string). Fortunately, Angus Wallace, a British orthopedic surgeon, was not afflicted with functional fixation when, on a May 1995 flight between Hong Kong and London, he was summoned to tend to another passenger who was suffering a collapsed lung as a result of injuries sustained in an accident just prior to boarding the British Airways flight. Wallace quickly determined that an emergency landing would only increase the chances of an irreversible crisis, so he elected to perform thoracic surgery midair. A check of the plane's first-aid kit revealed a few workable tools: a scalpel, scissors, some local anesthetic, and a sterile urinary catheter tube. Although the catheter tube would be useful for relieving air pressure in the chest cavity, it was too floppy to insert as it was. Wallace quickly solved this problem with—you guessed it—a coat hanger, which was sterilized with the five-star brandy British Airways keeps on board. Once the catheter had been inserted into the chest, tubing from an oxygen mask was used to link the catheter tubing to a partially drained Evian water bottle for displacement of the expelled air. The surgery was completed in flight, and the patient did so well that she was released from the hospital the next day.

So instead of taking the conventional approach of tightening controls or laying people off in hard times, the resourceful manager-leader might focus instead on greater efficiencies: high-performance teams, cross-functional efforts, more flexible work arrangements, or the development of new markets. The idea is to avoid being bound by what has worked before and to seek, instead, novel solutions and breakthrough opportunities.

For today's manager-leader, resourcefulness may take the form of exploiting new work processes and moving beyond traditional "fixes." For if the bad news is that money and people are in shorter supply, the good news is that diminished resources are forcing us to reexamine the ways we have structured our organizations and our work and to seek new ways of using the resources we have.

Humanity

Genuinely cares about, values, and responds to others; believes in human potential; is sensitive to individual differences.

First, you need to cherish, protect, and make life possible, and then work your way back to all the other issues.
—BELL HOOKS, "100 VISIONARIES WHO COULD CHANGE YOUR LIFE," *UTNE READER*

From time to time the authors still hear coworkers or seminar participants hold forth with that long-standing maxim of business, "One should keep emotions out of the workplace." It's no wonder. To say that the traditional workplace has not been entirely hospitable to the whole person understates the case. The primacy of efficiency as a corporate value, an obsession with the bottom line, and a business culture widely acknowledged as "macho" leave little room for those parts of the individual that operate outside of time clocks, and policies, and deadlines, and other such institutional mechanisms designed to impose a certain order and conformity on highly diverse beings. Managers have been taught for years to assiduously avoid crossing the line between business dealings and the personal lives of their employees. Derived from a mechanistic view of the organization, the rationale seemed sound: allowing the human condition—unpredictable, complicated, mysterious, and messy as it can be—to spill over into the workplace threatened to wreak havoc on the well-oiled machines we sought to craft.

Unfortunately, in shutting out what is deeply personal we have also disinvited the source of an employee's motivation, energy, and creativity—qualities that we have sought for decades to find a way to tap. The inability of traditional, machine-like organizations to thrive in current conditions and the need for a fuller contribution from all employees, however, have forced us to come to terms with employees as living, breathing people.

The emphasis on creating visions in organizations is a case in point. Most organizations have in recent years come to recognize the power of a shared vision as a force for aligning diverse efforts in the pursuit of a common purpose. But a vision can only become shared to the extent that it reflects the aspirations of the organization's members. So, too, with empowerment and diversity. In asking employees to become empowered we are asking them to value autonomy and risk, factors that have to do not just with performance per se but also with issues related to personal growth and development. As regards diversity, we cannot celebrate diverse gifts without recognizing the uniqueness of individuals, a perspective grounded in humanness and relationship. And we have little hope of successfully navigating the treacherous shoals of downsizing, reorganization, and other such disruptive events unless we can provide lifelines of support to those floundering with the profound personal transitions that accompany change.

Shared vision, empowerment, diversity, and sensitivity to personal transitions are all part of an emerging paradigm for work that acknowledges what De Pree (1989) describes as "covenantal relationships." As opposed to a contractual agreement, which deals with the formal terms of employment, a covenant "rests on shared commitment to ideas, to issues, to values, to goals, and to management processes." Covenants "fill deep needs and they enable work to have meaning and to be fulfilling. They are an expression of the sacred nature of relationships" (p. 60).

Few would argue with De Pree's sentiment; in fact, as organizations become more automated through technology, there is an even greater need for personal connection. Futurist John Naisbitt (1982) counseled us years ago that high tech requires high touch. But the reality of living out covenantal relationships in organizations can at times be like traversing a field studded with land mines. In an age of political correctness, when interpersonal sensitivities are highly idiosyncratic and managers are increasingly liable, it is not surprising if managers tread cautiously. As workplaces become more culturally diverse so, too, do values and expectations, requiring that managers take more factors into account when dealing with employees. And on the part of many employees there is a pervasive sense of entitlement that managers may fear they will only reinforce to the point of abuse if they readily accommodate individual needs.

Being a caring manager-leader does not mean being a resident social worker or amateur psychiatrist. And it does not preclude high standards for performance or corrective action when that is warranted. In fact, the truly caring manager will be guided by a respect for others that honors their interests and needs and that supports them as individuals in realizing their full potential—as workers, as family members, and as members of the community.

Embracing the value of humanity is a way for manager-leaders to help restore a sense of wholeness to people in the workplace. When people feel recognized for who and what they are, they usually bring more of themselves to the endeavor, become more fully engaged, and contribute more substantially. Irwin Federman (1992, p. 59) clarifies the link between humanity and leadership: "In order to willingly accept the direction of another individual, it must feel good to do so. This business of making another person feel good in the unspectacular course of his daily comings and goings, is in my view, the very essence of leadership."

This idea is by no means new. Evidence of the relationship of human factors to effective leadership comes out of the extensive studies (Hemphill, 1950) conducted at Ohio State University in the 1940s, which concluded that leadership consists of two dimensions: task and relationship. The task dimension, as the term suggests, is concerned with whatever is required of the leader to structure efforts toward the desired goal or outcome. The relational dimension, on the other hand, is concerned with providing for the human factors—fears, insecurities, needs for approval and inclusion, personal issues, talents and skills, hopes and dreams—that will affect how an individual or team functions in pursuing a goal. The leader who fails to appreciate those factors may limit the ability of followers, however capable, to participate in the effort with a high level of satisfaction and commitment.

Of particular relevance to today's manager-leader is the ability to deal humanely with change. The rash of downsizings, "right-sizings," reorganizations, outright layoffs, and assorted other change initiatives of all types and at all levels of the organization attests to the harsh realities of a business world in sweeping transition. There have been and will continue to be many casualties—those who lose their jobs not because of poor performance but because bloated, inefficient organizations suddenly find it necessary to become lean and mean. There are psychological casualties as well: those who are spared during a layoff but must live with "survivor guilt," those who are uprooted from important relationships with coworkers or colleagues because somebody rearranges the boxes and lines on the organizational chart, and longstanding employees who are rendered dysfunctional by a new wave of technologies they do not comprehend.

William Bridges (1991), author of *Managing Transitions*, points out that there is a difference between the external phenomenon of change, the implementation of which can be broken down into steps and plotted on a calendar, and the personal transitions individuals experience when change is imposed. By the time organizational change initiatives are announced they have usually been gestating in the minds of the change agents (managers and leaders) for some time and have been crafted into a master plan that its creators can readily champion. But those to whom the change is announced are generally at a very different point: they are facing not the promise of new beginnings the change agents have come to embrace but the many endings (read *losses*) any major change represents.

What kinds of endings? Depending on the nature of the change, endings can include loss of security, comfort, competence, and confidence; loss of political support; loss of personal investment in projects and programs; loss of collegial relationships, work partners, and teammates; and loss of community ties. More fundamentally, change can mean a loss of the way things were (which may not have been perfect but at least were known). As one worker commented, "It may be a jungle out there, but it's *my* jungle, and I know the trees!" And, reports Bridges (1991), endings is only the first stage of a process of transition that moves, in its own highly subjective way and time, to a second equally disconcerting place, the neutral zone—that limbo of uncertainty and confusion where the old is gone, but the new is not yet clear or comprehensible. The neutral zone might be compared with the awkward stage an athlete experiences when he or she is in the throes of trying to improve a skill. For example, the tennis player who seeks to improve her serve will undoubtedly suffer through a period in which nothing seems to work: she has unlearned the faulty serve she had developed but has not yet mastered the correct form.

It is only after individuals work through these first two difficult stages that they are able to bring themselves to new beginnings, the third and final stage of transition. As change agents we typically underestimate what any single person may feel he or she stands to lose in the face of change, the depth of individuals' struggles as they deal with transition, and the psychological toll this process takes, particularly if in the interest of moving the change agenda forward we fail to acknowledge or support people's needs during this time. Yet we're all familiar with the pressure to "get over it" and move on, perhaps best captured in the tough slogan "The train is leaving the station; you're either on the train or you're left behind."

Supporting people through the transitions associated with imposed change is one of the ways manager-leaders demonstrate humanity. Another way is by ensuring that they genuinely believe in and can stand behind the changes they have undertaken. Organizational theorists Patrick Connor and Linda Lake (1994), authors of *Managing Organizational Change,* conclude their book by recommending that managers who lead change need to be guided by ideals that transcend those that have traditionally served the organization, namely, rationality, technology, and efficiency. One of these new ideals is *commitment.* Because managing-leading change brings with it inevitable trade-offs, some of which undoubtedly serve the organization as a collective at the expense of its individual members, manager-leaders owe it to themselves and others in the organization to be very clear about what they have committed to and why. Another ideal is *stewardship.* Considering the profound impact organizations have on resources well beyond their internal systems, manager-leaders owe it to the larger community—no less the planet— to make responsible choices. Connor and Lake (1994, p. 207) remind us that "Managers . . . need to take into account the fact that they are changing, manipulating, and rearranging a variety of elements—human and nonhuman alike. They need to do so thoughtfully, carefully, and with respect."

Embracing the value of humanity creates an opportunity for manager-leaders: the chance to restore those parts of the individual formerly excluded from the workplace, in the interest of a more whole worker who can become more fully engaged and, as a result, make a more substantial contribution.

Self-Renewal

Takes time to develop, improve, and nurture self in the interest of achieving a sense of wholeness and well-being; discovers opportunities for ongoing learning; reflects on experience for what it can teach.

Learn to be quiet enough to hear the sound of the genuine within yourself so that you can hear it in other people.
—MARIAN WRIGHT EDELMAN, *THE MEASURE OF OUR SUCCESS*

The idea of self-renewal follows from the recognition that we are all in the process of *becoming*—a notion that in many ways runs counter to traditional American management culture. The hierarchical paradigm out of which management was born implied that by the time you made it into the ranks of management, especially middle or higher management, you had things figured out—you had paid your dues and earned your stripes; you "had it together" personally and knew the right answers professionally. In fact, knowing what to do and how to proceed (or at least appearing to) in virtually any circumstance has been one of the hallmarks of managerial success and a key criterion on which rewards are based. We value managers who are decisive; we question the savvy and competence of managers who, for whatever reason, come across as unsure. In a patriarchal system founded on the premise that those in authority—whether it's Father or the boss—know best, it shouldn't come as any surprise that managers have acted in their own interests and maintained this illusion—and in so doing have often insulated themselves from awareness of the need for self-development. Besides, the rungs of the corporate ladder by which success is measured have been credentials, titles, and promotions, not stages of growth and development. Skill in climbing the ladder has depended on what you *do*, how you *function,* and what bottom-line *results* you produce.

Another factor that inveighs against self-development is the historical role of the manager. According to John Kotter (1988), "managing" has only been around for the last one hundred years, and from its beginnings has been about control—control of budget, control of time, and, perhaps inevitably, control of other people. Implicit in such a model is a kind of self-sufficiency: it exalts the manager as a repository of power, information, answers, and authority. So it would appear that it is others, not the manager, who require direction and development.

The idea that self-renewal is at the heart of sustained effectiveness for the manager-leader enlarges our perspective of the role and its possibilities in light of current realities. *Enlarges* because we begin to address personal values as relevant and important to business enterprise. Enlarges because we recognize that lasting power derives not from a job title alone but from a sense of self-efficacy and an ability to influence that emanate from within. Without doubt there are those who are born with "the right stuff" to be effective manager-leaders, but equally without doubt, "the right stuff" is only potential until it is realized through a continuous process of development. Today's realities are too complex and too volatile for anyone to become complacent or to feel that at some point they have "arrived." New challenges require not only new tools and strategies but also often highly personal growth work and learning as well. In *The Fifth Discipline,* Senge (1990a, p. 14) reminds us that learning is a vehicle for re-creating ourselves: "Learning gets to the heart of what it means to be human. . . . Through learning we become able to do something we never were able to do. Through learning we reperceive the world and our relationship to it. Through learning we extend our capacity to create, to be part of the regenerative process of life—and to satisfy a deep hunger within each of us."

But even more fundamental than the need for growth and change is the simple need for maintenance and replenishment. We all know managers who use themselves up on a regular basis without ever finding a way to restore what has become depleted. These are the types who fight one brushfire after another, who are chronically overextended, who are never out from under, and who often, as a result, create stress in themselves and those around them. These types are always busy and work very hard, but what they seem not to realize is that frenetic activity in the absence of self-renewal will, over time, compromise effectiveness.

Covey (1989, p. 287) refers to the self-renewal process as "sharpening the saw," a metaphor drawn from his story of a man who has been sawing a tree in the woods for five hours; exhausted by the task and daunted by his lack of progress, he is nevertheless too busy sawing to stop and sharpen the saw, even though that would improve his efficiency. In *The Artist's Way,* Julia Cameron (1992) speaks of "filling the well" or "restocking the trout pond" as a means of ensuring that our reservoir of energies, ideas, resilience, efficiency, and creativity does not dry up and our efforts become sterile. "Overtapping the well, like overfishing the pond, leaves us with diminished resources" (p. 21).

How do we go about renewing ourselves? The process begins with self-examination, and it includes more than a single vantage point. We might begin by listening to ourselves: to the obvious, crying needs as well as to the voices that stir only dimly within us and are apt to be drowned out unless we can find a place of silence. We then proceed by opening ourselves to feedback from others in a variety of situations—at work, at home, in our social relationships—for there are some things we can't see about ourselves by looking into a mirror. Equally important is the response we make: do we view feedback as valuable information and a resource for personal growth, or do we find a way to rationalize feedback that is uncomfortable or at odds with our self-concept? Continuous learning is a part of self-renewal: the world we have known has picked up speed and is thrusting us forward into a new, electronic universe with virtually unfathomable possibilities that will change not only what we can do but the very nature of how we work. Unless we are willing to learn new skills—both technical and interpersonal—we will find ourselves aliens in a foreign place. Alvin Toffler (1970) predicted it three decades ago, and a recent study by the American Society for Training and Development confirmed it: knowing how to learn has become one of the highest-priority skills in U.S. corporations (Wall and Wall, 1995).

Self-renewal can occur through something as simple as a long, quiet walk or a weekend away, or as ambitious as pursuing a program of studies or working to change a lifelong behavior. The important thing is that we find ways to nurture ourselves so that we continue to thrive and move toward greater wholeness and completion in our work and in our lives. Erich Fromm (1947) reminds us that each human's main task in life is to give birth to him- or herself.

Balance

Integrates and harmonizes career, family, personal, and community responsibilities.

Life is not a rehearsal.

—ANONYMOUS

That we are inundated with choices, possibilities, and competing demands for our time and attention is a function of the times in which we live. For many of us, cultural and social change has meant more roles, more expectations, more pursuits, and more juggling! Our jobs are more demanding as a result of diminished resources, competitive pressures, new technologies, and relentless learning curves. Our family lives are more complicated as a result of dual careers, single parenthood, alternative lifestyles, and the prevailing realities of violence, drugs, homelessness, AIDS, and crime with which we and our children must contend. And we live in a society with a high cost of living and a philosophy of success that spawns such bumper stickers as "The one who dies with the most toys wins!" Notwithstanding these very immediate pressures, we are expected to give back to our communities and to develop rich and fulfilling personal lives—which in today's terms *starts* with finding the time to work out regularly at the health club, "introspect" with a therapist, make the daily trip to specialty markets for fresh fish and the day's supply of organic vegetables, and coach a recreation league soccer team.

For today's manager-leader the question of balance is especially unnerving. It would be difficult under any circumstances to apportion our energies so that the many expectations of life in the twenty-first century are all getting their just due. Functioning as a manager-leader compounds the problem. For it is difficult to contain the many and diverse responsibilities of managing and leading within the boundaries of an eight-to-five workday. Leadership by its very nature often engages us in pursuits that become compelling and take on a life of their own. And at a time when the competition is so intense and the focus is on customer service, we are all expected to make sacrifices. So we talk about quality of life and work-home balance but continue to gauge people's commitment by how late they stay at the office, how often they come in on weekends, and, in some organizations, whether they are willing to give up a family vacation to meet a pressing deadline.

The price of neglecting any of the important areas of our lives—work, family, self, or community—can be high in the long run and even devastating in the case of estranged relationships or ruined health. Yet the trap for many of us is in becoming driven by work, perhaps because in this arena accountability is so high and rewards and punishments so immediate. So we go in to the office with a raging flu or spend Sunday afternoon trying to catch up on paperwork before the onslaught begins all over again. Why? Survival, some would say. But, at least in part, it reflects a widespread and misguided tendency: we tend to measure ourselves and others in terms of professional credentials and accomplishments, not in terms of what we devote to creating happy homes, building vital communities, or achieving personal well-being.

Regardless of how much we are willing to sacrifice for corporate success, there will come a time when the organization will wave us good-bye (or push us out the door!) as it makes room for our successors. Given life expectancy these days, unless we have, as the Bible exhorts, stored up some other "treasures," the prospects for life after the corporation are indeed limited.

What constitutes balance is something that each of us must determine for ourselves, taking into consideration numerous factors, including temperament, circumstances, lifestyle, interests, family, and the shifting phases of our personal life cycles. One thing is true for all of us, however: we will enhance our leadership potential to the extent that we seek to become whole people who work to integrate and harmonize the important areas of our lives.

CHAPTER TWO

PERSPECTIVES

Habits of Mind

We are what we repeatedly do. Excellence, then, is not an act, but a habit.
—ARISTOTLE, *NICOMACHEAN ETHICS*

In Chapter One we examined values, those deeply held beliefs that determine to a large extent who we are and how we will engage with the world. Values, we might say, are at our core. Perspectives, the focus of this chapter and the second element of the Self-Leadership sphere, operate at a different level. Whereas values reside in our innermost being, perspectives flow out of the cognitive, conscious processes with which we respond to reality. Whereas values are steadfast and unchanging—the governing principles—perspectives are ways of dealing with our experiences and, as such, are influenced by prevailing models or theories, which are subject to change as new data challenge existing paradigms and we evolve in our understanding.

Thus, whereas the values in Chapter One may be thought of as having a certain permanence, the perspectives in this chapter—embracing change, testing assumptions, shifting paradigms, thinking holistically, tolerating ambiguity and paradox, trusting intuition, taking risks, seeking synergies, and modeling values—reflect a growing awareness of the particular "habits of mind" we will need in order to respond to the complexity of the coming age.

Embraces Change

Seeks new ideas and approaches; regards change as a source of vitality and opportunity; uses the energy and momentum of change to best advantage; goes *with* change rather than *against* it.

He that will not apply new remedies must expect new evils.
—FRANCIS BACON, *APOTHEGMS OF INNOVATIONS* (1624)

Conventional wisdom has it that people resist change—even when that change promises benefits. We naturally resist change, the theory goes, because no matter how beneficial the change may prove to be, the process of making any significant change necessitates disruption. At the least we must give up the comfort or security of what we are used to and adapt to something new. Beyond that, some kinds of changes require that we rout out deeply ingrained patterns of behavior or habits of thought and replace them with untried behavior or skills. In any case we are faced with an adjustment that can range from simple inconvenience to a profound sense of vulnerability and loss. True. But each of us can think of times when we have willingly—and with great enthusiasm—*chosen* change despite whatever the magnitude of the disruption could be expected to be: the decision to leave a secure job and strike out on our own, to move to an unfamiliar location, to change careers, to enter into a marriage, to renovate a house, to have a child. At some level, of course, we are aware that what we have embarked on will not be entirely smooth or easy, yet in these kinds of situations the unknown is generally perceived as full of promise. Our sense of a new beginning fills us with high hopes for what might be. Those of us who conduct executive development programs typically warn participants in extended programs about the dangers of "re-entry"—that is, going back filled with zeal about transforming both themselves and their workplaces overnight.

What seems to determine whether we will embrace change or resist it is the extent to which we are in a position to make a choice. It's one thing if we have chosen change: thus, the manager fresh from the executive development program goes back to the office the following Monday ready to undertake a long-overdue reorganization effort. Aware of the ordeal such an initiative represents, she is nonetheless energized by her own choice—her ability to make a conscious decision to determine change. It's quite another thing, however, if the change is imposed on us: as the direct reports of that manager who is fired up to reorganize, we are likely to retreat or dig in our heels at the prospect of changes with daunting and unknowable implications that are outside our control.

The truth is that much of the change we must embrace as manager-leaders of the future will not be of our choosing. Like it or not, change is *upon* us at an unprecedented rate and to an unprecedented degree. What we *are* in a position to choose is how we respond to changes that are externally imposed. We can capitulate to our deep-felt needs for safety and security and see change as the enemy: something that victimizes us, something to be feared. Or we can view change, with its accompanying ambiguity and chaos, as a revitalizing process—as an opportunity rather than as an ordeal. For many of us this will not be easy for all the reasons already mentioned—and then some.

In addition to the personal toll the disruption of change exacts, there is also the issue of the sheer time required to adjust to change—time that none of us has in ample supply. In an environment in which we are pressed to respond to increasing demands with fewer resources, the prospect of entering into an unsteady state, one that robs us of the orthodoxies we have come to consider our best defense against chaos, may seem untenable. Embracing change will sometimes require that we go against our grain, that we surrender our need for security to unrealized possibilities that will surely include loss as well as gain. Adopting a new approach, changing a behavior, abandoning a long-held belief may feel like pulling up the anchor at a safe port and setting sail on a sea that we know will at times be stormy and potentially dangerous. On the other hand, that sea is a pathway to new places and new opportunities, and if we choose not to embark on it we may find ourselves stranded on an abandoned and desolate shore.

One way to embrace change, even when we are not in a position to fully control it, is to focus on the possibilities inherent in change and to maintain our ability to make choices. Our fears of being victimized by change are most likely to be realized when we allow events or circumstances to happen *to* us and abdicate what Covey (1989, p. 71) calls our "response-ability." Because change is accompanied by energy and momentum, it opens up rather than shuts down possibilities. People who embrace change will anticipate and stay alert to these possibilities and thus leverage their ability to influence the direction of change. Take the case of William Mitchell (1993), an internationally known motivational speaker and author of *The Man Who Would Not Be Defeated*. Burned over 65 percent of his body in a horrendous motorcycle accident that obliterated his face and hands, he suffered through the agonies of a nearly miraculous recovery only to become paralyzed from the waist down a few years later when a plane he was piloting went down. Mitchell now tells his story from a wheelchair—a wheelchair that once felt like a prison but is now the vehicle of his calling and his entree to audiences all over the world. Mitchell's story is about choices: the choice to recover despite unbearable pain and incapacitation; the choice to find, within the limitations he couldn't control, opportunities he had never dreamed of for living out purpose and meaning in his life.

Or take the case of a colleague who spent years planning for children with his wife. They waited for just the right time to have their first, and they anticipated all that would follow—what they would teach their child and all of the ways they would guide their child to a bright and shining future of successes and accomplishments. But their child was born autistic, and suddenly all their plans meant nothing. Eleven years later, it is they who have been taught by a child who has brought needs and gifts beyond their understanding. By virtue of his struggles, the child has allowed his parents to discover their own unrealized strengths and has even helped to shape his father's academic research on vulnerability.

In both of these cases, individuals faced changes they would not have chosen. What they *could* choose, however, was how they would respond. And in both cases, in making the choice to embrace the change, they have found new possibilities.

The same is true for manager-leaders who remain mindful of making choices—even when those choices must operate within constraints over which managers have no control. The changes we are facing now and the ones that lie ahead will, most assuredly, involve disruption and sometimes even pain. But they are part of what we must learn to navigate in order to survive—and thrive—in the coming era. We might prefer to hang onto things as we have known them, but to do so in a high-velocity environment almost ensures that we will become immobilized or obsolete. If instead we engage with the tumult, we can maximize our maneuverability and avail ourselves of the rich opportunities inherent in change.

Tests Assumptions

Uncovers and examines underlying premises and encourages others to do the same.

A great many people think they are thinking when they are merely rearranging prejudices.
—WILLIAM JAMES

The nine dots puzzle, a well-known exercise in problem solving, requires that all nine dots be connected with no more than four straight lines and that those lines be drawn without raising the pencil from the page or retracing any line. The puzzle almost invariably traps the novice, who tries repeatedly—and unsuccessfully—to solve the problem within the limits of the "square" in which the dots are arranged. (Figure 2.1 depicts a typical failed attempt.) This is a literal example of thinking "inside the box": although nothing in the instructions prohibit problem solvers from operating outside the square, most impose their own constraint by *assuming* that the arrangement of dots represents boundaries that cannot be violated. In fact, moving outside the boundaries is the only way to solve the puzzle (Figure 2.2).

FIGURE 2.1. NINE DOTS PUZZLE.

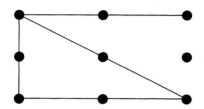

FIGURE 2.2. NINE DOTS PUZZLE SOLVED.

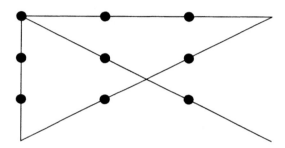

The nine dots puzzle is a powerful demonstration of the ways our underlying assumptions function—quite outside of our conscious awareness—to influence and sometimes limit our ability to see possibilities. This phenomenon is significant, because assumption making is integral to the way we perceive and interpret reality. For example, we know from Gestalt psychology that when numerous items or elements are presented to the senses, humans organize them into the simplest whole possible. A specific example of this phenomenon involves the principle of closure, whereby we fill in (or make whole) incomplete figures. Thus, in the nine dots example, the tendency is to perceive not nine dots but a square, and then to operate within the boundaries that the square *appears* to create (Figure 2.1). We have in effect acquired an assumption; that is, we now accept as fact or take for granted that what we perceive, a square, is true.

Whether or not a wrong assumption renders us incapable of solving a mind-teaser like the nine dots puzzle is of little consequence. What does matter is that faulty assumptions affect the perceptions we have, the positions we hold, and the decisions we make. The danger is not that we make assumptions but that once we have made them, they tend to remain invisible and therefore untested. In this case, because the effect of untested assumptions is insidious, what we don't know *can* hurt us. Even though, as Senge reminds us, "all we ever have are assumptions, never 'truths,'" our assumptions contribute to the development of what Senge calls "mental models" (1990a, p. 185). We develop mental models when we leap from observing behavior or events to interpreting them. In other words, we see an action or a situation and then determine, using whatever data we think we have, what that action or situation means. Often the only data we have are our previous experiences or generalizations—our existing mental models—which may or may not be relevant in a given situation but are likely to bias our perception of what is "true." Unless we are able to bring our assumptions or mental models to the surface and examine them, we are limited by them.

Learning to test assumptions will involve, for many managers, not only a new skill but also a new behavior. The new *skill* consists of consciously laying bare the premises or assumptions that underlie our positions, decisions, and even statements insofar as they frame reality in a particular way and then examining the data on which those premises or assumptions are based. For example, a manager's decision to reduce costs by cutting headcount may rest on one or more unexamined assumptions: that a smaller staff will be capable of, and perhaps even more efficient in, managing the workload without compromising quality; that cutting staff is less costly than other kinds of economies; or that staff reductions are what we've always done in tough times, and we should continue doing what we've done before.

The new *behavior* consists of acknowledging, sometimes publicly, that our interpretations and inferences may be faulty or incomplete, and of engaging with others in reflecting on not just *what* we are thinking but *how* we are thinking. Although most of us are skilled in advocating our ideas and positions, we need to start at a prior place—at the source of those positions. We need to learn the skills of reflection and inquiry, and to recover the art of dialogue. We need to admit the tenuousness of our personal "truths." We need to open ourselves to the vulnerability of not knowing and of being changed in ways that enlarge our understanding.

Shifts Paradigms

Is open to new ways of viewing things; adapts own thinking to accommodate emerging ideas, recent discoveries, new insights; avoids undue reliance on the way things have been done in the past.

I know that most men, including those at ease with problems of the greatest complexity, can seldom accept even the simplest and most obvious truth if it be such as would oblige them to admit the falsity of conclusions which they have delighted in explaining to colleagues, which they have proudly taught to others, and which they have woven, thread by thread, into the fabrics of their lives.

—LEO TOLSTOY

In his book on paradigms, futurist Joel Barker (1992) cites compelling examples of organizations that failed to take advantage of breakthrough opportunities because they were so locked into a particular way of doing something that they could not see a new possibility: the Swiss watchmakers who dismissed quartz crystal technology and went from being the major players in the industry in the 1960s to having only a sliver of the market share and the profits a short ten years later; the photographic processors who rejected—out of hand—xerography, clearly one of the most significant inventions of the twentieth century.

The problem is that we rely on paradigms as models of how things are. Barker (1992) explains that paradigms provide us with "rules" that guide us in determining what to do in order to succeed in a given situation. The risk is that our paradigms, once established, can blind us to ways that the world is changing, cause us to leave assumptions untested, and paralyze our ability to make an appropriate response. In our own time we have seen paradigms shift more rapidly than ever before as accelerated social, cultural, and technological changes have necessitated new ways of thinking and behaving.

An obvious example of a paradigm shift involves the meaning of the term *family*. Not so long ago the Ozzie and Harriet model—two married, Anglo-Saxon, heterosexual parents with two offspring in a single-income home where roles were well defined—was representative of the American family. Today a mere quarter of the American population fits that traditional family model. Today's "families" include divorced or unmarried parents, gay couples, "blended" parents with their respective children (the "Brady Bunch" model), a single person's circle of close friends, children produced through artificial insemination or surrogate pregnancy, and children who are likely to become "latchkey kids" because, partly as a result of a shift in the male-female paradigm, both parents now go off to work each day.

Similarly, at work we can find countless examples of paradigm shifts: a radical departure from "paper and pencil" methods to computerization; the flattening of tall, vertical organizations; a movement away from hierarchy and toward personal empowerment. These paradigm shifts are broad in scope and heralded in ways that no one can miss. We may not always agree with where things are headed, but at least we are aware that the tide is turning in the case of large-scale social, cultural, political, and organizational changes as they become organized into full-scale movements.

More difficult to detect and reckon with are those paradigms we have so internalized that we are unable to see them as separate from ourselves. Hence we may cling to them—without realizing we are doing so—beyond the point at which they have outlived their usefulness. Several years ago one of the authors became aware that a good friend and highly sophisticated cook (Carla) who baked her own bread was routinely storing it in the refrigerator. When she informed Carla that research showed that storing bread in the refrigerator actually hastened the chemical processes that cause bread to become stale, she was indifferent: "I just do what my mother always did." Carla's message was clear: she was going to continue to do what she has always done, right or wrong, because of a well-established paradigm.

The challenge for manager-leaders of the future will be to become sufficiently open to new ways of thinking and behaving that they can strike a balance between maintaining an appropriate degree of continuity while also proactively moving forward with change rather than struggling in vain to withstand it or to recover from its onslaughts. Clearly a risky leap of faith is required for manager-leaders to be out in front of shifts that have not yet proven themselves, especially when the decisions the manager-leader makes based on emerging paradigms stand to affect many other people and sometimes even the company's fortunes as well. On the other hand, manager-leaders will not always be in a position to wait and see. The kind of moderation Polonius recommended, "Be not the first by which the new is tried; nor yet the last to lay the old aside," may still work in some arenas, but not in today's competitive business environment.

Peter Drucker claims that we are living in an age of "sharp transformation" in which our society has so rearranged itself in terms of worldview, values, structures, arts, and key institutions that it has taken on a new identity. In this new society, according to Drucker, knowledge replaces land, capital, and labor as *the* primary resource, and organizations, which have been conserving institutions, must become destabilizers—organized for the constant innovation that changing knowledge warrants. In this society, says Drucker, "it is safe to assume that anyone with any knowledge will have to acquire new knowledge every four or five years or become obsolete" (1992, p. 96). Hamel and Prahalad speak directly to the problem of what they call "managerial frames[:] . . . the assumptions, premises, and accepted wisdom that bound or 'frame' a company's understanding of itself and its industry and drive its competitive strategy" (1993, p. 76). Hamel and Prahalad argue that managerial frames more than anything else determine competitive outcomes and that failing to reckon with these frames— a kind of blindness—is inexcusable in a global economy. Inexcusable perhaps, but no less insidious a pitfall. And there can be no more striking example than Apple Computer, a model of creativity and innovation—of thinking outside the box—whose slide from glory is being attributed, ironically, to its failure to get beyond its own paradigms. Here was an operation that started out as a "skunks works" run by two young iconoclasts, Steve Jobs and Steve Wozniak, who worked out of a garage, played rock music in the background all day, and flew a pirate flag from the building. But, as Walter Mossberg of the *Wall Street Journal* points out, Apple began to believe its own PR. Its business operation became insular and rigid: suggestions weren't heeded if they weren't consistent with the "Mac

Way" (interview on National Public Radio, Jan. 27, 1996). According to a *Washington Post* analysis, Apple never "figured out the basic rules that govern this new market" (James Moore of GeoPartners Research, cited in Corcoran, 1996, p. H1). Whereas Apple continued to look at the world as "Apple versus Microsoft," the playing field had long since shifted to the solitary Macintosh team versus the Win-Tel (computers configured with Microsoft Windows software and Intel chips) community (1996). Apple continued to go it alone, refusing to license its designs and resting on its graphical laurels at a point when their competitors were catching up in that arena. Thus, a bird that once soared free is now threatened with becoming the proverbial dinosaur. For, as Hamel and Prahalad (1993, p. 76) remind us, "Just as the health of biological species depends, over time, on genetic variety, so it is with global companies: long-term competitiveness depends on managers' willingness to challenge continually their managerial frames." Or, in the words of Marcel Proust, "The real voyage of discovery consists not in seeking new landscapes but in having new eyes."

Thinks Holistically

Sees the "big picture"; uses an interdisciplinary approach; appreciates how the parts affect the whole.

Not only is there but one way of doing things rightly, but there is only one way of seeing them, and that is, seeing the whole of them.
—JOHN RUSKIN, *THE TWO PATHS*

Most would agree that seeing the big picture—another way to describe holistic thinking—is important. The reality is, however, that we have generally not had a lot of experience seeing the big picture. The Western worldview influences us to analyze reality, to divide it up and understand it in terms of its parts. So, for example, we divide knowledge into disciplines, school curricula into subjects, medicine into subspecialties, and organizations into functions. Think for a moment about the way the traditional organization has operated: information has been hoarded and selectively shared on a "need to know" basis; functions have been segregated in "silo" or "stovepipe" arrangements that promote parochialism and tunnel vision. The result is segmentation between and sometimes even within functions. Managers, for example, often inadvertently dig their own functional foxholes by becoming focused exclusively on those concerns that directly apply to them or their work unit. They make decisions, solve problems, implement programs, and develop policies without regard to the impact their actions will have on the rest of the organization. These isolated interventions can create as many problems as they solve. You may recall the Sufi tale about the man who noticed an unsightly bump under his rug. He immediately set about smoothing it with his foot, only to discover when he turned around that a new bump had appeared at another spot. Each time he smoothed out a bump a new one would surface somewhere else. Curious and frustrated, he finally lifted the rug, and a very angry serpent crawled out. Fixating on the particulars—a specific task, the narrow limits of *my* job or *our* department—can not only limit our ability to contribute to synergistic outcomes but may also result in redundancy, duplication, or worse, divisiveness and internal competition.

One of the authors is responsible for an executive development program that focuses, in part, on helping potential leaders broaden their business perspective in the areas of strategic and systems thinking. This is an experiential, distance learning program that lasts approximately ten months and requires that participants internalize learning through applications on the job. Initially, the program works to break down the insular tendency to view everything in the context of the company's products or services. Working in teams, participants build a number of business models using current data on industries and companies that are not associated with their own organization or its competitors. This requirement is usually met with much groaning and grumbling about how spending time in such an activity is impractical and irrelevant. Only later, when these managers go back inside their units to work on their own critical strategic issues, do they discover the benefits—business opportunities in the areas of new products and services, new customer sources, or innovative approaches to strategic problems—of seeing connections to their business that, on the surface, seem to have no relevance.

Russell Ackoff (1981) argues that we are currently in a profound shift away from Machine Age thinking, with its focus on the parts, to Systems Age thinking, whereby we seek to understand the parts in relation to the whole. Evidence of this shift in the business world has taken the form of new kinds of alliances. Companies are forming partnerships with vendors, with customers, and even with competitors. The health care industry is refocusing its approach in a more holistic direction—to a more team-oriented, integrated effort in caring for and supporting the wellness of the whole person, as opposed to treating gall bladders and broken legs. The traditional organizational chart, with its emphasis on the boundaries of boxes and lines, is being replaced in some organizations with a more weblike arrangement designed to foster relationships *across* boundaries. The effort to reengineer business processes (despite the somewhat limited, Machine Age connotations of the term) involves looking at how the parts can best interact to maximize value. And many organizations have become much more proactive in their efforts to create more sustainable communities, both at the local and global levels.

"Messy"

The very premise of this book is that the manager-leaders of the future will need to cast their nets broadly, to draw on the seemingly unconnected, to listen to voices from many different disciplines and endeavors, and to tap the richness of their own life experience. For it is only in this way that they can hope to discover solutions of sufficient power, scope, and sustainability to meet the challenges of the twenty-first century.

Tolerates Ambiguity and Paradox

Functions effectively in "messy" situations where information, goals, values, or direction is uncertain or apparently conflicting, or where processes cannot be tightly structured; is able to live with questions that allow for discovery; resists premature closure and pat answers.

[B]e patient toward all that is unsolved in your heart and . . . try to love the questions themselves. . . . Live the questions now.
—RILKE, *LETTERS TO A YOUNG POET*

As we witness the astounding speed of technological progress and the new frontiers it opens to us, we also mourn the loss of a slower, simpler way of life. We are caught up in a fast-moving, highly volatile, and increasingly complex environment in which nothing stays in place long enough to be certain. This is clearly at odds with what makes most of us comfortable and with the ways we typically use to come to terms with our world.

Michael McCaskey, author of *The Executive Challenge*, explains that our minds act as "inference machines": faced with a need to make sense of a world that is ambiguous, we organize reality through a process McCaskey calls "conceptual mapping," by which we draw on our personal experience to explain what might be going on in any given situation (1982, p. 18). The problem, of course, is that our frameworks for perceiving reality are highly personal and therefore idiosyncratic: we are selective in what we take in, and in how we interpret it. Coupled with our limited vantage point and limited processing capabilities—we have no way of perceiving and apprehending all the data simultaneously; especially if they are changing rapidly, the resulting maps may be considerably distorted. Yet once we have developed a conceptual map we are likely to cling to it, to confuse the map with the territory: we assume that what we hold to be true *is* reality. Through what Argyris and Schön describe as a "self-sealing" quality (cited in McCaskey, 1982, p. 21), individuals or groups may come to rely on a map in such a way that it is reconfirmed, despite its implicit distortions, even as it circumscribes the perception of subsequent events.

That our minds are so eager to resolve perceptual loose ends suggests how unsettling the experience of ambiguity can be. We all need "answers" in order to negotiate reality so that we gain a sense of control over our environment. And some of us more than others feel best when situations are highly structured and the answers are clear up front. However, by insisting on answers in a time of rapid change we may be foreclosing on possibilities. A simple example will serve to illustrate this idea. One of the authors recently facilitated a simulation designed to produce experiential learning about complex systems. One of the participants, who was clearly unhappy to be there, demanded to know, up front, what the objectives of the exercise were. When she was informed that articulating objectives in advance would diminish the learning value of the experience, she became incensed—so incensed that she openly expressed her anger, confronted the facilitator when she should have been participating in a reflective learning exercise with her team, and summarily disavowed the potential learning value of the session, thereby *ensuring* that she would not benefit from the day.

The question is, can we become open to engaging life as more of a discovery process, in which some answers are allowed to emerge (spin themselves out) over time? The discomfort we feel when we find ourselves in ambiguous situations—having to make our way through a social event unescorted, for example, or being on our own in a strange city to attend a conference—often challenges us to operate in new ways and to call forth resources in ourselves that enhance our feeling of self-efficacy. Consider alternative approaches to planning a trip to a foreign country you have never visited before: you can nail down every detail before you go, or you can leave some things unresolved to allow for serendipity or the unforeseen. Although the former option is safer and more comfortable, the latter is likely to allow for more interesting possibilities and discoveries.

McCaskey (1982) suggests a number of specific strategies that will help us come to terms with ambiguity. First he recommends that we learn to *invite* ambiguity rather than shun it or buffer ourselves from it in an attempt to maintain stability. Instead, we should respond with increased flexibility. And, recognizing just how tenuous our individual maps are likely to be, he encourages us to make them explicit and test them against the maps of others who can offer additional data and alternative interpretations. In so doing we enlarge and refine our own maps. McCaskey offers, as well, several "skills and virtues" for managing ambiguity, which include Janusian thinking—comfort with acknowledging and using seemingly contradictory beliefs; controlling and not controlling—knowing when to be the captain and when to ride the waves; and humor—a means of regulating stress and encouraging unusual juxtapositions. The idea, then, in tolerating ambiguity and paradox is not simply to give over all direction and "go with the flow" but rather to maintain an openness to what is unfolding, to respond in real time, to live with questions, and to honor discovery as we pursue the vision.

These are unusually confusing times. As life becomes more complex, it presents us with more options, more dilemmas, and more paradoxes. We can choose to become overwhelmed by a world that makes us feel suddenly out of control because it doesn't fit with our old structures; or we can expand our own comfort zone for dealing with paradox and ambiguity, recognizing that the answer may lie within the struggle and confident that if we are open to them, answers will present themselves when we may least expect them.

Trusts Intuition

Relies on informed judgment and well-developed instincts in lieu of conclusive proof in making decisions; balances need for data with confidence in personal knowledge and experience.

It is only with the heart that one can see rightly; what is essential is invisible to the eye.
—SAINT-EXUPERY, *THE LITTLE PRINCE*

According to one of their recent ad campaigns, the best reason for buying a Mazda is that "it just feels right!" We all know the experience of *feeling*, at a very intuitive level, that something is right. We may not be able to prove it with data; in fact, sometimes we know it is right *in spite* of what the data might suggest, because we know it not in our heads but in our guts and in our hearts—or, as some are fond of saying, in our "heart of hearts," a measure of just how deep and sure that knowledge is.

Yet despite whatever personal truth we have discerned by listening to our hearts, we live in a culture that has placed far greater value on what can be proved than on leaps of faith. This is especially true of organizations, which are famous for amassing and analyzing facts, crunching numbers, quantifying data, and otherwise relying on logic to point the way. Being able to bring science to bear on our decisions gives us confidence, whereas going on a hunch is viewed as risky business. It's a question of "hard" versus "soft"—and hard wins out on the basis of sheer respectability. So we have taught our MBA students mathematical formulas for determining probabilities as a means of making the right decisions, we conduct exhaustive market research to guide new product development, and we re*engineer* business processes in the hopes of achieving breakthroughs.

Even in the hard sciences, however, the really breakthrough ideas do not appear to be entirely the product of logic or cognition. Mozart is said to have written his best symphonies while traveling; Einstein's theory of relativity finally came together while he was riding on an elevator; and chemist Francis Kekule discovered the structure of the benzene molecule in a dream. There are plenty of business cases to match these. One of the most famous is of Ray Kroc, founder of McDonald's, who flew in the face of his lawyer's counsel and paid what seemed an untenable amount to purchase an operation that has become one of the greatest entrepreneurial success stories of the twentieth century. Similarly, such innovations as frozen food, the fax machine, the VCR, the microwave oven, the cellular phone, and Federal Express would never have come into being if initial consumer data had been heeded. Needless to say, in each of these cases considerable experience and cognitive effort led up to the point at which the innovator's conscious mind gave itself over to some process beyond cognition that allowed the answer to present itself.

Some call this process "incubation." To get a sense of how it works, try this simple exercise: choose an object in the room on which to focus your gaze. Fix your attention on this object by looking directly at it for several seconds. Now shift your attention to something several feet to the right or left of the object. Can you still see the original object? The fact that the original object is still apparent at some level is analogous to the way intuition works: we consciously attend to a problem or we directly experience something that doesn't disappear entirely when we turn our attention away from it. Rather, the problem or experience begins to "work" at an unconscious level, generating connections that may not be possible while we are consciously controlling it. Then, perhaps when we are least expecting it, we experience the "Aha!" Thus, the writer who is blocked leaves the typewriter and goes to a movie, or the poet struggling with a line that won't resolve takes a long walk, and—voila!—the muse returns.

Viewed in this way, intuition might be thought of as *another way of knowing* that informs raw data with the wisdom of experience—what Ross Perot described as thoroughly "knowing your business" (cited in Rowan, 1986, p. 9). For the manager-leader, intuition is a most powerful—and critical—capability. We generally acknowledge that leadership is an art, and there is ample evidence that managing effectively depends largely on keen sensibilities and seasoned judgment. We also know that as much as we want the security of being sure, excessive analysis results in paralysis or in the kind of plodding, stunted thinking that dulls creativity and innovation. Management consultant Tom Kuczmarski reports (in Martin, 1995), for example, that as a result of slavish reliance on demographics, focus groups, and other types of market research, all but 10 percent of new products are nothing more than extensions of existing lines despite the fact that the real profit potential lies in truly original offerings. And any number of products that seemed like sure bets according to market research—New Coke, lean burgers, and pump baseball gloves, to name a few—have failed miserably. Conversely, such truly visionary innovations as Chrysler's minivan, Compaq's Systempro (the first PC server designed to link desktop computers into a network), and the HeartMate (a device developed by Thermo Electron to sustain a diseased heart until a transplant can be performed) were brought into being despite customer ambivalence or outright resistance (Martin, 1995).

Given the rapid rate of change in so many arenas, the value of trusting intuition is obvious: we simply won't be able to count on having in place all the pieces we need to perform a complete analysis. We will have to work with what we have, including our best instincts. If we are attentive to our experience and our environment, at both the very immediate and the more global levels, our intuition will serve us well.

Takes Risks

Tries things even when the possibility of failure exists; makes experiments in the interest of discovering new opportunities and solutions.

Scorn trifles, lift your aims; do what you are afraid to do.
—MARY MOODY EMERSON, DIARY ENTRY, 1805

The sheer act of being alive involves at some level, albeit inadvertently, risks. *Choosing* to take risks is quite another matter, particularly in the context of our professional lives, where, in an unforgiving world governed by short-term measures and bottom lines, a failed risk may jeopardize my career.

It is popular today to advocate risk taking as an inherent part of the entrepreneurism and innovation necessary for organizations to survive in today's crowded and competitive marketplace. In a cover article in *Fortune* magazine on failure (Sellers, 1995), Roberto Goizueta, CEO of Coca-Cola, claims that intolerance of mistakes (read risks) accounts for America's failure to remain competitive: "The moment you let avoiding failure become your motivator, you're down the path of inactivity. You can stumble only if you're moving" (p. 45).

And risks that do fail? These have now become "learning opportunities," as if the pain of failure could be sanitized semantically. "Baloney!" says Peter Block, author of *The Empowered Manager* (1987). The reality is that no one wants to fail, no matter how powerful the potential learning opportunity, because, according to Block, none of us wants to be responsible "in case there's a jury someday. . . . If there's a jury, and I'm responsible, then I'm going to be in trouble" (Jackson, 1991). For most of us there *is* a jury—not someday but now—and not a disinterested one: an organizational culture that punishes boldness, an insecure boss who doesn't tolerate mistakes, a client who shoots the messenger.

Yet implicit in the definition of leadership is the requirement to take risks. For if we define leaders as those who take others where they might otherwise never go, then leaders must push the boundaries and forge ahead into the unknown with all its attendant risks. This is part of the anxiety of leadership—and something that no amount of planning or preparation or skill or analysis can finally eliminate. When we sign on to the role of leader we are assenting to a course that is not ultimately safe. And it just may be that failure itself is becoming legitimized. John Kotter, Harvard Business School professor, describes the scenario of a group of executives twenty years ago dismissing a candidate for a senior spot *because* of a big failure: "Yep, yep, that's a bad sign." Today that same group might say just the opposite: "What worries me about this guy is that he's never failed" (Sellers, 1995, p. 49).

On the other hand, effective leadership is not about rash, irresponsible behavior. It is not about taking foolhardy risks that create danger or unnecessarily destroy the existing order of things. Manager-leaders take *appropriate* risks; they find ways to do the right things so that new possibilities become viable. Manager-leaders aren't afraid to experiment, because they recognize that playing it safe can be the biggest risk of all—it denies them an important opportunity to push the limits of success or to fail and learn.

No one can challenge the exceptional performance over the years of 3M. James Collins and Jerry Porras (1994), authors of *Built to Last,* put them at the top of their list of visionary companies—"'the best of the best' in their industries . . . role models—icons, really—for the practice of management around the world" (p. 3). A cornerstone of the 3M culture is risk taking, which is considered so vital that new trainees are told that they will be expected to disagree from time to time with their superiors in the interest of bringing new ideas forward. In addition, as part of their training, they are presented with a graphic test: once they have successfully walked a plank positioned on the ground to reach a sum of money placed at the other end, they are challenged to consider whether they could perform the same feat if the plank were suspended midair, seven stories high (Stewart, 1994, p. 98). Should a participant begin to ruminate over "the downside risk," reports Stewart, the leader counters with, "What risk? You've already proved you can do it."

On the other hand, most of us are aware of countless examples of companies in which risk taking is systematically discouraged—where following the rules or deferring to existing structures is valued over innovation, where testing the winds is the preferred mode of action, where the fence is the only safe place to be, or where stepping up to issues or trying new things involves paying a price. But when risk taking is perceived as dangerous or unacceptable and people become governed by excessive caution, they lose the ability to make decisive moves and to take bold action—what Collins and Porras (1994, p. 9) call "Big Hairy Audacious Goals," a hallmark of the most visionary (read *successful*) companies.

For the manager-leader, the importance of being able to take risks personally and to encourage others in taking risks cannot be overstated, as it underpins other critical leadership behaviors—most notably, pursuing a vision, acting with courage, and embracing change. The challenge for the manager-leader, of course, is to find ways of creating space for risk taking when the organizational culture or a particular boss is not supportive.

Several years ago, when her children were in a small, rural elementary school, one of the authors came up with the idea of volunteering to develop a fine arts program. Her thought was to draw on resources in the community to provide the children with workshop experiences in various forms of visual and performing arts. She had never undertaken such a project but felt confident that she could offer the school a unique contribution. What she hadn't counted on was a very conservative principal who was uncomfortable with anything that varied the routine or that could raise the level of scrutiny of the administrative office to which he reported. Needless to say, his reaction to the idea of a fine arts festival was less than favorable, which was exacerbated by an obvious difference in the personal styles of the principal and the author. Having developed a strong commitment to the project by this time, the author's first task was to develop some tolerance for the experiment. Over the next several weeks she worked to provide the principal with what he needed to keep the conversation alive and, eventually, to agree to a trial event. As the program evolved over the ensuing months, what became most evident to the author was that creating the space for risk meant understanding and satisfying what others who must participate in or sanction the risk need to make it reasonable on *their* terms (which may be very different from what the risk taker himself or herself needs).

What were the specific lessons learned? Build credibility so that the risks you want to take are viewed in light of a proven track record; be patient; and pay attention to providing sufficient data, being sensitive to timing, involving others in planning, managing the process, coordinating efforts, developing contingency plans, and, most important, accommodating personal style. In these ways, manager-leaders can increase the likelihood that the risks they feel they must take will not only have a chance but also that as the prime movers they have not isolated themselves—that both the success and the responsibility of the risk becomes shared.

Finally, it must be acknowledged once again that the very term *risk* implies the potential for failure and loss that in organizations can translate into loss of approval, of clout, of promotion, or even of a job. But of all the possible losses, none is as damaging as the loss of integrity, the loss of spirit, or the loss of heart.

There may be times when no amount of skill or effort to prepare the way will be sufficient to ensure a safe path for a risk we feel we must take to preserve the core of ourselves and to preserve our capability to lead.

Seeks Synergies

Encourages and practices collaboration; works with others to achieve breakthrough outcomes.

None of us is as smart as all of us.
        —BLANCHARD TRAINING AND DEVELOPMENT (APPEARS ON A PROMOTIONAL BUTTON)

Something powerful can happen when good minds come together to generate ideas, solve a problem, or make a decision. There is a bonus effect, as in "two heads are better than one," but *better* not just in an additive sense. The real bonus is the capability of producing *synergistic* outcomes—outcomes in which the total is greater than the sum of the parts—when 2 + 2 equals more than 4. In a collaborative effort, synergy results in outcomes that exceed in quality and creativity what any single individual could achieve or what the same group of individuals could achieve working collectively. Participating in a well-functioning group or team is a little like being one of several elements in a chemical reaction: diverse resources—information, thoughts, ideas, perspectives, and styles—mix, sparking an energy that takes on a life of its own and is amplified through the interaction.

In 1993 the floods that ravaged the Midwest literally buried the town of Valmeyer, Illinois, whose residents were left with two options—either disperse to other communities or relocate their town to a site that was out of the Mississippi flood plain at a projected cost of $22 million and a projected time frame of eight to ten years. Despite such formidable projections, Valmeyer residents, committed to restoring their community, took the project on with a vengeance, forming committees to deal with everything from street lights to social services. The former mayor quit his job to work more than full-time on the project, including going to Washington, D.C., to leapfrog federal paperwork and funding hurtles. Just two years later, families began to move into new houses in the new Valmeyer, and the first public structures opened for business. By spring 1996 schoolchildren were scheduled to move into their brand-new building, and by the end of the year two-thirds of the original residents were expected to have settled in (Watson, 1996). The story of Valmeyer is a remarkable story of guts, heart, determination, and, most important, synergy.

The potential for synergy is a powerful resource at a time when tangible resources are diminishing and demands are increasing. On the other hand, working collaboratively requires that we go against the grain of rugged individualism that runs so deep in our culture and in the institutions that have formed us. We learn as young schoolchildren that we are in competition with others for grades—recall the familiar classroom scene of boys and girls nearly falling out of their chairs to be first with the answer—and that working together is considered cheating. The competitive instinct is reinforced in adults in the workplace through ranking and reward systems based on individual achievement. We may therefore be reluctant to participate in a process in which our contributions are not necessarily visible or credited. We fear that becoming a team player will mean giving up personal identity, interests, opportunities, and rewards. These are legitimate concerns at a time when many organizations are making a very awkward transition from a "Lone Ranger" mentality to espousing collaboration, often in the absence of systems and structures to support this shift. The classic example is the organization that decides to become team based but makes no changes in its performance evaluation criteria or its formal reward system. Informal reward systems can also undermine synergy—for example, the boss who plays favorites or who recognizes only the most visible outcomes at the expense of supporting efforts.

Yet evidence for the need to seek synergies is clear. Increasing specialization, highly complex issues, and a proliferation of information mean that no single individual can possibly have all the answers or solve every problem. As we struggle to become more responsive to customer requirements and more timely in our delivery of products and services, we will need to capitalize on a resource that has not yet been fully realized—the capability of working together to produce breakthrough results. David Asman, editor of *The Wall Street Journal on Managing*, pronounces synergy *the* lesson of the eighties, a decade that despite dire predictions and pervasive fears—of takeovers, the deficit, foreign competition, and so on—pulled through with strong enterprise and remarkable expansion. The common link to the successful strategies of the eighties lay in managers' ability to combine seemingly incompatible elements in bold ways. Thus the fear of being frozen out by foreign competitors gave way to efforts to do business *with* foreign interests; labor and management began to explore synergies between their goals; the "rusting" industrial sector found synergies with the management techniques of the service sector and with state-of-the-art technology; and the zero-sum game of market share gave way to a view of the market not as a fixed pie but as something that can expand to accommodate any number of products to the extent that they add value. Video stores, for example, instead of cutting into the Hollywood market as was originally feared, have resulted in exponential growth in both video and film because of the synergy between the two products (Asman, 1990), and the synergies continue as satellite television now joins the partnership by offering current movies sponsored by video retailers.

For the manager-leader, seeking synergies involves a broad view, a personal investment in relationship building, and an ongoing effort to build a culture in which highly collaborative efforts are facilitated and valued. Synergies rarely just happen. Typically they occur when people have developed an appreciation of what others bring to the table, an interest in exploring and exploiting interdependencies, high levels of trust and information-sharing, and a process for working together that accommodates individual priorities. This last condition is especially important because of the vulnerability people feel in today's organizations: at a time of increasing workloads, higher personal accountability, and recurrent downsizings, it can go against our sense of survival to respond to a colleague's request for "a minute," when that minute is likely to turn into an hour that we don't feel we have to spare because contributing to someone else's project is viewed as separate from our real work. To promote synergies we must create a shared sense of "we" so that the contributions of diverse individuals extend what each of them can achieve alone.

Models Values

Communicates values and acts accordingly; demonstrates personal convictions; "walks the talk."

Example is not the main thing in influencing others, it's the only thing.
—ALBERT SCHWEITZER, *OUT OF MY LIFE AND THOUGHT*

Communication scholars tell us that messages come more through the nonverbal signals we send than through the words we speak. Consider, for example, that the statement "Close the door" can send a message that is quite cheerful or mildly irritated or blatantly hostile depending on the way the words are intoned. But vocal inflection, body language, and facial expression are only the most obvious types of nonverbal cues. More subtle and profound are the actions we take and the extent to which these reinforce—or contradict—what we say.

Take, for example, the CEO who promulgates a vision of customer service and employee satisfaction but bases every decision on the bottom line, or the executive director who pays lip-service to the value of employee input but whose calendar allows no time for meetings with field personnel. The gap between word and deed in these and similar instances indicates a failure to internalize or act on what is claimed as a belief.

In some cases this amounts to blatant hypocrisy. In others it reflects a common problem to which we are all susceptible to some degree despite how committed we may think we are to a particular belief, idea, or approach. Harvard professor Chris Argyris describes this phenomenon as "espoused theories" versus "theories in use" (cited in Senge, 1990a, p. 175). What he means by this is that although we may buy into something intellectually, we are often unable to translate it into behavior or even to recognize that we have failed to do so.

This problem may be common and quite understandable, yet its impact is significant—especially in the case of leaders, because they represent role models for others. If the recognized leader fails to live out the values he or she espouses, followers are not likely to take the leader's words very seriously, for as we sow, so also shall we reap. Employees may react to new initiatives predicated on those espoused values with confusion or cynicism (or both) and thus become stalled and even resistant rather than mobilized.

This topic, "models values," or "walking the talk" is a fitting conclusion to this chapter and this section of the book, as it is in this attribute that all of what we have been talking about heretofore comes together. At a time when there is so much chaos in both the external environment and in organizations in transition, we need something that won't go away, something in which to place our confidence. Harsh business realities force difficult decisions that at times may feel capricious. Whole plants or departments are shut down. Competent people are laid off. Disruptive changes are imposed. The one thing that people must be able to count on, in any arena, is that their leaders will not abandon or compromise their values for the sake of expediency. For example, employees ultimately can come to terms with their organization's need to downsize, although it might involve tremendous personal pain and loss; what they can't accept is their leaders' failure to handle downsizing in a humane way.

We wish that learning to model values were as simple as making a decision to resist expediencies and consistently act in accord with one's beliefs. We'd like to be able to count on the idea that if our hearts and instincts are right and we pay attention to them, we will have reliable guides. But if we heed what Argyris tells us, we understand that sometimes, despite our best intentions, we won't even realize the subtle ways that we inadvertently violate our own beliefs and in so doing send confusing signals to others. Learning to model values, then, is more than a decision. It requires a willingness to consciously monitor our behavior and to seek and listen to feedback from others. T. S. Eliot (1970, p. 177) talked about "the still point of the turning world." Leaders' commitment to core values—their own personal values and those the organization chooses to embrace—must be the still points in the turning worlds of their organizations.

PEOPLE LEADERSHIP
FOSTERING EMPOWERMENT

If the sage wants to be above the people, in his words, he must put himself below them;
If he wishes to be before the people, in his person, he must stand behind them.
Therefore,
He is situated in front of the people, but they are not offended;
He is situated above the people, but they do not consider him a burden.

LAO TSU, TAO TE CHING

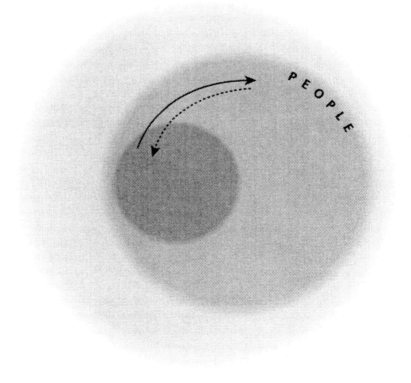

CHAPTER THREE

ENABLING INDIVIDUALS
AND TEAMS TO PERFORM

*I have a theory that talent is very common. What is rare is the environment that allows
talent to flourish.*

—MARY VINTON FULBERG, *A WOMAN'S DAY-BY-DAY ENGAGEMENT CALENDAR*

It would be hard to find an organization that didn't subscribe to the notion that
"people are its most important resource." The phrase is incorporated into
vision statements, company objectives, employee orientation programs, and so
on. Yet the phrase has taken on the hollowness of a cliche. Only recently have we
begun to understand just how untapped the "people resource" is and how critical the role of the manager-leader is in enabling an individual's or a team's full
contribution.

The first consideration to be addressed in the People Leadership sphere is
the changing role of manager-leaders in relation to their people—a shift away
from the traditional model of directing and controlling to an approach that supports and facilitates individual and team performance.

The skills discussed in this chapter—setting parameters, re-presenting the
organization, expanding access to information and new knowledge, cultivating
diverse resources, promoting continuous learning, facilitating contribution, and
advocating feedback and recognition—form a new paradigm for creating a partnership with employees as a means of fostering personal and professional empowerment and, as a result, enabling higher levels of contribution.

Sets Parameters

Assists employees and teams in developing a clear understanding of both desired performance outcomes and the boundaries and conditions within which they are free to make choices about how they achieve those outcomes.

It is of great importance to the sailor to know the length of his line, though he cannot with it fathom all the depths of the ocean.
—JOHN LOCKE, *AN ESSAY CONCERNING HUMAN UNDERSTANDING*

A division chief in a county agency, when asked what her philosophy of her work was, responded, "I believe that people are basically good and that my role as a manager and leader is to facilitate that goodness in my people's work." Her statement reflects McGregor's now widely held Theory Y (1960). Most of us would probably agree that believing in people is the right starting point for managing and leading, but it is *only* a starting point. We cannot simply take the intrinsic goodness of people's motives and intentions for granted and assume these will automatically translate into excellent performance. The challenge for many manager-leaders is not to their ability to *believe* in people but to their ability to *facilitate* people's efforts in a way that combines focus and purpose with freedom and self-expression.

Take, for example, the story told to one of the authors at a training conference in 1986 by a consultant who, in preparing to leave for an extended business trip, entrusted the chore of caring for the lawn and garden to her teenage son. She was very specific about exactly what tasks to do and how to do them, to the point of writing up a lengthy checklist. On her return she was distressed to find the lawn and garden in poor condition despite her son's assurances that he had done everything on the checklist. She pondered the gap between expectations and results and experimented with a different approach prior to leaving on her next extended trip. "While I am gone," she advised her son, "you are in charge of maintaining a healthy lawn and garden." To ensure that her son understood what "healthy" meant, she outlined a few criteria about the length and color of the grass, the absence of weeds in the mulch, and so on. But she didn't write a checklist. To her delight, on her return she found both the lawn and garden in fine shape. When she queried her son about his efforts, however, she discovered that he had taken quite an entrepreneurial approach: he had hired out the mowing, he had rigged up a sprinkler on a timer, and so on. In other words, by being helped to focus on the desired outcome—the *what*—he had been able to be very creative and engaged about the *how* in a way that produced the desired results.

The lawn care story is a story of empowerment—that elusive concept that so many subscribe to but so few seem able to implement. This dilemma is not surprising. For although empowerment is clearly an idea whose time has come, implementing it remains a potentially treacherous proposition: there are many ways to "do" empowerment wrong. And when empowerment efforts are implemented poorly, they often produce the very effects that skeptics fear in the first place. For example, if a leader fails to communicate clear expectations and to define the parameters within which the individual can act, what is produced may be unacceptable and may discourage the leader from subsequent efforts to share authority and responsibility, even though it was the leader's deficiency in structuring the project that inadvertently undermined its success.

The following is a classic story of empowerment gone awry, despite everyone's good intentions. The leader of a church music ensemble decided to give one of its members, Sarita, responsibility for choosing the music for the Easter Sunday liturgy. Sarita was delighted to have this opportunity, as she had a strong interest in liturgical music and had been especially frustrated at the lack of aggressiveness on the leader's part to introduce new music at weekly liturgies. Sarita spent considerable time making her choices, selecting music that she felt would not only be fitting for the occasion but that, because they were new pieces, would revitalize the congregation.

On the evening of the Holy Week rehearsal, however, there was a palpable undercurrent of tension as the leader surreptitiously pulled various members aside on their arrival and urged them to protest Sarita's choices. "Tell her there's no way for us to learn all that new stuff," the leader whispered gruffly, "and besides, the congregation won't be able to participate if everything we sing is new." Meanwhile Sarita was enthusiastically announcing her program, only to see it meet with unanticipated resistance. Within moments she was feeling defeated and ready to give up. Although one member tried to encourage consensus building, it was too late. Sarita was too frustrated; her energy was gone, and one got the feeling that it would be a long time before she took on such a responsibility again.

Presumably the leader of the ensemble really did want to give Sarita the opportunity to take a leadership role. And, clearly, Sarita rose to the occasion with great energy and creativity. What the leader failed to do, however, was set parameters. If there were conditions that had to be met—such as that at least a portion of the musical selections be familiar to the congregation and to the music ensemble—then these needed to be identified up front. As it was, Sarita felt blindsided by critical information that was not made available until after the fact.

Did Sarita have some responsibility to *seek* such information as a way of ensuring that she would be aware of any parameters or constraints that might apply? Ideally, yes, in an environment where everyone understands the customer-supplier relationship (broadly defined). On the other hand, the burden is on the manager-leader to take the initiative in helping employees know where the boundaries lie.

In an organization these may be governed by highly specific constraints, such as budget, time frame, and a host of other considerations we now refer to as "customer requirements." Boundaries should also be governed at a more global level by the organization's core values and the shared vision the organization has agreed to pursue. Sometimes boundaries are determined by external conditions such as laws or precedents, and sometimes they arise from the manager's personal biases or preferences that may be no less valid because they are personal but that need to be acknowledged as such. For example, the music leader might have said to Sarita, "Including some new music is fine, but my strong preference would be to do some of our favorites from years past that everyone is familiar with." Manager-leaders should avoid, however, what author and consultant Rick Maurer labels "details to the 10th power"—direction that takes the form of "a massive pile of spirit-breaking directives," which has the effect of sapping rather than energizing (1992, p. 94).

Skeptics of empowerment fear the anarchy of scores of workers turned loose to "do their own thing." Rightly so, if employees are given carte blanche. Fears about empowerment are usually fears that have to do with loss of control. But empowerment is not really about loss of control in any ultimate sense; rather, it is about shifting the *locus* of control. In the old paradigm, control was externally imposed in a hierarchical system where the boss was boss, structures were imposed, and rules and policies were enforced. In the new paradigm of empowerment, control is largely internalized through individuals' commitment to a few governing ideas—such as the core values and the vision of the organization—and to a clear understanding of how their work can contribute to the realization of those ideas.

One of the most important roles effective manager-leaders serve is helping their employees connect the work they do as individuals to the organization as an interdependent system and to the larger purposes that system serves. Thus the focus is not so much on rules and policies (beyond those necessary to ensure that legal, security, safety, quality, and other such considerations are maintained) as on developing a shared sense of purpose and a mutual understanding of expectations and of the boundaries within which employees are free to make choices. By developing this sense of purpose and understanding, managers are focusing attention on the "what" and providing a context within which employees can take initiative in determining the *how*, thereby maximizing their contributions.

Re-Presents the Organization

Actively conveys the organization's and work unit's history, culture, missions, values, and visions; ensures that employees and teams understand how their efforts contribute to the larger purposes of the organization.

*The leader's job is to energetically mirror back to the institution how
it best thinks of itself.*

—DONALD KENNEDY, FORMER PRESIDENT OF STANFORD UNIVERSITY
(CITED IN KOUZES AND POSNER, 1987, P. 190)

As described in the previous section, the manager-leader's role in clarifying expectations and setting parameters relative to a specific job is crucial to ensuring that employees can function effectively day-to-day. If, however, our goal is to develop employees who are fully empowered to add value, the manager-leader's role in helping employees connect what they care about and what they are doing with the larger world of the organization is equally crucial. For example, a clear understanding of what the mission, values, and vision of the organization and the work unit are provides employees with a set of governing ideas that enable them to act in a way that is at once consistent and creative: *consistent* in the sense that choices and decisions reflect commitment to core values and a clear direction; *creative* in the initiative and self-expression with which that direction is pursued. Similarly, being aware of the history and culture of the organization helps employees to become grounded in what the organization is all about and to see how what each individual brings to the organization (experience, skills, talent, perspective, personal meaning, and so on) contributes to and enlarges the whole. In the absence of this kind of connection and perspective, of knowing how they and their work fit into a larger and—one hopes—more ennobling purpose, it is easy for employees to succumb to the inevitable tedium, hassles, frustrations, and, at times, *perceived* limitations of their jobs with a resulting loss of energy, spirit, and sense of opportunity.

Consider the case of the receptionist for a boat dealership that specialized in rare vintage boats. One evening a prospective buyer called in search of a specific model that he knew was a long shot. To his amazement, the dealership had the boat. He was astounded at his good fortune and told the receptionist that he was in the area and could be there by eight o'clock that evening. To his utter chagrin, the receptionist replied perfunctorily, "I'm sorry, sir, we close at seven." On his subsequent visit to the showroom, he relayed his frustration to the salesperson, who took it upon himself to follow up with the receptionist. "What is your job?" the salesperson asked the receptionist.

Somewhat predictably she replied, "I greet people when they come through the door, handle incoming phone calls, and do some typing."

"Your job," countered the salesperson, "is to *sell boats!* That's what we *do* here!"

The point is obvious: had the receptionist seen her job as selling boats and had she been more clear and engaged about the vision of accommodating the customer, she would surely have recognized the opportunity in this call and could have acted more creatively than just quoting the standard closing time. In other words, she would have been empowered to *think* and to *respond* rather than to proceed mindlessly on the basis of rules or routine. Could she have promised the customer that the showroom would stay open all night if need be? Of course not: that's where setting parameters comes in. But she could have offered to find out what, if anything, they could do to accommodate this customer's needs (for example, check with the sales staff to see if someone was able to stay late).

We have all dealt with employees who seem to miss the point of what they've been hired to do: the airline ticketing agent who is insolent in responding to our request for flight information, the waitress who challenges our dissatisfaction with a poorly prepared meal, the clerk who ignores our need for assistance in favor of continuing to chat with a coworker. Sometimes this kind of behavior is a result of individual human factors, such as attitude, temperament, or style; personal problems; or just the proverbial bad day. Often, however, employees have not been encouraged to see beyond the immediate activity of their jobs to the higher purposes their efforts might serve or the legacy they have been bequeathed. As a result, employees may have little stake in their jobs and lack the sense that what they do at work and how they do it does have an impact—that it has the potential to be important, enduring, and meaningful for them personally, for their organizations, and for society.

The power of understanding this kind of connection is wonderfully illustrated by the well-known story of the man who passed by a construction site and asked of a laborer, "What is that you are doing?"

"Why, as anyone can see, I'm just laying brick—one on top of another," the laborer idly replied. The observer posed the same question to a second laborer, who answered somewhat more thoughtfully, "I'm building a wall." A third laborer, however, responded to the very same question with a truly inspired sense of purpose and role: "I'm helping to create a cathedral!"

In today's complex and dynamic organizations it is up to the manager-leader to help employees see the cathedral as well as the bricks. In general, we are requiring that our employees juggle more and more responsibilities as resources diminish and workloads increase. We need, as well, more and more of their energy, thought, and creativity, which are easily dulled by too tight a focus on simply completing routine tasks from one moment to the next or responding to multiple demands. It thus becomes incumbent upon the manager-leader to make employees aware of what needs to be front-and-center in both the long and the short term, and to communicate those messages in a way that allows employees to internalize and act on their importance. The organization's and work unit's vision, for example, ought to be part of an ongoing conversation, so that it serves as a reference point for decisions, goals and priorities, assignments, and resource allocation, and so that the vision itself evolves in a way that is truly shared. In addition, the organization's identity should be fostered and celebrated through stories and commemorations that allow employees to develop a sense of history, belonging, and loyalty.

Arguing against the trend of making shareholder interests the primary focus of a company, John Kay (1997, p. 133), director-designate of Oxford University's new School of Management Studies, makes the point that a business consists of more than its physical assets: "A company is its history, its structure of relationships, its reputation. These are the things that allow the company to add value." Kay asserts that the essence of any company is its "corporate personality" and concludes that the key to GE's sustained effectiveness has been its ability to maintain its identity and apply it "in an array of changing businesses and changing environments" (p. 134).

This same capability served Johnson & Johnson well when it was faced in 1989 with the Tylenol crisis. Committed to its longstanding credo of putting the customer first, Johnson & Johnson pulled all Tylenol capsules from the U. S. market and launched a massive public information campaign—at a cost estimated at $100 million—when it was determined that some bottles had been laced with cyanide. What Johnson & Johnson lost in dollars it more than regained in public confidence.

More recently, State Farm Insurance Companies has been put to the leadership test of re-presenting the organization at a defining moment in its history. In the spring of 1997, State Farm corporate headquarters received an anonymous letter alleging wrongdoing related to the company's Matching Gift program, whereby associates' donations to eligible colleges and universities are matched up to $1000. The scheme involved an attempt by one agent to involve several other agents in misrepresenting themselves as donors to a single institution, using cashier's checks that he had purchased, and applying for matching funds amounting to a total of $50,000. Following an initial investigation, contracts with fifty-three agents across twelve regions were terminated subject to appeal. As a result of further review of each case by an appeal board and the president of the company, the terminations of twenty-four agents were upheld and twenty-nine rescinded based on evidence of an ability to rebuild a relationship of trust with the individual.

Beyond taking the very real and visible leadership action of terminating dishonorable members of the company's sales force, president Ed Rust made a point of communicating, via e-mail (April 25, 1997), the significance of this incident to every agent and employee at State Farm. Citing the uniqueness of this situation in the company's history, he spoke of his endeavor to deal with the problem in a way that was consistent with the company's core values of honesty, integrity, and mutual good faith. He quoted the pronouncements of the founder of State Farm, George Mecherle, on the difference between character and reputation: " 'Character is what we are. Reputation is what others think we are. And while it's well that we have a favorable reputation, it's imperative that our character be above reproach so that we invite the confidence necessary to success.' " Rust closed his letter by reiterating that the standards by which State Farm operates "go beyond the letter of the law," that character is the company's "most valuable asset," and that character *is* its "future." By reaffirming the company's core values and by linking the company's future with the legacy of its past, Rust was helping people make the connection between their individual actions and the collective identity they participate in. He was reminding them, as well, of the privilege of that shared identity and of the responsibility and honor that must attend to it.

In *Images of Organization*, Gareth Morgan (1986, p. 135) argues that "organization rests in shared systems of meaning, and hence in the shared interpretive schemes that create and recreate that meaning." Morgan views organizational culture—the guiding ideologies, values, and beliefs as communicated through language, norms, ceremonies, folklore, and other social practices—as the " 'normative glue' " that holds the organization together (p. 135). So, for example, the many stories of Nordstrom's exceptional customer service are now the stuff of legend; hearing the tale of how Nordstrom took a return on snow tires—which they don't even sell—may make a cost accountant's blood run cold, but it is a part of the mythology that gives Nordstrom the aura of being larger than life.

Robert Haas (1993, p. 4), CEO of Levi-Strauss, observes that "the most visible differences between the corporation of the future and its present-day counterpart will not be the products they make or the equipment they use—but who will be working, why they will be working, and what work will mean to them." If this is true, then one of the most important functions the manager-leader can perform is that of shaping a context to which people can respond because it has meaning for them. To accomplish this, Juanita Brown and David Isaacs (1996–1997), senior affiliates at the MIT Center for Organizational Learning, emphasize that manager-leaders will need to dedicate time and attention to telling stories—including compelling scenarios of the future—framing a common language, and evoking imagery and metaphors as a way of translating organizational experience into shared meaning.

We frequently talk about tapping the unrealized potential of employees, typically referring to skills, ideas, talents, and the like. As manager-leaders we must also seek to tap the *meaning*, often latent and unformed, that lies within individuals, and to provide a context that allows this meaning to be transformed collectively for the larger purposes of the enterprise.

Expands Access to Information and New Knowledge

Establishes an information-rich environment in which employees and teams are encouraged to understand relevant business factors, make connections, develop insights, share learning, and respond dynamically to rapidly changing conditions.

In an economy where the only certainty is uncertainty, the one sure source of lasting competitive advantage is knowledge.
—IKUJIRO NONAKA, "THE KNOWLEDGE-CREATING COMPANY," *HARVARD BUSINESS REVIEW*

In addition to ensuring that employees have a sure grasp of what the organization is all about and where it wants to go, manager-leaders must also be willing to share information with employees in a completely new way. Historically, managers have intentionally withheld access to information—sometimes as a way of protecting the integrity of the information, sometimes as a way of protecting the employees, but perhaps most often as a means of maintaining power over others. However, limiting the information employees have to work with renders them less able to contribute fully and more likely to misjudge or question management's intentions.

Without information, employees are often unaware of business pressures, risk factors, and what the company is really up against; the myopic view that results may cause employees to entertain unrealistic expectations and to feel betrayed when they are not met, and to assume that it is up to management to make the enterprise work. A case in point is the Alameda Naval Depot. In the popular video, *Excellence in the Public Sector* (Starr and Cram, 1989), Tom Peters facetiously describes this unit as "eighth out of six" on virtually all measures at the point that it was threatened with closure. In a desperate effort to save the unit, management tried a radical approach: they went to the workers and told the bad news like it was. Instead of sparing employees, they leveled with them—and succeeded in pulling off a remarkable turnaround (reaching second out of six across the board) in only six months. By providing information, managers helped employees recognize their personal stake in the survival of the agency. Employees became motivated to respond to the crisis in a way that produced extraordinary results.

Without information, employees are often unable to understand or accept the decisions of management or to make good decisions themselves. Without information, wrong assumptions proliferate and the rumor mill kicks into high gear. Without information, people rely on their own best guesses to figure things out, or they make up what they need to know.

Most important, without information, people are confined within the boundaries of a job at a time in our society when some believe that the traditional job is quickly becoming a "social artifact." According to William Bridges (1994), the conditions that created the need for jobs at the time of the Industrial Revolution no longer apply. Instead of the routine, repetitive tasks that were easily isolated and packaged as jobs in larger manufacturing organizations, much of today's workplace is best characterized as a "field" of highly complex, nonroutine, ever-changing "work situations" (p. 64). What will it take to make "de-jobbed" organizations work? From his study of companies that have begun to make the shift effectively, Bridges (1994) derived a recipe for success that requires giving workers the information they need in order to make the operating decisions that managers used to make and to understand the kind of high-level business and financial issues that used to be the sole province of owners and executives.

In examining the role of information in systems, Margaret Wheatley (1992) concludes that systems become self-organizing—that is, able to grow and develop in response to external realities through the creation of temporary structures—as they are "perturbed" by information. Wheatley (1996) also speculates that the kind of self-organization we have observed in times of crisis—whether in our homes, in our neighborhoods, or on the job—is a function of an enormous amount of information passing among highly intimate relationships—the kind of spontaneous synchronization that flocking birds are able to achieve. Information, according to Wheatley, is the fundamental organizing principle. As such it ought to flow freely (Wheatley and Kellner-Rogers, 1994).

So instead of being guardians of information, manager-leaders need to find ways of *creating access* to all kinds of information and of thinking differently about where knowledge lies and what it means to "create" knowledge. Ikujiro Nonaka (1991), professor of management at the Institute for Business Research of Hitotsubashi University in Tokyo, points out that Western managers are conditioned by a long and deeply held view of knowledge as something formal and systematic, consisting of data, valued by quantifiable metrics, and arrived at through "information processing" (p. 96).

Many of our most successful Japanese competitors, on the other hand, have become distinguished for their ability to serve customers, capitalize on new markets, and develop emerging technologies precisely because of the way they manage the creation of new knowledge. Their secret lies in the way they go beyond information processing to making available the more subjective, intuitive, "tacit" knowledge of individual employees as a resource for the entire organization. Images, symbols, and analogies are valued as sources of inspiration—no less powerful because the inspiration is serendipitous—for new products. And shared self-knowledge—a collective sense of what the organization is, where it is heading, and what it wants to create—is valued as the basis of innovation. In this kind of company, the creation of knowledge is not a specialized activity but a way of behaving that involves the company and everyone in it in a "nonstop process of personal and organizational self-renewal" (Nonaka, 1991, p. 98).

A case in point: in 1985, when Matsushita was having difficulty developing a bread-making machine that would bake bread evenly and had analyzed the problem exhaustively with no success, they moved to a novel approach: they apprenticed software developer Ikuko Tanaka to the chief baker at the Osaka Hotel, renowned for baking the best bread in Osaka. After observing, over a period of months, the baker's unique twisting technique for kneading the dough, Tanaka worked with project engineers to design ribbing inside the cylinder of the machine that would replicate the twist method. This unique feature resulted in a product that achieved record sales in its first year on the market (Nonaka, 1991).

This example makes several points about sources of knowledge and the ways in which new knowledge can be created within an organization. For example, the chief baker's knowledge of how to knead bread was tacit, that is, the kind of internalized know-how a master craftsperson has "at his fingertips" or "in her bones" but may not be able to articulate. Explicit knowledge, on the other hand, is articulated knowledge. New knowledge is created when either of these types of knowledge is transmitted, combined, or extended in some way.

For example, tacit knowledge can be transmitted as tacit knowledge through observation, imitation, and practice. Explicit knowledge can be created from explicit knowledge through the synthesis of discrete bits of data into a larger whole, as in the case of an analysis or report. More powerful knowledge creation occurs when tacit knowledge is converted to explicit knowledge—such as when the Matsushita developer was able to articulate what she had internalized through observation. Explicit knowledge can be made tacit (Nonaka, 1991) as someone internalizes information in a way that develops or extends it—when, for example, a company vice president uses the results of available research to develop a new approach to performance evaluation, or when a reader of this book uses data from the personal assessments to initiate significant behavior change.

Notwithstanding the importance of an information-rich environment, an obvious problem all of us face in this age of information proliferation and instantaneous communication is that of becoming overloaded with more data than we can manage or make useful. How to cope? This is a challenge for which simple time management and prioritizing skills are probably not sufficient; we also need to take into account the overarching values, vision, and strategy of the organization, as well as specific performance expectations. On the other hand, if we limit ourselves only to information that appears to have immediate relevance, we constrain our ability to make novel connections from seemingly unrelated things—a source of "new" knowledge and the well-spring of creativity and innovation. Somehow we must learn to manage information in a way that couples what we think we need with what allows us to make discoveries.

Cultivates Diverse Resources

Views individual differences as potential strengths and seeks to understand, appreciate, and tap the unique capabilities of each person.

*Grown-ups love figures. When you tell them that you have made a new friend,
they never ask you any questions about essential matters. They never say to you,
"What does his voice sound like? What games does he love best? Does he collect
butterflies?" Instead, they demand: "How old is he? How many brothers has he?
How much does he weigh? How much money does his father make?" Only from
these figures do they think they have learned anything about him.*

—SAINT-EXUPERY, *THE LITTLE PRINCE*

In recent years the issue of diversity has gained sudden prominence in organizations, due in large part to the rapidly changing demographics of both the workforce and the customer base, as well as to the increasing liability organizations and
individual managers face in the areas of discrimination and harassment. These
trends have spawned a proliferation of sensitivity training programs intended to
raise consciousness, bridge gender and cultural gaps, and reform offensive or unacceptable behavior. The approach, often packaged in a half-day format, goes something like this: at a time when both our workforce and our external customers are
becoming more culturally diverse, it is important that we come to terms with
diversity as a source of potential strength and competitive advantage rather than
allow our differences to result in the friction, misunderstanding, and divisiveness
that ultimately diminish productivity and profits.

The intended effect of such programs is that, armed with an understanding
of diversity issues, the opportunity to exchange perspectives across genders or
races, and some tools for avoiding such classic blunders as sexist language, offensive jokes, or stereotyping, we will at best collectively transform our organizations
into meccas of harmony, equality, and mutual respect, or at the least avoid lawsuits. The effort is good as far as it goes, although it doesn't go nearly far enough.
Yet it's not uncommon to hear from someone who has sponsored or been through
such a program, "Oh, we've *done* diversity."

The myth implicit in such a statement is that a single program can undo our
human tendency to view what is different as inferior or threatening, and can undo
the generations of social and cultural programming that have reinforced that tendency in very profound ways. Diversity is a highly complex social, moral, and
organizational issue at this time in our history; despite our efforts over the last several decades to come to terms with diversity, it continues to confound us.

Start with the cultural metaphor that has guided our evolution: America as
the great melting pot—a vision of assimilation in which value was placed on fitting in and minimizing or altogether suppressing differences. Then consider the
monumental and uneasy shifts we as a nation have struggled to make in recent
years from *discriminating against* to *tolerating* differences. In the sixties the civil rights
movement introduced major cultural upheaval in its efforts to end discrimination
and achieve freedom and equality for blacks. Then the women's movement gained

momentum, and since that time we have been subject to any number of efforts by disenfranchised or underrepresented groups to claim their due. As a result of these phenomena we have been forced to come to terms with a long history of oppression or neglect of those who were different, particularly those of a different race or gender. Because these movements were driven by such fundamental issues as equality and fair treatment, we focused initially on what we had in common as the rationale for securing guarantees of basic rights for all; differences were regarded as something that we *had* to learn to live with, painful as that might be (and it was and continues to be very painful for many). Yet, notwithstanding that the dust has hardly settled from the commotion of those times and that, in some quarters, only negligible progress can be said to have been made on those agendas, the conversation today has moved to a whole new level: now we talk about *valuing* diversity, which involves not tolerating but *celebrating* differences as the basis for a richness and strength that sameness does not afford.

These kinds of shifts require deep personal growth work for virtually all individuals—work that can only be accomplished at a very internal level and through a sustained effort over time, for "We have all been raised with prejudice," as one manager puts it, or, in the words of another, "We are all recovering racists" (Copeland-Briggs Productions, 1990). And to some extent, what can be said for racism can also be said for other kinds of prejudice. So we find ourselves today, almost a half-century later, still deeply immersed in the psychic chaos of a collective and wrenching transition that shows no signs of abatement: there is confusion and disorientation and disagreement; there is bashing and bullying and blaming; there is guilt and backlash.

Attempts to redress the ills of the past—such as affirmative action—have complicated matters further with quotas and charges of reverse discrimination. And then there's the recent preoccupation with political correctness, an attempt to arrive at socially acceptable ways of speaking that in objectifying phenomena can rob things of their identity or become impossible to get right. Witness the following scenario from an article in *Training* (Gordon, 1992, p. 29):

> Joe learns that he must never forget himself and use a term like "salesman" or "chairman" around Betty, and he must always refer to Maya as a "woman of color," to Diana as "black," and to Sam as "Chinese American" rather than as "Asian American." Betty, Maya, Diana and Sam learn to call Joe a European American but never to call Bob one because Bob thinks the term is extraordinarily silly, although he must never say so or laugh at it because that would transgress against Joe's diversity.

Gordon (1992, p. 29) comments: "These are not people who will like one another, trust one another, be comfortable with one another or do any creative work together. These are porcupines, bristling, with hyperacute sensitivities, circling one another warily and on tiptoe."

This raises the critical point that valuing diversity does not equate with political correctness, equal employment opportunity, affirmative action, or training programs. Nor is it up to the personnel department to achieve diversity through changing the company's hiring statistics. The word *valuing* implies something far beyond getting the words or the numbers right.

Truly valuing or cultivating diversity in today's workplace requires a very different approach, a way of thinking and operating that does not rely on a self-protective or defensive posture as a hedge against lawsuits and is not limited to protected classes, but instead embraces and acts on a vision of full inclusion. Cultivating diverse resources means recognizing and appreciating the unique gifts, talents, and potential that each individual—young or old; white, black, or Asian; male or female; able bodied or disabled; gay or straight—brings to the organization, and consciously seeking to create an environment in which these capacities can be most fully realized. The fundamental diversity issue, which is often overlooked as a result of the focus on subcultural differences, is that *all* individuals differ as a result of family values, temperament, personality type, work style, professional orientation, and the like.

Making the workplace hospitable to all is, to some extent, everyone's job. But manager-leaders bear an added responsibility, since *valuing* diversity and *managing* diversity are not the same thing. R. Roosevelt Thomas Jr., president of the American Institute for Managing Diversity at Morehouse College, goes so far as to say that learning to manage diversity is really about learning to manage in the first place, considering that until recently, managing consisted mainly of enforcing a corporate "mold"—how to look, what to do, what to say, and so on—and rewarding those who fit that mold. Managing diversity, says Thomas, is not ultimately a moral or social issue: "You can learn to respect each other, you can like each other, you can minimize racism and sexism, you can have better interpersonal relations. You can do all that and still not know how to manage diversity" (cited in Gordon, 1992, p. 24). Rather, managing diversity is a business issue: "It's about human performance. It's about making a profit. It's about remaining competitive" (p. 24).

Manager-leaders who want to create a work environment in which diversity is truly valued must begin by examining the subtle or not-so-subtle ways in which they respond to others—and not just others who are different in obvious ways (gender or color) but *all* others. Needless to say, these differences pose increasingly complicated challenges for managers. For the differences that represent the potential strength of diversity also mean that there are fewer common frames of reference. Although it has always been a mistake to stereotype, whatever similarities might have been assumed in an environment that was more homogeneous and in a time that was less complex, no longer apply. Nor is it sufficient for managers to school themselves in the characteristics typically associated with various cultures, because in the global village that we are fast becoming, there may well be more variations *within* subcultural groups than across them. Manager-leaders must go well beyond becoming sensitive to cultural differences: they need to learn about and respond to *individuals* regardless of their cultural origin, gender, age, and so on, and regardless of the fact that, as Thomas reminds us, many of them "aren't like you and don't aspire to be like you" (cited in Gordon, 1992, p. 23). In this regard James Autry (1991) challenges the long-standing management wisdom that no one deserves special treatment. On the contrary, claims Autry, *everyone* should get special treatment as a way of acknowledging their uniqueness.

Managing diversity means learning to maintain the critical tension between the need to honor individual differences and the need to create a cohesive whole, and between the need to deal with people both as individuals and as members of groups. For example, looking for opportunities to promote minorities and women takes into account an imbalance in the current system that needs to be addressed if we are to achieve organizations that are more representative of our society. This is an example of taking the special needs of a group into account. It is equally important, however, not to allow sensitivity to a group to interfere with a manager's ability to provide the kind of honest, direct feedback, coaching, or even corrective action that individuals, regardless of their race or gender, need and deserve.

It is common today to suggest that we will have bridged cultural gaps when we become truly "color-blind," a metaphor that speaks most obviously to race but that can be extended to other kinds of differences as well. In one sense *color-blind* is right: we need to become able to see past superficial markers that, based on inaccurate stereotypes, may predispose us in a way that limits our ability to perceive, value, and cultivate the uniqueness of the individual. On the other hand, valuing diversity is not about color-blindness at all, but in fact just the opposite: it's about seeing more clearly the various colors of diverse individuals and cultures and groups, and appreciating the way each contributes to a veritable garden of human and organizational possibility. The challenge for manager-leaders, as Gordon poses it, is "Can we achieve *unum* without asking the *pluribus* in the melting pot to do so much melting?" (1992, pp. 23–24).

Promotes Continuous Learning

Actively encourages employees and teams to pursue new ideas, new ways of thinking, and appropriate behavior changes in a variety of ways (for example, formal training, on-the-job development, mentoring, reading, feedback, and reflection); creates an environment that fosters experimentation and learning from experience collectively as well as individually.

When old words die out on the tongue, new melodies break forth from the heart; and where the old tracks are lost, new country is revealed with its wonders.
— RABINDRANATH TAGORE, *GITANJALI*

Earlier in this chapter we talked about a shift away from the traditional job, which was based on the notion of work that could be divided into clearly defined, repetitive tasks, to "a field of work needing to be done" (Bridges, 1994, p. 64). Bridges says that in such an environment individuals need to reevaluate their assumptions and strategies, focusing their resources, both individually and collectively, on doing what needs to be done and in changing as what needs to be done changes. In the de-jobbed organization, according to Bridges, hiring will be less about filling slots than about finding people who can function effectively in the absence of cues derived from job descriptions and who can move from project to project, performing a variety of tasks as they present themselves. The shift Bridges describes clearly requires continuous learning, as workers are forced to become more vendor-minded—thinking of the company as their customer and selling not so much formal credentials as their ability to maintain a learning curve consistent with the changing demands of markets, products, and rapidly evolving technologies.

What Bridges describes at the level of the individual worker plays itself out at a more global level for organizations: in the face of high-velocity change and intensifying competition, there is only one way for an organization to remain a viable player in the marketplace: by learning continuously, staying current with changes that range from the highly technical (for example, new technology or new developments in the field), to new concepts and processes (what a self-organizing system might look like or how to reengineer a work process), to more subtle changes (emerging trends and new directions). Given the unprecedented challenges of the era that is upon us, the need to learn continuously would seem unquestionable, yet many factors in the workplace can undermine our ability to do so.

Take, for example, our obsession with the bottom line and with the kind of frenetic activity that is generally associated with high productivity. When was the last time employees in your organization were encouraged—or, for that matter, *permitted*—to read or study or simply reflect at their desks or engage with coworkers in a spontaneous dialogue at the break station about organizational issues? A reluctance to value the critical if sometimes "inefficient" work of learning is borne out by the experience of one of the authors in her work as a meeting facilitator. In the interest of results, almost invariably the participants' focus in a meeting is on satisfying the agenda and getting to closure regardless of what unresolved issues deserve further reflection or exploration before a sustainable solution can be achieved. So unless several action items appear on a flipchart within the first half hour of the meeting, people begin to feel that they are "off-track" or wasting their time. Similarly, in her efforts to introduce the process of dialogue to organizations, this author has found on more than one occasion that even when the heart and soul of the organization begin to be revealed in such a forum, a check-in with the participants at the end of the dialogue reveals that many in the group feel frustrated that "we haven't gotten anywhere."

The other author, who facilitates a distance learning program for high-potential managers of a Fortune 500 company, has observed a similar phenomenon in the way some of the participants have handled learning activities related to the program. Because the program extends over a period of ten months and requires approximately ten hours per week on independent assignments, participants have had to make decisions about how, where, and when they would complete these assignments. Initially some members of the group made a point of doing their "classwork" at home, assuming that to do it during business hours when their staff were devoting themselves to company business would send the wrong message and create resentment. Others, however, approached the situation in just the opposite way, believing that *not* to incorporate these learning activities into their normal workday was to send the message that this kind of learning was not a high priority. For the first group there was also the issue of balancing work and home life if, in addition to long days at the office, all the requirements of the program had to be satisfied during what should have been family time. Ultimately both groups determined that what was important was not whether or not they worked on learning assignments during the workday but *how* they involved their employees in the learning process. They found, in fact, that employees wanted to know what the program was about and what their manager was learning. When managers began to include their staff in demonstrations of their new learning and in dialogues about some of the issues related to their learning—including the difficulty of finding time for completing assignments—employees often began to participate in the process at some level by expanding their knowledge base, becoming more efficient as teams, or picking up some of the manager's work to buy him or her more time for program-related efforts.

Peter Senge (1994), author of *The Fifth Discipline* and one of the foremost proponents of learning organization theory and practice, observes that in trying to create learning organizations we confront a core paradox: at a time that calls for deep shifts in our mental models and organizational infrastructure—changes that can take years to accomplish—our organizations are set up to do just the opposite: focus on the trivial and the short-term, and relegate learning to the human resources department via a menu of training modules. Certainly training is a part of learning, but it is only a part, and in today's environment it is probably not the most important part.

What Senge and others mean when they talk about a "learning organization" is a place where learning occurs collectively as well as individually and where a "deep learning cycle" (Senge, 1994, p. 21) is embedded in the infrastructure of the organization so that learning becomes systemic. More specifically, Senge (1990a) proposes five disciplines—mental models, personal mastery, systems thinking, shared vision, and team learning—as the cornerstones of a learning organization. Others who have built on Senge's work concur with the need to go beyond training modules and traditional skill-building activities in the way we think about learning.

Harvard professor David Garvin (1993), for example, claims that continuous learning is essential to continuous improvement, a "basic truth" that he believes most companies have failed to grasp. "Solving a problem, introducing a product, and reengineering a process," observes Garvin, "all require seeing the world in a new light and acting accordingly" (p. 78). Garvin believes that the term *learning organization* necessarily implies the modification of behavior in response to new ideas, knowledge, and insights. Thus, although some organizations have been effective at acquiring new knowledge, they have not successfully integrated this knowledge into their work processes; as a result, the potential for lasting improvement remains unrealized. True learning organizations, on the other hand, regularly engage in systematic problem solving, experimentation, and learning from their own and others' experiences; they create an infrastructure that supports these activities, builds them into day-to-day operations, and ensures that new learning is disseminated throughout the organization. Garvin (1993) credits the success of these practices to the establishment of a particular mind-set that expresses itself in attention to accuracy and detail, in disciplined thinking, and in probing, testing, and analysis.

Should we have any doubt about the importance of continuous learning, we have only to look at the fate of organizations that have failed to learn. A study by Royal Dutch/Shell found that a full one-third of Fortune 500 companies listed in 1970 had disappeared by 1983 (Senge, 1990a). Senge attributes the premature demise of organizations to organizational learning disabilities that prevent the organization from adapting, changing, and growing in response to its environment. The same Shell study also identified several companies that had demonstrated remarkable longevity, owing to their ability to run "experiments in the margin" (p. 288) and in so doing create new knowledge and new opportunities for growth.

Shell itself is testimony to the power of learning. The weakest of the big seven oil companies in the early seventies, it emerged as one of the strongest following the OPEC oil crisis. The key to Shell's success was an innovative form of planning as learning called "scenario analysis," which required operating managers to envision a variety of scenarios for the future and to consider the management implications of each rather than assume that the future would be an extension of the past. This process helped managers test their mental models and make explicit various sets of assumptions as a means of preparing for discontinuous change. When the oil crisis became a reality, Shell was poised to respond with strategies they had already anticipated (Senge, 1990a). This example bears out Senge's belief that we need to engage in not just adaptive learning, which enables us to cope, but also generative learning, which enables us to create.

The conditions Garvin (1993) sets forth for collective learning and the Royal Dutch/Shell experience (Senge, 1990a) suggest that manager-leaders must

- Encourage and make safe the kind of risk taking associated with experimentation: employees are unlikely to try things if they fear reprisals for unsuccessful trials or if the organization is unduly focused on results.
- Free up employees for reflection, dialogue, and assessment, and model openness and attentive listening to customer feedback and to the best practices of other organizations.
- Provide training in tools, skills, and methodologies that enable critical, disciplined thinking and a consistent approach.
- Seek to institutionalize structures and mechanisms that support ongoing learning; in the interest of seeing that learning becomes a way of life, manager-leaders must be willing to invest time in processes that don't yield short-term results.
- Develop appropriate measures for evaluating learning, regardless of quantifiable outcomes.
- Articulate guiding ideas and model the norms and behaviors that will transform the culture into a learning organization (Senge, 1996).
- Examine their own management practices with respect to how they foster or inhibit learning.
- Create subcultures—virtual laboratories for sustainable experiments that test the relationship of new learning capabilities to business results (Senge, 1996).
- Function as the *ecologist for the organization,* according to Phil Carroll, CEO of Shell Oil; that is, recognize the company as a living system connected to the larger system within which it is embedded (cited in Senge, 1996, p. 53).

Juanita Brown (1994) encourages manager-leaders to become "knowledge gardeners," cultivating the generation of knowledge within individuals and the sharing of it among individuals. The point is to "actively manage the learning process to ensure that it occurs by design rather than by chance" (Garvin, 1993, p. 81) and to ensure that people are able to move from superficial knowledge to deep understanding.

Simply put, all of the aforementioned requirements constitute what Senge (1990b) refers to as the "new work" of the manager-leader as designer, teacher, and steward. *Designer* in the sense of creating the kind of organizational architecture that supports ongoing learning in the service of shared purpose, values, and vision. *Teacher* in the sense of facilitating employees' ability to become increasingly clear about, and to focus attention on, current reality and their own mental models at a level that reveals the underlying causes of today's problems and new possibilities for shaping the future. And *steward*, the most subtle of all, in the sense of serving both the larger, ennobling purposes and values of the enterprise as well as the people who, in a learning organization, have committed to those values and share ownership for their success.

Facilitates Contribution

Expands capability of employees and teams to contribute to the organization in a variety of ways, ranging from providing input on decisions to owning and developing their work; provides management direction and support appropriate to what individual employees and teams require in order to continuously improve performance.

[I]n a world-class organization, everybody in the company has to be thinking every day about ways to make the business better.
—WILLIAM BYHAM, *ZAPP! THE LIGHTNING OF EMPOWERMENT*

Recent discoveries about the behavior of the natural universe and, more specifically, the emergence of chaos theory have prompted people like Meg Wheatley, Erich Jantsch, and Ikujiro Nonaka to focus considerable attention on the idea of self-organizing systems. Self-organization, the ability to organize from within, is a phenomenon evident in nature that suggests a new model for human systems. For example, we have all witnessed the spectacle of hundreds of individual birds flocking—taking flight in a way that is marvelously aligned and synchronized, without any apparent external structure or control. Somehow each bird is able to respond to local cues moment-to-moment in a way that produces an overall pattern that has focus, integrity, and direction. Similarly, a certain species of termite, when in proximity with others of its kind, changes its behavior from the simple boring of holes to the building of elaborate towers complete with arches and bridges and positioned to take advantage of prevailing breezes for ventilation, all without an organizational chart or layers of managers. The obviously important differences between termites or birds and humans notwithstanding, it is useful to consider how such self-organizing behavior might provide insights for human organizations. Clearly these examples of self-organization, which appear to be highly efficient and productive, involve all members of the community in a highly dynamic effort that depends on access to information and on *full* participation.

Yet as promising as this new theory may sound, the prospect of moving from the leader-as-hero model to a more shared experience of leadership in organizations poses threats to both managers and employees. The manager fears loss of identity and control, and employees often fear heightened levels of responsibility and accountability. After all, what is comforting about the leader-as-hero, if we put ourselves in the employees' place, is that the leader shoulders the burden *for* us. In trusting the leader to get it right on our behalf, we absolve ourselves of personal responsibility for making choices and decisions and for initiating action, as the following story illustrates so well.

Having finished her grocery shopping at a local food chain that touts its consumer advocacy program, one of the authors approached the checkout counter only to find a large case of windshield wiper fluid obstructing her access to the conveyor belt—so much so that she was forced to lob her items onto the belt. When she reached the cashier she offered the young man some customer feedback.

"You know, that windshield wiper fluid is in a very bad place. I could barely reach the conveyor belt to unload my groceries."

"Oh, I know," he replied. "You're right—it's a terrible idea. And they want to put them at every checkout stand!"

"Well, can you please tell your manager," the author rejoined. "Because it's sure not going to get me to buy the fluid. It just annoys me."

"Oh, they won't listen to me," he said. "They'll just think I'm trying to get out of work."

"Would it help if I talked to the manager?" she asked.

"Oh, yeah. That's what you should do."

So she did. But, after hearing her complaint, the manager replied, "Oh, I agree. It's a dumb idea. But they [upper management] won't listen to me."

"But you are the store manager, right?"

"Yeah, sure, but they won't listen to me."

She was finally encouraged to put her complaint in writing—"then maybe they'll listen."

The question is, how many "theys" are there? And the answer? Always one more!

So in redefining the role of the leader in organizations we are also calling for employees to claim their autonomy, resisting the temptation to automatically shunt responsibility to the anonymous "they." But we should not be surprised when we meet with resistance.

In a video based on AT&T's attempt to implement empowerment in its retail stores, vice president Bob Martin observes that he assumed people would jump at the chance to have more power if they were offered it. But just the opposite occurred: many employees, if not most, were reluctant to operate outside existing boundaries (Jackson, 1991).

There are many reasons people fear becoming empowered—some personal and some organizational, some legitimate and some, for the most part, unfounded. Personal obstacles to empowerment (or to owning one's contribution more significantly) often have to do with highly individual needs for safety and security. Some people never move beyond dependency on others for structure and direction. These employees want rules and want someone else to make them. Some people accept hierarchy as desirable and view deferring to higher authority as a way of demonstrating respect, a value they have been taught to observe since early childhood. Others eschew the concomitant responsibility of empowerment and prefer to limit their involvement on the job; their view is that they are paid to do a particular job, and they have no interest in taking on continuous improvement, relationship-building across functions, or the larger concerns of the organization, thank you. And there are those who are just plain cynical enough to assume that there is nothing to be gained—and maybe something to be lost—by investing themselves at a higher level.

This latter point brings us to some of the organizational reasons people resist greater involvement. Probably the most significant is that mechanisms to gain employees' participation are often lacking or are implemented so poorly, so capriciously, or with such little staying power that people don't take them seriously. "This, too, shall pass" is the common plaint. And because people frequently don't trust such initiatives—either to survive or to be carried out in good faith—they are reluctant to take on the disruption or the risk of making the required efforts or changes in their own behavior. If, from past experience, I have reason to expect that initiatives come and go, I am hardly motivated to do more than wait for the latest program to spend itself and disappear from the reader screen. People brought up in a hierarchical world also have very real fears when suddenly they are encouraged to do what amounts to killing formerly sacred cows. Without the proper groundwork and without repeated, visible indications of support (both of which are rare in the authors' experience), it's hard for people to believe that an invitation to think outside the box, to speak up about issues and concerns, to provide authentic feedback, to challenge management, or to take risks is for real.

Correctly or not, people assume that these kinds of overtures are gimmicks or that the first time they cross a manager, make a mistake, or take a risk that fails, they will pay a price—too high a price at a time when there is very little job security. Finally, some people limit their contribution because they lack confidence in their own abilities; as a way of staying safe on their terms, they prefer to do just what they already know or what someone else directs them to do.

Much of this resistance reflects the long-standing patriarchal character of most organizations, whose hierarchical structure separated thinking from doing and thus fostered what were essentially parent-child relationships. People were taken care of by the organization in return for doing what they were told. This was the fundamental exchange, with its implicit expectations: management would figure things out, and staff would implement what came down to them.

Today, however, organizations must respond quickly and creatively to a highly volatile marketplace; they must customize products and services; they cannot afford to be encumbered with bureaucracy and with employees who are conditioned not to think or take initiative. So organizations today are striking a "new deal" in which employees take responsibility for finding ways to add value on an ongoing basis, for learning continuously, and for regarding the company as a customer rather than as a caretaker. In short, organizations are seeking to become less paternal and more partner-like in relation to their employees, and to foster adult-adult relationships in which everyone shares responsibility—and accountability—for the success of the enterprise. The idea of working "smarter not harder" implies that all workers will need to become not just more efficient but more savvy as well.

Accomplishing this shift will not be easy; employees who have been insulated from critical information about forces affecting the business will have difficulty appreciating the urgency of the situation and the need for fundamental change. And, despite their best intentions, managers may miss the mark in trying to involve others. Chris Argyris (1994) exposes this delusion of empowerment in "Good Communication That Blocks Learning." He describes the current management practice of soliciting employees' ideas about what needs to be improved in the organization and then assuming full responsibility for developing and implementing solutions. Apparently we have learned to allow and even encourage participation, but only to a point—a point that stops far short of ownership, which we may wish for in our employees but may be systematically undermining by our own behavior, however well-intended. The net effect is that something as encompassing as empowerment is reduced to token efforts, which clearly will not suffice.

Organizations today are leaner, meaner, and flatter; spans of control and workloads are greatly enlarged; time frames are compressed; change is volatile; customization and timely responses carry the day. For all these reasons, the

manager-leader's role in facilitating individual and team contributions
hardly be overstated. The good news is that manager-leaders who want to
the shift to a more facilitative approach often find they have plenty of resou
to draw on, including underdeveloped relationships with colleagues
untapped talents in their staffs. The challenges, on the other hand, can be
midable. One lies in being patient and persistent as we make our way in
new workplace: we are all learning new behaviors and renegotiating relatio
ships, processes that take time and may require considerable reassurance. I
tiatives to empower may initially appear to fall flat, perhaps not so mu
because employees aren't interested as because they aren't sure. They may loo
for repeated cues that it really is safe to speak up on an issue, give honest feed-
back, or take the initiative on a decision before they will risk taking those steps.
Exhibit 3.1 offers a framework for considering the various factors likely to affect
the success of empowerment efforts.

One way to signal your genuine desire to facilitate employees' contributions
is to make the process of sending things up the organization easy for them. The
Seaboard region of State Farm Insurance Companies has instituted the F.L.U.I.D.
(Flow Up Idea Development) program, available to all agents and employees in
the region, as an express lane for receiving and recognizing ideas and solutions
related to the major strategic initiative. The hallmark of this program is that it's
simple and straightforward: there are no special forms, procedures, or approvals
required. To date the program has generated a wealth of ideas from across the
organization and has resulted in countless time- and cost-saving innovations as
well as access to better information for employees and a greater variety of products
for customers.

Another challenge to manager-leaders lies in breaking down long-standing
barriers—among departments and across lines of authority and, at a deeply per-
sonal level, within ourselves. This internal barrier, erected by the part of us that
fears not being in control, prevents the self from becoming truly open to others'
ideas and to a more emergent (rather than externally imposed) kind of order.
If employees are being asked to claim more autonomy, managers must reclaim a
measure of the vulnerability too long suppressed in trying to live up to the old and
sometimes misguided ideal of needing to be in control.

Consider the contrast in management approach illustrated by the following
scenarios. The vice president of a major division in a large corporation would not
permit reporting managers who were unable to attend senior staff meetings to
send substitutes. The effect was to distance the senior staff from the rest of the
organization and to limit developmental opportunities for less senior staff; meet-
ings took on the aura of an exclusive club in which secrets were shared and pri-
vate decisions were made. A human resources (HR) vice president in the same

EXHIBIT 3.1. IMPLEMENTING THE "E WORD" (EMPOWERMENT) SUCCESSFULLY.

Environmental Considerations

What external constraints and liabilities are we subject to (for example, laws or regulations)?

Organizational Considerations

What is the current context for action?

Is the mission clear?

Is there a shared vision?

Do core values inform thinking and behavior?

What is our history regarding autonomous behavior?

What systems and structures influence behavior, and in what ways?

What processes and norms govern decision making?

Are thinking outside the box and risk taking rewarded or punished?

How are mistakes and failures dealt with?

Are there factors particular to our products, services, or operations or to a specific project or task that necessarily limit freedom of action?

Individual or Team Considerations

What is the level of knowledge, talent, skill, or experience?

What is the level of understanding of environmental and organizational considerations?

What is the level of personal or team commitment to the larger purposes and goals of the organization?

What is the level of interest in personal growth and autonomy?

Self Considerations

What personal factors may affect my ability to truly share power?

---

company, on the other hand, held quarterly network meetings with HR managers across the country and encouraged any managers who were unable to attend to send a delegate fully empowered to represent their unit in offering viewpoints and casting votes. This approach yielded several positive outcomes: participating units were always represented and apprised of information and decisions; meetings became a developmental vehicle for delegates, who were exposed to a broader perspective of the company and their work; and organizational levels and boundaries were transcended, allowing for greater access among members of the HR community.

There are many ways manager-leaders can and should facilitate individual and team contributions, most of which are elaborated in other sections of this book. What follows is a brief summary of some of the most important of these mechanisms.

- *Keep mission, vision, and values front-and-center.* Ensure that individuals and teams remain aware of the larger purposes of the organization and of how their individual and team efforts play a role in helping to realize these purposes.
- *Create conversations about business issues.* Make a point of engaging employees one-on-one and in groups about the larger questions related to the future of the business. Encourage individuals to pay attention to forces of change, emerging markets, new opportunities, and so on.
- *Clarify the parameters within which people have freedom to act.* Avoid the trap of appearing to hand something off only to reclaim it because the individual or team misunderstood the scope of their authority or failed to take into account such critical factors as budget, time frames, legal liabilities, or customer requirements.
- *Provide support and direction as needed on an individual or team basis.* One way to encourage individuals or teams to realize a high level of contribution is to ensure that they continuously develop both the skills and the confidence to act autonomously. As you encourage greater participation or new roles, be sure to provide adequate direction and support.
- *Respect the uniqueness of each individual.* Take care to discover, appreciate, and nurture what each person brings to the table.
- *Provide and seek ongoing feedback.* People need to know how they're doing, particularly when they are trying out new behaviors or undertaking unfamiliar roles or tasks. Let people know what's working and what's not, and how what's not working could be changed or modified to make it more effective. And let your employees know you welcome the same kind of feedback.
- *Follow up on input.* Nothing so convinces people of the value of participating as seeing the input they offer get results. Although this does not mean that everything employees propose should necessarily be accepted, they need to know that their suggestions and recommendations will not fall into a black hole. Where appropriate, act quickly to implement employee recommendations; where it is determined that a suggestion or recommendation cannot or should not be implemented, provide a rationale so that at least employees know they were listened to and can gain an understanding of relevant factors in management decisions.
- *Remove barriers.* Look for ways to free people to do the right things, be creative, realize their talents, and so on. Periodically reevaluate existing rules, roles, policies, and structures to ensure that they still make sense and are not discouraging people from taking risks or exploring new possibilities. Ensure that programs

designed to solicit input do not become so encumbered with bureaucracy that they discourage ready participation.

• *Create safe places and practice fields.* Find ways of giving people confidence that they can challenge ideas and try out new behaviors with impunity.

• *Reinforce desired behaviors.* Develop metrics and incentives that reward people for adding value, taking initiative, learning new skills, and engaging in healthy dissent.

• *Encourage individual and collective learning.* Provide individuals and teams with the resources and mechanisms they need to make experiments, to share information, to have developmental opportunities, to reflect on successes and failures, and to implement change on the basis of their discoveries.

Earlier we referred to the work of McGregor, whose Theory Y suggests that talent is widely distributed in the population. We have long paid lip-service to the idea that the members of any organization are its most important resource. Having acknowledged that, it is only fair to acknowledge as well the formidable challenge managers face in reckoning with the sheer messiness of the human condition—with values and styles that don't match their own, with baggage and personal agendas and crises and treachery, with distractions and limitations and slumps. These human factors plague our lives and our organizations at some level over time, no matter how clear our vision or how inspired our leadership. Facilitating contribution is not about eliminating those sometimes disagreeable variables that are part of what make people human; rather, it is about creating conditions in which the capabilities of a workforce rich in diversity and in largely unrealized potential can be more fully applied to ends that align the values of the organization with those of its members.

Advocates Feedback and Recognition

Exchanges feedback with peers, superiors, and direct reports on an ongoing basis to mutually enhance performance; appropriately acknowledges good work; guides employees and teams in actively giving and seeking feedback, and in valuing one another's contributions.

Few men are wise enough to prefer useful criticism to treacherous praise.
—LA ROCHEFOUCAULD, *SENTENCES AND MORAL MAXIMS*

The role of today's manager-leader is, without a doubt, multifaceted, highly complex, and somewhat ambiguous as a result of numerous shifts in organizational structure and processes. On the other hand, the *essence* of the manager-leader's role remains simple and clear: to facilitate effective employee performance. How is this accomplished? In a number of ways: by marshaling resources, setting direction, coordinating tasks, providing training, and, most important, offering feedback and recognition. For it is only when employees are given useful information about how they're doing that they are in a position to strengthen what is working well and to improve what is deficient. And to the extent that they feel their contribution is valued, employees are encouraged to extend themselves and to commit at deeper and deeper levels. Yet feedback and recognition seem to be especially tough areas for managers: feedback can be very sensitive and therefore difficult to convey so that it is received as constructive, and recognition can easily be overlooked or mishandled. Nonetheless, manager-leaders must strive to make giving feedback and recognition an integral part of the way people work together— ongoing processes that everyone participates in and that are woven into the fabric of day-to-day activity.

It is fair to say that feedback is the bane of many, if not most, managers' professional existence. Witness the plaint of one HR director of a telecommunications firm, who described the typical scenario of a manager at his wit's end coming in to report that one of his workers (we'll call him Stan) "is incompetent in x function."

"How long has this been the case?" the HR director queries.

"Oh, he hasn't been effective since the day he walked in!" is the response. However, when the HR director reviews Stan's performance appraisals from the last several years, what he finds is one "Good" after another, including the most recent appraisal written less than six months ago *by the very manager who has come to complain.* "But why haven't you *told* him his performance isn't up to standards?" the HR director asks.

"Because I didn't want to demotivate him," is the manager's predictable (and chagrined) reply.

No question about it, feedback is a loaded proposition. And regardless of how well we come to terms with the concept intellectually, some of us may never feel entirely comfortable giving or receiving feedback, especially when it is corrective. Or we may give corrective feedback effectively about certain kinds of issues but disregard other equally important ones. For example, we have no problem addressing problems strictly related to performance, but back away at the point where personal characteristics or behaviors become involved: we can discuss missed deadlines or the failure to pay sufficient attention to detail, but we are reluctant to bring up an employee's abrasive manner, despite the negative effect it is having on coworkers. Sometimes we focus only on quantifiable results or technical capabilities and fail to deal with more subtle, less easily measured process issues, such as how an employee functions on a team or interacts with peers.

Despite the difficulties associated with corrective feedback, there are some practical steps we can take to understand and value feedback and to approach it in a way that serves both individuals and the collective enterprise.

First, it is important to understand the term *feedback* in its broadest and most impersonal sense as a function of any system—mechanical, electronic, ecological, human, or otherwise. For example, a "system error" message on a computer screen lets the user know that a component or program is malfunctioning, or that, for example, the user forgot to remove a disk from the A drive before booting up. An increase in natural disasters or evidence of a hole in the ozone layer tells us, as a people, that some of our practices may be resulting in irreversible damage to our planet. At a more personal level, we receive feedback anytime we try to develop a new manual skill, such as riding a bike. A seven-year-old child making the transition from training wheels to a two-wheeler is entirely dependent on feedback from a system that includes the bike, the terrain, the weather conditions, the surroundings (for example, pedestrian or road traffic), and the child herself. If the handlebars wobble, the child learns that she may not be holding them tight enough; if the bike begins to tip, she learns she may not be balancing properly or pedaling fast enough. The point here is that in our relationships with mechanical, electronic, or other kinds of impersonal systems, we recognize feedback as essential to knowing that we are succeeding or to determining what corrective measures we may need to take.

Observed in this light, feedback is *information*—valuable, *critical* information—and in this light it is virtually inconceivable that organizational systems could thrive over time without intentionally cultivating feedback of all kinds, including interpersonal. We know, for example, that in an age of consumer activism and intense competition for market share, organizations that do not seek feedback from their customers are likely to find that they have defected to competitors. Less visible—but sometimes equally or even more costly—is the price of failing to attend to systemic feedback available within the organization, or failing to institutionalize interpersonal feedback norms and processes.

Systemic feedback may elude us because we don't know how or where to look for it. For example, our tendency to become mired in the present and what is close at hand often results in our inability to see causes and effects that are separated in time and space. So, although we acknowledge that experience is the best teacher, we miss some of its most important lessons because we perceive it in such a limited way. Without mechanisms for monitoring systemic feedback, organizations impair their ability to learn collectively. Feedback, in a very real sense, is the foundation of the learning organization.

Feedback is also the foundation of individual growth and development. Lacking appropriate feedback mechanisms, we pay personal costs, such as the psychological defections that come about when individual issues remain unresolved. We know the scenario well: because David doesn't feel he can broach a sensitive issue with a coworker, he may vent his frustration by gossiping or complaining to other coworkers; or he may go directly to his or the coworker's boss (a form of political maneuvering); or he may suffer in silence, diffusing his own energies and allowing the unresolved issue to fester and distance him from his coworker. In any case there is a cost: in energy, in relationship, in trust, and, very likely, in productivity and in the potential for synergistic endeavors. Productivity losses also occur when we are uncomfortable giving corrective feedback to our direct reports and allow a performance deficiency or counterproductive behavior to become increasingly problematic. For that matter, an entire career can be derailed if blind spots or "fatal flaws" go unaddressed (McCall and Lombardo, 1983).

Despite its value, corrective personal feedback is generally difficult for us to hear: unlike other kinds of feedback, it carries with it certain risks—of exposure, vulnerability, and disapprobation. These are very real risks, especially in organizational cultures where feedback is not valued, occurs erratically, or is conveyed in an unskilled way. Yet, ironically, we put ourselves more at risk to the extent that we avoid or disregard feedback. In some ways it's a question of paying now or paying later—but paying later is usually a lot more expensive.

The alternative to avoiding feedback or leaving it to chance is for manager-leaders to develop the giving and receiving of feedback as a shared norm and a skilled process within the work unit. Constructive feedback is an unusual gift— one that can be as difficult to give as it is to receive. Nonetheless, it is an invaluable gift that all of us need and cannot give ourselves. Manager-leaders thus play a crucial role in creating the kind of environment in which that gift is able to be both offered and received as such. When feedback is approached in this way, both individuals and the organization stand to gain. The tangible benefits include higher productivity, greater efficiency, increased customer satisfaction, higher levels of competence and creativity, and more collaborative outcomes. Intangible benefits include continuous learning, higher levels of trust, better working relationships, an enhanced sense of community, and mutual support for personal and professional growth.

One of the roles the manager-leader can play to ensure that feedback is beneficial is to provide individuals and teams with training in appropriate feedback techniques. Giving and receiving constructive feedback is a disciplined process that requires attention to details of time, place, language, and intent. Another role involves facilitating the development of some agreements among members of the work unit about what the parameters of feedback giving and receiving should be. In *Feedback Toolkit*, Rick Maurer (1994) advises, for example, that feedback in the workplace should be tied to a business reason and not used as a vehicle for clearing the air or venting. Agreements should also be made about what approach might be used to initiate feedback—a kind of code, if you will—so that the recipient has an opportunity to consciously prepare himself or herself to listen and to avoid defensive, knee-jerk reactions that typically occur when an individual is caught off-guard. Agreeing on a code as simple and straightforward as "I need to (I'd like to) give you (offer you) some feedback" or even a single term (such as "reality check") that has meaning for the group or adds an element of humor can serve to depersonalize the sting of corrective feedback by signaling that the sender is about to invoke a process that all members of the unit have agreed to and helped to develop. Ensuring that the giving and receiving of feedback is a skilled, responsible process is critical if we want individuals and teams to open themselves to the risks of having their blind spots revealed.

It is equally critical that feedback become a truly shared *norm*. For no matter how much skill an individual brings to the feedback process, if he or she is the only one engaging in it, it can feel like a high-risk behavior that isolates that individual from others. On the other hand, when everyone actively seeks and gives feedback on an ongoing basis, there is reciprocal permission granted to work together in a way that acknowledges individual strengths and needs and that invites openness, dialogue, collective learning, and continuous growth.

Establishing effective feedback as a shared norm is partly a function of dedicating both time and resources to training in skills and to developing a workable process, as described previously. But to become truly integrated into day-to-day activity, feedback must be modeled, practiced, and incorporated into formal and informal interaction on a daily basis, and appropriately rewarded. So, for example, a time might be routinely set aside at the end of staff and team meetings for feedback. And feedback skills might become a criterion for performance evaluation. However, modeling good feedback involves more than just setting up mechanisms: it requires as well that manager-leaders monitor their own communication behavior to ensure that they are not subconsciously undermining others through subtle verbal and nonverbal messages. If I am the manager-leader, how I position myself in relation to you spatially, how much eye contact I accord you in conversations and meetings, how long it takes me to respond to your request—all send signals that can dramatically affect your sense of your value. We tend to live up to expectations: in situations where the expectations are high and the feedback we get affirms our ability to meet those expectations, we rise to meet them; however, when the feedback, however subtle or inadvertent, suggests that others disregard us or have little confidence in our capabilities, then we diminish our own expectations for ourselves with a consequent loss in confidence and self-esteem. (This is popularly known as the "Pygmalion Effect.") Delivering feedback effectively must become not just a process but a "habit of being."

Up to this point we have been focusing on corrective feedback. Equally important—and powerful—is positive feedback or recognition. All of us know from personal experience that it means a lot when others let us know that we are valued for ourselves or for some contribution we have made. But just *how* powerful recognition can be was demonstrated quite dramatically at a conference break-out session when the facilitator sensed that energy in the room was waning. He digressed from his presentation to make an odd request of the audience: turn to the person next to you and for the next minute take turns giving each other thirty seconds' worth of the most affirming feedback or recognition you can come up with. In response to the question of what to do if you were seated next to a stranger (which most of the audience were), the facilitator said, "make it up . . . tell lies if you have to . . . for thirty seconds." At the end of that minute the change in the room was palpable: people were bright, animated, and energized. It really hadn't mattered *what* they had been told; it mattered simply that they had been affirmed.

We all need affirmation, some of which we can provide for ourselves, but some of which we are truly dependent on others to bestow on us. Just as physical touch is important for human development, so too are psychological strokes. And in today's leaner, meaner workplace, we all need them more than ever. Unfortunately, however, the very stresses that make recognition so essential—steep learning curves, heavy workloads, pressure to continuously improve products and increase productivity—may cause recognition to fall low on the list of managers' priorities. We tend, as parents, teachers, journalists, managers—as humans—to focus on what's *not* right rather than what is. Ken Blanchard calls it the "leave alone–zap" style (1982, p. 13): we are much more likely to catch someone doing something wrong than we are to catch him or her doing something right.

We also tend to think of recognition in terms of programs and awards. Although these are an important part of recognition, they are only two of many ways recognition can be bestowed. In fact, some of the more personal, informal ways of recognizing others can be as powerful as institutionalized programs, if not more so. Jotting positive comments on work that another has submitted for your review, seeking another out to verbally acknowledge a special effort, soliciting another's counsel on a difficult issue or decision, taking another into confidence about an impending development, providing a developmental opportunity or a chance for greater visibility, responding to another's concerns, even showing an interest in the things that are important to another, both at and away from work, are all ways of letting that person know that he or she is valued in a very personal way.

Just as it is not the sole province of the manager-leader to initiate feedback, so it is with recognition. The video *Excellence in the Public Sector* (Starr and Cram,

1989) features a recognition program developed by a timber cutter in the U.S. Forest Service. The program involves a check in the amount of $32.50 ($25.00 net) that each employee is given each year to award to a coworker who is especially deserving. Remarkably—or maybe not so remarkably—a woman who had received several of these over a period of years commented that although she had also been the recipient of sizable cash bonuses, none of them meant as much to her as these less grandiose endorsements from her fellow workers. The program has been so successful that management has sought to become part of it—only to be told that they would have to start their own.

What this story illustrates so clearly is that the key to meaningful recognition lies less in its material content than in what it signifies and how it is given. The story also suggests that when recognition programs become institutionalized they can also become depersonalized through the bureaucracy and politics that sometimes attach to them. Our guess is that the reason Forest Service workers responded with such enthusiasm to the Groo Award is precisely because it was outside the formal system and hence had an authenticity that programs within the system did not. This is not to say that organizations should dispense with formal recognition programs or that special efforts should not be honored with tangible rewards—time off, a thoughtful gift, a significant cash award. What's most important about recognition is that it should be timely, personal, and genuine, whatever form it takes.

Feedback and recognition may seem largely personal, but they are the underpinnings of an individual's, team's, or system's ability to be accountable and make corrections, build capacity, and satisfy customers and other stakeholders over time. The free exchange of skilled feedback enhances both honesty and trust: there are fewer "undiscussables," and both dialogue and healthy dissent become more possible. And when corrective feedback is balanced with appropriate recognition, people are able to trust the process even when the message may be difficult to hear. For all of these reasons, one of the manager-leader's most important priorities should be ensuring that feedback and recognition are part of the day-to-day conduct of the business and part of accomplishing continuous learning, both individually and collectively.

CHAPTER FOUR

MANAGING ACROSS BOUNDARIES

Manage the organization "horizontally"—that is, insist that "vertical" obfuscating be replaced with proactive (no checking "up"), "horizontal," front-line cooperation.
—TOM PETERS, *THRIVING ON CHAOS*

According to John Kotter (1988), one of the most critical skills for thriving in the organization of the future is the ability to build a network of strong relationships. Kotter's claim addresses the organizational imperatives that flow from current changes in our society. If, in response to a more global, competitive, customer-driven market, organizations must become more flexible and responsive in the way they develop and deliver products and services, then diverse individual efforts will have to be coordinated across functions in a more timely way. If resources are diminishing, then people will have to negotiate their needs more collaboratively. If problems are more complex and far-reaching, then solutions will have to be more synergistic.

These changes require our working together in new ways that extend our ability to create partnerships throughout the organization. For example, we must actively push to extend the boundaries of conventional work encounters by building collaborative relationships. We must develop our ability to negotiate win-win solutions by achieving integrative agreements. We must broaden our organizational perspective by engaging in dialogue. These are the skills we explore in this second chapter devoted to the People Leadership sphere.

Builds Collaborative Relationships

Seeks out others as a means of generating information, ideas, resources, opportunities, synergies, and so on; takes into account the concerns, needs, and interests of others within the system; extends the boundaries of conventional work relationships to achieve value-added results.

The way to do business with people is to do business with people. . . . Business exists only among people and for people.

—JAMES AUTRY, *LOVE AND PROFIT*

In the video based on her highly successful book *Leadership and the New Science* (Mehal and McCarey 1993), Margaret Wheatley makes a very bold claim: "Relationships are all there is." *All* there is?! However far we've come in acknowledging the importance of relationships in a business culture that is typically hostile to anything "touchy-feely," we are hardly prepared to accept the idea that relationships are *all* there is! A means to something, perhaps . . . higher sales or better morale. But hardly all there is.

What Wheatley is proposing is not a management guru's pipe dream but a discovery grounded in the natural universe and demonstrated in the work of modern physicists who describe physical phenomena as waves of potential. Wheatley believes that we, too, are waves of potential that only become realized in and through relationships—with ideas, with situations, and most important, with other people (Mehal and McCarey, 1993). Thus it is that each of us can be said to play a role in helping others realize the fullness of their capabilities to the extent that we are able to elicit their talents, perspectives, ideas, knowledge, and skills. In other words, when we engage in a conversation with someone from a different discipline or unit, we trigger the possibility of new connections.

Our experience in human relationships supports this phenomenon. Take, for example, what we call "chemistry." Each of us has found that we can be different selves in different relationships. We have probably been in relationships from time to time that just don't seem to work. We see ourselves behaving in ways that even we don't like: we become withdrawn or self-conscious, petty or adversarial. For whatever inexplicable reason, the dynamics don't play to our strengths. If we are fortunate we have also experienced relationships that somehow bring out the best in us—we're wittier or brighter or more compassionate. As one friend commented to another, "I like who I am when I'm with you."

Most of us have also had a chance to observe, whether we realized it at the time or not, that the essence of any system is the relationships among its parts. Think about the last really disappointing all-star game you viewed: all the right parts, but no developed relationships. For a system to work well, it's what's possible *among* the parts, not the parts in isolation, that matters most.

In organizations, this connectivity is expressed through the quality of personal relationships and their effect on our ability to achieve results. A case in point is the story of Justice Antonin Scalia's career as a member of the Supreme Court. In a recent article in the *Los Angeles Times*, David G. Savage (1996) describes the way in which Scalia's "caustic personal attacks" have alienated his colleagues and so diminished his influence—despite expectations for his leadership when he ascended to the Court—that although the high court is still predominantly Republican, its major rulings have "a decidedly liberal bent." According to Savage, when Scalia was named a justice in 1986 he was viewed as someone who by virtue of his "intellectual drive and personal charm" would take the lead role in shaping the Reagan revolution in the Supreme Court. However, his self-righteousness and his need to castigate his fellow justices' positions as "irrational . . . preposterous . . . [and] comical" have, in the words of Stanford professor Kathleen Sullivan, "scared away all the allies" (Savage, 1996, p. 16). Sullivan facetiously nominates Scalia for the "Felix Frankfurter award," referring to Scalia's illustrious predecessor, a Harvard law professor and former Supreme Court justice who, destined for greatness when he became a justice in 1939, could not resist lecturing his "dimwit" colleagues on the Court, thereby eroding his ability to offer meaningful dissents (p. 16).

Leadership potential obviously can be undercut by disrespect; it also can be greatly enhanced by leaders' overtures of genuine interest and respect—not only toward allies but in all of the various types of relationships manager-leaders are likely to encounter as they pursue their visions and goals. Peter Block, author of *The Empowered Manager* and *Stewardship*, refers to this attentiveness to relational dynamics as "positive politics." "We become political," says Block, "at the moment we attempt to translate our visions into action" (1987, p. 132). Considering the inevitability of competing interests among diverse stakeholders, we cannot assume automatic or universal support, and we may encounter outright antagonism from time to time, regardless of the merit of our ideas. Yet there is much we can do to develop respectful relationships and to work at negotiating agreement or trust (or both). At best this allows us to broaden our influence; at the least, to minimize the risk of alienation.

Block (1987) describes five types of stakeholders: *allies*, with whom we share both agreement and trust; *opponents*, with whom we share trust but not agreement; *bedfellows*, with whom we share agreement but not trust; *fencesitters*, who are driven by political expediency and are therefore reluctant to commit; and *antagonists*, with whom we share neither agreement or trust. Positive politics involves acknowledging the dynamics of organizational relationships for what they are—a predictable fact of organizational life—and approaching each type of stakeholder with the intent to negotiate as much agreement and trust as possible. The cornerstone of this approach is openness—both in being clear about what our purposes are and in listening to the interests, needs, and concerns of the other. If the other is an ally, we nurture a supportive relationship; if an opponent, we take into account an alternative point of view; if a bedfellow, we seek to expand trust; if a fence-sitter, we encourage commitment; and if the other is an antagonist, we work to defuse covert destructiveness.

For today's harried manager the imperative to *build* relationships may seem like an overwhelming task; building relationships takes time and energy, both of which most managers feel are in short supply as it is. How does one accomplish the multiple tasks and objectives that fall to the manager and still manage to build relationships? This is a dilemma. Relationships do require dedicated effort, and as humans we are finite beings with a limited number of hours each day to meet seemingly limitless expectations. In today's competitive environment we are pushed to perform (read *produce results*), not build relationships. However, we are mistaken if we regard relationship building as something separate from our real work instead of recognizing that it provides the means by which we can get more and better things done. We also may assume that relationship building requires a lot of *extra* time when in fact much of it can be done moment-to-moment during our daily interactions with employees, peers, customers, and others, through simple behaviors that value and affirm others or at the very least demonstrate respect, courtesy, and professionalism. Is it sometimes necessary to do much more than that? Yes. The typical work arena includes a variety of people—some who are collaborative and easy to work with, others who are difficult, angry, suspicious, and untrusting. Our inability to control any more than our half of a relationship can be exceedingly frustrating. We may find that our best efforts are rebuffed or ignored, or that great patience is required to bring someone around, or that sometimes nothing we do ultimately makes a difference.

Relationships are, in a very real sense, investments—the yield may not be immediate, but over time they can pay very big returns. The ability to cultivate and sustain mutually supportive relationships raises the manager-leader's credibility; it lends "referent power" (cited in Shaw, 1981, p. 295)—the more sustainable power that derives not from title or position but from being liked and admired; and it garners a type of "idiosyncrasy credit" (Hollander, 1958, p. 118)—tolerance on the part of others in a group for deviation from group norms, in this case for mistakes, tough decisions, or the stresses of hard times. When people have satisfying relationships with their manager-leader they are more willing to pull together to make things happen, even when that involves dealing with extra pressure or giving more of themselves.

Beyond these very personal benefits, the effort to encourage and build strong relationships across the system can pay significant organizational dividends, as the following story illustrates. Because the training and development department in a large company was minimally staffed, the company routinely used external facilitators to teach core management development programs, thereby freeing up the internal staff to concentrate on curriculum development. As a result of a highly collaborative relationship with the internal staff, external facilitators had assumed a significant role in updating and adapting the curriculum they taught and took great pride in contributing to the quality of the programs. Feedback and ideas for new program content flowed freely between facilitators and developers. However, when a new manager took over the department he decided to create greater separation between staff and facilitators. When he was asked by the staff developers about the facilitators' reaction to a proposed curriculum change, his response was, "They facilitate the program and get paid to do what we tell them to do." This approach has resulted not only in the loss of valuable feedback from the people who deal daily with the department's primary customers but also in a loss of trust. Whereas mutual problem solving had involved both parties in finding the best solutions, now issues are documented and escalated; whereas facilitators had volunteered their time and ideas toward making each program the best, now every minute is billed.

The preceding story makes clear that building and maintaining strong relationships can benefit the organization in tangible ways; and failing to create or strengthen bonds can cost the organization. The ability to build relationships has, in fact, become an increasingly critical skill for today's manager-leaders. Partnerships have become the model for successful enterprise: former competitors increasingly seek alliances with one another as a way of expanding their capabilities, mapping out new business territories, and capitalizing on emerging markets; companies work to form tighter linkages among vendors, suppliers, retailers, and others. Robert Haas (cited in Howard, 1990, p. 136), chairman and CEO of Levi-Strauss, conjures up the vision of a "seamless web of mutual responsibility and collaboration" reflected in "interrelationships and mutual commitments, straight through the chain" that he believes would not have been possible formerly but now are essential: "You can't be responsive to the end-consumer today unless you can count on those kinds of collaborations at each step along the way" (p. 136). Consistent with a systems approach (see Chapter Five), manager-leaders today need to think more broadly than they did in the past, taking into account many different types of stakeholders at various levels both within and outside the organization. Involvement tends to be more widespread because of multiple and competing interests, and roles are less clear—circumstances that create an opportunity for manager-leaders to extend their influence beyond a limited span of control.

Many factors make it incumbent upon manager-leaders to act as bridges across relevant units and beyond them to the larger systems of which the organization is a part. Today's organizations are leaner, with resulting pressure to find greater synergies. Players and stakeholders come and go and change roles within a project life cycle. And a "new deal" with respect to employment places the burden of adding value to the organization on the individual. Thus manager-leaders must be more concerned than ever before with marketing their units to other parts of the organization, fostering collaborative efforts, negotiating for resources, satisfying internal clients, maintaining high levels of communication, synthesizing multiple needs and interests, managing expectations, developing partnerships with vendors, and ensuring that their workers have information, input, access, and visibility relative to other parts of the system—all of which depend on the ability to build successful relationships.

The bottom line is that building relationships is the most fundamental of all the attributes and skills required for effective management-leadership. It is the foundation on which all of the other capabilities are built.

Engages in Dialogue

Initiates exploratory conversations as a means of examining assumptions, beliefs, "what ifs," and so on; willing to suspend the need to know, the need to win a point, the need to judge or decide, in the interest of allowing greater understanding to emerge through shared inquiry.

AND SO IT WAS
That the People devised among themselves
a way of asking each other questions
whenever a decision was to be made . . .
We sought to perceive the flow of energy
through each new possibility. . . .

— PAULA UNDERWOOD, *WHO SPEAKS FOR WOLF*

Alan Webber, former editor of the *Harvard Business Review,* asserts that "the most important work in the new economy is creating conversations" (1993, p. 28). For many this notion will come across as disconcerting, if not a bit incongruous. *Conversations* connotes an informal, leisurely, and often unfocused exchange at odds with the pace, pressure, and task orientation of current enterprise. Yet the connotations of the word may underlie its potential impact. Physicist Werner Heisenberg observes, "Science is rooted in conversations" (cited in Senge, 1990a, p. 238).

If we think about our personal experience of conversations, we are likely to discover that on more than one occasion a conversation has been particularly meaningful, significant, or insightful, or has even, in no small way, changed our life. With these possibilities in mind, Brown and Isaacs (1996–1997), senior affiliates at the MIT Center for Organizational Learning, exhort us to consider that the numerous encounters—across cubicles, in the hallways, at the proverbial watercooler, via e-mail, or through the grapevine—which we typically assume are distractions from work and try to shut down, may in fact be rich sources of organizational learning. Drawing on the discovery by the Xerox Institute for Research on Learning that knowledge creation is largely a social process, Brown and Isaacs propose that "thoughtful conversations around questions that matter might be *the* core process in any company—the source of organizational intelligence that enables the other business processes to create positive results" (1996–1997, p. 1). The key elements in this proposition are *thoughtful* conversations and *questions that matter*. Brown and Isaacs are talking about dialogues.

Dialogue is a word that has become a part of the vernacular in recent years; the very casualness with which the word is used today suggests that we may have lost an appreciation of exactly what it signifies. The word *dialogue* comes from two Greek roots—*dia* meaning "through" and *logos* meaning "word." Thus *dialogue* literally stands for "meaning coming through the word." Dialogue does not necessarily occur just because two or more people are involved in a verbal exchange. Rather, it represents a very specific *mode* of communication—with ancient and venerable origins—that is in some respects almost antithetical to the way we live and the way we do business today. Author and consultant Judy Sorum Brown (1993, p. 1) compares dialogue to "good conversations . . . over the back fences of our lives . . . under the apple tree . . . in rocking chairs on front porches. . . . It is continued, thoughtful exchange about the things that matter most." Brown quotes both Maya Angelou and poet Paula Underwood in describing dialogue as a means of hearkening back to "that which we have forgotten to remember" (p. 1).

David Bohm (1989, p. 1), a theoretical physicist and a major proponent of dialogue, refers to dialogue as a "*stream of meaning* flowing among and through and between us" (italics in original). It is like a meandering stream that moves easily between two banks. The stream itself represents a collectivity of ideas and knowledge that drifts back and forth in an open, uncontrolled way in no particular hurry to get somewhere. There is the sense of opening up, exploring, diverging, considering. Entering into the stream means putting aside preconceived ideas and agendas, and becoming open to the flow of ideas and to unfolding meaning. The wisdom that emerges in a dialogue is that of the collective, not of any single individual, be that person the tribal elder, the senior manager, or the loudest voice.

Dialogue, according to Senge (1990a), is grounded in two skills: inquiry and reflection. Inquiry skills are specific capabilities that come into play when we interact with others, especially with respect to complex or difficult issues. When we enter into a dialogue, for example, we pose speculative questions, invite others to examine our assumptions and beliefs, and suspend premature judgments or decisions. We literally think out loud together. Reflection skills involve monitoring our own internal processes—we consider not just what is being offered but also how we are receiving it; William Isaacs, director of the Dialogue Project at MIT, uses the term "listen to your listening" (1996–1997, p. 3) to describe how individuals should seek to become aware of the way they take things in, form judgments, make sense of the world—and of how these processes influence their actions. The intent is to enlarge our mutual understanding. The following excerpt from a dialogue illustrates the flow of ideas and the emergence of new directions:

Speaker A: So when we use the term *trust* with respect to organizations, what are we really talking about?

Speaker B: I guess what first comes to mind for me has to do with knowing that the decision makers can be counted on.

Speaker C: Counted on . . . in what way?

Speaker B: Oh, that they're motivated by the right things . . . that they're not going to sell us out . . . that sort of thing.

Speaker A: I think, for me, trust has to do with personal relationships. Like how open people are in their dealings with one another or how much people can be counted on to live up to what they promise. . . . Which complicates the issue—that last part, I mean, about living up to promises, because now that I think about it, I'm not sure people who don't come through are not so much untrustworthy as that they feel pressured, so they overpromise. I don't know.

Speaker C: I think that's right, and I wonder how many facts of organizational life—like pressures to say yes even when you know you can't deliver, and accommodating your boss when you don't agree—erode trust among otherwise well-meaning people.

Speaker B: Meetings are the worst . . . when you find yourself sitting there *not* saying what you know should be said, or not raising critical issues because the consequences are just too big a price to pay.

Speaker A: That hits pretty close to home.

Speaker C: So are we saying that we, personally, contribute to the lack of trust? And that people are perhaps unable to operate with trust in organizations? . . . Are we all victims of the institutions we've created?

Speaker B: I wonder to what extent the ability to maintain trust among people has to do with the size of the group . . . ? I mean I think it's easy to trust the people whom you know the best and have close relationships with, but trust is something that people build, and how do you build trust with people in the organization you hardly know?

In this dialogue, coworkers are exploring the broad issue of organizational trust; their willingness to stay *in* the question, to speak authentically, to range freely within the topic, and to bring their existing notions to the surface for mutual reconsideration—without feeling a need to drive to a conclusion or to accept or reject specific points—leads them to new ways of looking at and thinking about the topic and its implications, to greater mutual understanding, and possibly, eventually, to new strategies for engendering trust within their organization. (This just as easily could have been a dialogue about something more concrete—a specific project or decision, for example.)

If dialogue is like a meandering stream, Bohm (1989) compares its counterpart, discussion, to a ping-pong match. Discussion is often a contest that involves debating ideas, making points, arriving at a decision, and emerging victorious. Bohm reminds us that the etymology of *discussion* shares with *percussion* and *concussion* the notion of striking against. Discussion in its purest sense denotes a mode of communication that is largely closed off and competitive. Whereas dialogue is about entertaining questions, discussion is about determining answers. Whereas dialogue encourages divergence of thought, discussion works to achieve convergence in the form of a decision. Whereas dialogue focuses on inquiry, discussion focuses on advocacy (Senge, 1990a).

Although both modes of communication are essential, it is fair to say that in our culture and in our workplaces dialogue has been relegated to the status of an all-but-lost art. We are, by all assessments, a driven nation—a nation of doers not thinkers. Nowhere does this action orientation show up more powerfully than in our workplaces, where the axiom "Time is money" translates into pressure to produce more and more outputs in less and less time. Couple this pressure with the emphasis in our culture on individualism and competitiveness, and it becomes obvious why we tend to be impatient with a process that requires that we slow down and reflect, that we subject our beliefs to scrutiny and reconsideration, that we suppress self-interest in order to think collectively, and that we live with unanswered questions.

Taking the time to explore our tacit assumptions is critical, since these underlie our positions. Indulging the pressure for quick decisions, our need to be right, and our tendency to rely on discussion in the absence of dialogue often results, however, in flawed outcomes: false consensus, inadequate decisions, winners and losers—a failure to discover the common ground that would allow for more creative, sustainable solutions.

Dialogue can take many forms. As an outgrowth of work currently being developed at MIT, facilitators are convening formal dialogues with increasing frequency, in which participants representing multiple interests come together to explore ways of working or being together. These dialogues include members of highly diverse communities, for example, or members of different organizational interests such as labor and management.

Formal dialogues are intended to provide a forum for a more intimate and reflective mode of communication. To that end, participants are seated in chairs in a circle, often with nothing in front of them (tables, desks, and so on) that might function as a barrier to interaction with others in the circle. This arrangement reinforces a sense of equality and recognizes the importance of each person's contribution. The resulting inner space is referred to as the "container" and is intended to serve as a safe place for testing ideas, challenging assumptions, and offering reflections or speculations. Occasionally, participants are encouraged to wear blindfolds, especially when they are being introduced to dialogue, as a means of heightening their awareness of *what* is being said (as opposed to *who* is saying it) and of minimizing anything in the environment that might detract from reflection.

The conversation is initiated with a focused, important question; it may be a question that poses a dilemma or challenges the group, or it may be one designed to tap the wellsprings of the participants' own knowledge and experience. Someone skilled in the dialogue process generally provides a low level of nonintrusive facilitation to ensure that the setting is conducive, that participants are provided with some assistance in understanding and entering into the spirit of the process, that they stay in the dialogue mode, and that they periodically attend, very consciously, to the process elements of the dialogue. This conscious attending not only allows participants to build skill in the interactive elements of dialogue but also, in Edgar Schein's words, to "shorten the internal feedback loop as much as possible" (1994, p. 3) so that they become more aware of how their individual thoughts and reactions are influenced by past experiences, existing biases and beliefs, and of events or comments that trigger these influences.

For manager-leaders these kinds of dialogues can serve many purposes within a work unit, task force, or team. They allow difficult issues to be brought to the surface and examined; create an opportunity for collective, generative learning; foster a sense of team and encourage collaborative thought; offer an escape from the routine pressures of the workplace and allow people to take a longer view and a more thoughtful approach—to go deep; and provide an opportunity to assess, to reexamine, and to mine the insights of experience. In creating a level playing field in which each person's voice is invited and welcomed, dialogue serves the goal of heightening the participants' awareness and appreciation of diversity even among those who, from all outward appearances, may seem to be the same. In providing a forum for reflective conversation, dialogue offers a means of focusing attention on larger, more fundamental issues such as mission, values, vision, and core business strategies and processes. And, according to Brown (1993), because dialogue allows for a more natural process of change through an unfolding and emergence of meaning and direction, it may facilitate change efforts and reduce resistance we have assumed was inevitable as a result of our experience with more instrumental, mechanistic change approaches.

In some ways equally valuable and infinitely more accessible to the manager-leader on an ongoing basis are the many day-to-day opportunities to engage informally in dialogue with superiors, peers, direct reports, and other stakeholders across the system. As discussed previously, these exploratory conversations can take place spontaneously in person—while at lunch or on a break, when walking down the hall or traveling to an off-site meeting, as a regular feature of "managing by walking around"—or remotely, via e-mail exchanges or phone interactions. In addition, dialogue should be systematically built into business meetings of all types—where many are gathered to evaluate a project or ponder a decision, or even where two people put their heads together to formulate a plan—as a means of ensuring that outcomes are informed, thoughtful, inclusive of diverse perspectives, and, as a result, more sustainable.

Most accessible of all are the internal dialogues manager-leaders can engage in with themselves on an ongoing basis. One young student of organizational leadership suggests that manager-leaders make a practice of struggling with a weighty issue, unresolved dilemma, or difficult concept. In this way they learn to live with questions, acknowledge complexity, engage their intuitive capabilities, and hone their sensibilities.

Viewed as an ongoing process, dialogue is much less a methodology than an approach that holds great promise. In recent years we have seen a shift from more authoritarian models of decision making to models that emphasize consensus decision making. In part this shift is in response to the benefits of taking into account diverse points of view and of arriving at a decision that everyone truly owns. But the process of dialogue suggests that there may be a model of decision making beyond consensus, the possibilities of which we have only begun to explore: consensus seeks to reconcile differences through a synthesis of *existing* positions; dialogue, on the other hand, seeks the emergence of *new* meaning and direction. Manager-leaders who make dialogue a part of the way they involve others demonstrate not only respect for individuals but also a desire for inclusiveness; a willingness to address thorny issues openly; a trust in an inherent organizational intelligence; and a recognition that whenever diverse people come together to exchange ideas, new possibilities can come into being.

Notwithstanding the power of dialogue—in fact, *because* of its power—some cautions are in order. Because dialogue has the potential of tapping into the deep recesses of people's thoughts and feelings and because people present themselves in very different ways, dialogue must be regarded as a privileged conversation; thus, it must be managed in a way that affords safety, sensitivity, and respect. Under no circumstance should a dialogue become coercive or manipulative.

A second caution involves recognizing, as mentioned earlier, that dialogue is highly countercultural. We and members of our organizations are used to operating in a context that is high powered, high pressured, and otherwise focused on results, so many people will, at least initially, feel awkward and uncomfortable with dialogues. Because dialogue is not an analytical, task-driven process, and because it is very likely to spawn confusion long before any discernible meaning emerges, some people will regard dialogue as a colossal waste of time. Some will resist opening themselves to a process that requires them to go deep, to suspend certainty, and to embrace ambiguity. And for some, a process as exploratory as dialogue will appear to be nothing more than fluff with absolutely no connection to their work or to the goals of the organization. Brown (1993) compares the frustration with dialogue with the frustration Western negotiators experience in accommodating the culture and style of their Asian counterparts: although there may be a very protracted, seemingly unproductive time—from the Westerner's point of view—invested in preliminary conversations, by the time the implementation stage has arrived, there is a high level of accord, and implementation proceeds quite smoothly, whereas in the United States, implementation typically involves major challenges and resistance.

These reactions are predictable, and they point up the need for the manager-leader to be mindful of people's fears and concerns, to create the space and safety for meaningful dialogues to occur, to function as a teacher and role model in helping individuals see the value of such conversations, and to commit to making dialogue an intrinsic part of doing good business.

At a time when we are desperately seeking answers and efficiencies, our learning to value dialogue is one more exercise in letting go: letting go of certainty, letting go of being right, letting go of the need to judge meetings exclusively in terms of measurable outputs. If today's manager-leaders are to come to terms with complex issues in meaningful ways, they must be willing to take a longer, wider, and deeper view. They must be open to learning not only how to communicate more effectively but also how to communicate in new ways.

Achieves Integrative Agreements

Works to produce win-win solutions—outcomes that reconcile differences and mutu-ally satisfy the needs and values of self and others.

*Joint undertakings stand a better chance
when they benefit both sides.*

—EURIPIDES, *IPHIGENIA IN TAURUS*

Many of us were raised to believe that compromise was the preferred method for resolving conflicts. Sometimes it is; sometimes it is the best we can do. However, although compromise may produce an amicable and fair settlement, it is unfortunately a settlement in which both parties have to give up part of what they want or feel entitled to. In the classic example (Pruitt, 1983), two individuals who claim a single orange solve the dispute by cutting the orange in half, each of them both losing and gaining—perhaps unnecessarily. Suppose that individual A had actually wanted the orange to use the zest in making a cake, and that individual B had wanted the pulp of the orange to make fresh juice. Had they uncovered this information, they would have easily been able to solve the dispute in a way that gave each individual all of what he or she wanted.

This kind of outcome is known as a *win-win* or what Dean Pruitt calls an "integrative agreement" (1983, p. 35). Win-win agreements have become an appealing alternative to the competitive win-lose model also known as the zero-sum game. The win-lose model assumes that if one party wins, the other, *by necessity,* loses. What makes a win-win or integrative agreement possible is a willingness on the part of those involved to explore, collaboratively, beyond their initial positions ("This orange is *mine.*" "No, it's *mine!*") to the values and needs that underlie those positions. Why, after all, do we consider Solomon so wise? Not because he was willing to cut the baby in question in half but because he recognized that such a proposal was a means of discovering the true motives of the parties involved.

If ever there was a time for integrative agreements it is in the current climate of multiple competing interests. Regulatory considerations, consumer demands, customer requirements, employee expectations, budgetary limitations, and political interests are just some of the factors in the mix of what most manager-leaders must reconcile in accomplishing objectives, launching an initiative, or successfully competing in an increasingly challenging marketplace.

We are rarely (if ever) in our organizational lives dealing with something as simple as dividing an orange between two people. More typically we must wrestle with a welter of complex issues in attempting to arrive at a mutually satisfying agreement. Yet this very complexity can actually serve the process of a win-win solution because it offers us much to work with: as we consider with others the many factors that must be taken into account, we are likely to find trade-offs that can then be packaged in a mutually acceptable agreement. In multifaceted situations it is likely, for example, that some of one party's high-priority items are another party's much lower priority items; these gaps can be leveraged. Pruitt calls this logrolling (1983, p. 39), a technique that one of the authors has successfully employed with vendors. When she has found herself heading toward a deadlock on price, she intentionally moves away from trying to fix price and instead explores other considerations such as billing, delivery, storage, and training. Very often she is able to discover a way of making up the price difference for both parties: she might agree to pay up front or take delivery earlier than needed; the vendor might agree to train facilitators for no charge or at a reduced rate, to handle the storage of materials, to adjust billing to accommodate budget cycles, or to customize materials at no additional cost.

Logrolling is only one of several techniques that Pruitt (1983, pp. 36–41) recommends. Others include "expanding the pie," finding a way to increase available resources or opportunities; "nonspecific compensation," repaying a concession by one party with something unrelated but of equal value; "cost cutting," finding ways of making one party's requirements less odious or difficult for the other party to accept; and "bridging," devising a new option that does not grant either party his or her initial demands but nonetheless satisfies the underlying interests of both.

Roger Fisher and William Ury (1981) of the Harvard Negotiation Project have also contributed significantly in this arena. In their best-seller, *Getting to Yes,* they offer a new win-win model of negotiating that is based on principle rather than on the traditional "hard" (too adversarial) or "soft" (too accommodating) negotiating styles. In his sequel, *Getting Past No,* Ury (1991) has provided additional strategies—such as "go to the balcony," "step to their side," and "build them a golden bridge"—for dealing with difficult people.

These are useful techniques that suggest very practical steps for producing more satisfying and sustainable solutions. More important for manager-leaders than techniques, however, are the attitude and spirit that must inform the use of the techniques. Achieving truly integrative agreements requires a high level of openness; skills of inquiry and a willingness to engage in authentic dialogue; an appreciation of the larger system and a genuine respect for and interest in the needs, concerns, values, and even styles of other players within it; and often a goodly measure of patience and persistence.

Openness and strong inquiry skills are crucial because they allow for the uncovering of possibilities that may not be initially obvious. In the preceding section ("Engages in Dialogue") we described dialogue as a collective inquiry in which new meaning emerges *through* the deliberations of individuals who allow *questions*—rather than their own predetermined answers or positions—to guide the conversation. So although some models of negotiating encourage our coming to the table with a clear notion of exactly what we want to walk away from the deal with, manager-leaders may be better served by taking a more open-ended and exploratory approach, especially in the early stages of a negotiation, however formal or informal.

Appreciating the larger system and respecting the needs and concerns of other players within the system speak to the need to achieve agreements that are sustainable and that build relationships for the sake of facilitating future transactions. If we behave parochially, concerning ourselves with only what serves us personally or our department or work unit, we may succeed in maximizing our situation in the short term at the expense of the larger system and, ultimately, of our own long-term survival. For example, in the popular simulation "Friday Night at the ER" (a board game developed by Bette Gardner at Breakthrough Learning), participants, who play the roles of department heads, quickly discover that unless they work out agreements that take into account the entire operation—at times even suboptimizing their own unit temporarily—the system quickly breaks down, which puts everyone, even those departments that had positioned themselves most strategically, at risk.

In today's international marketplace, operating successfully across the larger system may require a global perspective and an understanding of another culture. These sensibilities are a part of working with others, and when we work *with* rather than around or against others in the system, we are also investing in future endeavors. Fisher and Ury (1981) point out that with few exceptions (dealing with a used car salesman would be a stereotypical example), the relationship itself should be as much—if not, in some cases, more—of an interest than the substantive content of a negotiation. At the very least, maintaining a good relationship throughout a negotiation increases the chances of a mutually satisfying outcome; at best we build trust and establish a collaborative context for subsequent negotiations.

Dealing with the relationship part of negotiating agreements involves some simple things, such as being sensitive and responsive to others and employing effective interpersonal behavior in our face-to-face dealings, and some not so simple things: recognizing that often what is really important to the other has nothing to do with what is being talked about; being willing to come to terms with the concerns and interests of others, rather than glossing over them in the interest of a quick resolution, even when those concerns and interests are messy or difficult to resolve; or accommodating someone else's personal style. Extroverts, for example, may be comfortable working things out, out loud in real time, whereas introverts often need time to deliberate by themselves before they are ready to make a decision. For example, for years one of the authors resented her physician spouse's frequent recalcitrance when it was time to get ready for a social engagement that he had previously agreed to attend. She subsequently realized that almost invariably on those occasions she had pressured him to assent, on the spot—"if the hospital is quiet"—despite his expressed preference for not making social plans when he was on call, and that his yes was entirely perfunctory, given mainly to pacify her; hence, when it was time to get ready he was unmotivated and virtually immovable. She had not only failed to appreciate his need to think about and get comfortable with a situation before he gave an answer, but had also disregarded, in the interest of satisfying her own need, his very real and legitimate concerns.

This brings us to the last of the cluster of negotiation skills we have recommended: patience and persistence. These are important because of the role timing often plays in another's ability to come to genuine agreement; although we may be ready to move forward directly, others may be struggling with unresolved issues that impede their ability to make a full assent, or they may just need more time to process ideas. If we force the issue, we may get the answer we are seeking but find that the support and commitment we need to implement the agreement are lacking.

Patience and persistence can often pay big rewards, as one of the authors discovered in her dealings with her children's grade school principal about hosting a group of folk singers as part of a fine arts program that she had initiated (also discussed in Chapter Two). Although the author had accommodated the principal's requests for information about the group for a recording of their music and for extended time to think about the event and discuss it with faculty, she could tell as she approached him on the day the decision had to be made that he was on the verge of saying no because he had to be away from the building that day and was uncomfortable about allowing something out of the ordinary to take place in his absence. Sensing his hesitation, she intentionally suggested that he not give her an answer just yet but wait until she returned at noon to pick up some materials due from the teachers. When she returned at noon he was resolute: the answer was no—he had told the administrative office that the day would be routine, and that's the way it was going to stay. The author, very disappointed, told him that she regretted his decision for the children's sake but accepted his right, as principal, to make that choice . . . and she then decided not to leave right away. She hung around and chatted with the principal and his secretary, realizing that although the principal had shown his strength, he might still be somewhat ambivalent, and she had decided to buy some time for him to reconsider. Sure enough, within a short while and with almost no warning, he gathered himself up and almost exploded, "All right! You can have your concert! I guess I'm not much of a principal if I can't leave my school for one day without worrying!" What seemed to have made the difference was the author's measure of patience in accepting the original decision and allowing the principal the time and space he needed to come, on his terms, to a different choice; and her persistence in keeping the issue open even after it appeared to be closed.

We talked at some length earlier in this chapter (see "Takes a Systems Approach") about the fundamental, irrefutable truth that we—individuals, corporations, countries, members of the universe—are all connected. We know, as well, that when we consistently operate out of self-interest we may get away with it in the short term but are generally undercutting our long-term ability to thrive or sometimes even to survive. Considering these basic truths, the only approach that makes sense—certainly the only choice for those who want to call themselves manager-leaders—is for us to work to achieve the kind of agreements that maximize gains for the entire system.

ORGANIZATIONAL LEADERSHIP
SHAPING THE ENTERPRISE

We must learn how to see the company as a living system and to see it as a
system within the context of the larger systems of which it is a part. Only then
will our vision reliably include return for our shareholders, a productive environment
for our employees, and a social vision for the company as a whole.

PHIL CARROLL, CEO OF SHELL OIL,
"LEADING LEARNING ORGANIZATIONS," *LEADER OF THE FUTURE*

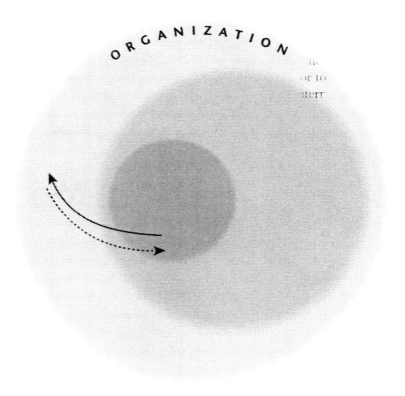

CHAPTER FIVE

CREATING A CULTURE

If they [modern organizations] do not search for ways to provide a context for meaning and community, as well as for worthwhile purpose beyond self and wealth, they may unwittingly be "killing the goose that has laid the golden egg."
— JUANITA BROWN, "CORPORATIONS AS COMMUNITY:
A NEW IMAGE FOR A NEW ERA," *NEW TRADITIONS IN BUSINESS*

In commenting on the usefulness of the culture metaphor for describing organizations, Gareth Morgan (1986, p. 135) clarifies this metaphor's implications for the role of the manager-leader: "Whereas previously many managers have seen themselves as more or less rational men and women designing structures and job descriptions, coordinating activities, or developing schemes for motivating their employees, they can now see themselves as symbolic actors whose primary function is to foster and develop desirable patterns of meaning."

As important as any other activity that may fall to manager-leaders, it is their role to help develop a culture in which others are encouraged and allowed to do the right things. In today's organization, developing that culture means ensuring that all employees share a set of beliefs about what the organization stands for and can act in accordance with those beliefs. Developing that culture also means recognizing the interconnectedness of elements within the organization and being able to use that understanding to identify high-leverage opportunities for making significant organizational change. And developing that culture means building a stronger sense of community within the work group and across functional boundaries.

In this chapter we discuss the first aspect of the Organizational Leadership sphere, namely, creating a culture; we explore the skills and attributes related to developing core values, taking a systems approach, and building community.

Develops Core Values

Facilitates consensus around a set of shared beliefs about what the organization or work unit stands for; works to ensure that these beliefs are reflected in the systems, structures, choices, and decisions of the organization as a means of shaping its organizational culture.

A company's values—what it stands for, what its people believe in—are crucial to its competitive success. Indeed, values drive the business.
—ROBERT HAAS, CHAIRMAN AND CEO OF LEVI-STRAUSS,
"VALUES MAKE THE COMPANY: AN INTERVIEW WITH ROBERT HAAS," *HARVARD BUSINESS REVIEW*

In the section on self-leadership, we talked about the importance of manager-leaders' modeling personal values. Values are equally important at the organizational level, although for many decades they have been virtually ignored by business practitioners who have been trained to focus on the numbers and that most important of measures, the bottom line. Instead of concerning ourselves with what we stand for, we have obsessed about what percentage of market share we can claim and how much profit we can make, often at the expense of fundamental values. Our customers are reduced to market research statistics and our employees to "headcount." Even in those companies that acknowledged a role for values, values were the "soft stuff." Robert Haas, chairman and CEO of Levi-Strauss, admits: "The soft stuff was the company's commitment to our work force. And the hard stuff was what really mattered: getting pants out the door" (cited in Howard, 1990, p. 134).

Yet values are central in shaping the identity of an organization and in informing its members' work with meaning and purpose. Because values answer the question, What do we believe in? they express what Kouzes and Posner (1987, p. 115), authors of *The Leadership Challenge,* call the "collective yearnings"—the common ground or shared sense of what we want, believe in, and are willing to work for. Robert Haas comments: "What we've learned is that the soft stuff and the hard stuff are becoming increasingly intertwined" (cited in Howard, 1990, p. 134).

Why this newfound recognition of the importance of values? Precisely because of the way "permanent white water" requires that organizations respond. If organizations are to thrive in an environment of rapid, volatile change, intensified competition, globalization, and technological revolution, they must transform themselves to become quicker, lighter, more agile—able to ride the waves and shoot the rapids. That means moving beyond the limitations of hierarchical structures and relocating power at all levels of the organization within a context that aligns efforts and choices. Values are central to creating that context.

Some question the need for organizational values, assuming that the personal ethics and good intentions of the organization's members should be sufficient. There is an understandable reluctance to devote the kind of time and resources required to identify and commit collectively to core values—which some fear ultimately may *not* make a critical difference—in light of intense pressures to perform and, in the case of public agencies, greater accountability for taxpayer dollars.

These are legitimate concerns, yet the potential significance of organizational core values cannot be overstated. Are they different from *personal* values? Yes. Do they make a difference? Yes, *if* the processes of determining them and integrating them into the business are accomplished well. Will that take a lot of time and resources? Yes.

Let's start with what core values are. Core values answer the question, What do we believe in? After the mission question (Why do we exist?) it is perhaps the most important question an organization must answer, for it determines *how* the organization will live out its mission in terms of a few—and it is very few—well-considered, fundamental beliefs. Collins and Porras (1994), authors of *Built to Last: Successful Habits of Visionary Companies,* define core values as the organization's "essential and enduring tenets" (p. 73) that are not compromised for the sake of expediencies or financial gain and that withstand changes in the environment over time. Core values represent a deliberate choice that the organization makes about how it will *be* and what it will become *known for.* In that respect, although core values must be congruent with the personal values of the organization's members, they transcend individual values: they are tied, very specifically, to the enterprise, and they function at a collective level. Core values are the soul of an organization.

In answer to the question, Do core values make a difference? we have only to consider Collins and Porras's six-year study (1994) of twenty companies they defined as "visionary"—the premier institutions or crown jewels in their respective industries by virtue of their impact and the esteem in which they are held by peers. Collins and Porras found that visionary companies are guided by a core ideology that encompasses core values and that plants "a fixed stake in the ground" (p. 54). It is interesting to note that the core ideologies of these companies varied widely in terms of focus (for example, a focus on customers, employees, products or services, or a particular trait such as risk taking or innovation) and were not necessarily geared to how the ideologies might be received by outsiders. In other words, "the critical issue is not whether a company has the 'right' core ideology or a 'likable' core ideology but rather whether it *has* a core ideology . . . that gives guidance and inspiration to people *inside that company*" (p. 68). So, for example, a company like Merck becomes known for integrity and social responsibility, 3M for innovation, and Disney for magic.

As for the investment required to institutionalize core values, it can be formidable, particularly if an organization is starting from scratch. In some organizations core values are handed down from its founders. Such is the case with George Merck, who had a deep belief in "preserving and improving human life," or the "HP Way," developed in the late fifties by Bill Hewlett and Dave Packard and still the basis for the company's operation today. When an individual joins an organization that has a strong set of identifying core values in place historically, the individual buys into those values when he or she signs on to become a member of that organization. In the absence of such a legacy, organizations must seek to discern values that are meaningful and intrinsic.

There are two kinds of core values. Those that are driven by the nature of the products and services the organization provides are generally obvious and straightforward. For United Airlines, safety is paramount, whereas for Ben & Jerry's, flavor carries the day; Wal-Mart and Hyundai subscribe to economy, whereas the Four Seasons Hotel and Lexus are all about luxury.

The second kind of core value is about more generic issues related to the organizational culture and what it will hold dear. Because these kinds of values— such as partnership, respect for the individual, social responsibility, individual initiative, and fun—are less intrinsic to the business, they represent deliberate choices and are therefore less easy for a large number of people to agree on. The organization must find a way of gaining the buy-in of existing members. This takes considerable time and involvement, as we are tackling very fundamental questions and asking people for a very deep commitment, one that will inform their work on a day-to-day basis.

Core values in the absence of commitment not only are hypocritical but can be destructive as well. James F. Barry (1996), a coach and professor at the U.S. Naval Academy, laments the numerous scandals that have plagued the Navy in recent years and suggests that at least part of the reason is the "ethically corrupting system" at the Academy (p. C1). Although the school has maintained academic excellence, the values articulated in its mission—the highest ideals of duty, honor, and loyalty—have become thoroughly compromised, claims Barry. Sexual harassment, favoritism, and covering up are tolerated to such an extent that students have come up with informal "rules of the road" that include such maxims as "The administration is the enemy," "The system is basically punitive," and "Loyalty is more important than truth" (p. C1). The consequence is that bright, highly motivated students—the "pick of the litter," according to Barry—learn behavior that undermines true leadership, operate out of fear of retaliation, and often become disillusioned to the point of leaving the Academy (p. C4).

For the manager-leader, undertaking the development of core values in an organization or work unit of any size, in a way that builds true commitment and a supporting culture, is like going on a journey that at times will seem long and discouraging, maybe even futile and endless. And, like any journey involving large numbers of people, there are bound to be stragglers and dissenters along the way. The litany of challenges to the process is likely to include any or all of the following:

- *Are We There Yet?* "We've already spent a day-long retreat and a half-day work session, and we *still* don't have core values. This process must be flawed."
- *Just Send Us a Postcard.* "Why doesn't the senior VP just close the door of her office, spend a couple of hours, write the damn things, and let us know what they are. That would save all of us a lot of time and effort and the department a lot of money. Besides, in the final analysis they're going to be what she wants anyway."
- *Journey As Side Trip.* "This has nothing to do with our real work," or "This is a waste of taxpayer dollars," or "This won't really make a difference," or "We need to get back to solving the *real* problems" (or any combination of these).
- *Led down the Primrose Path.* "This is the consultant's agenda, not ours, and we're allowing ourselves to be bamboozled."
- *Getting Nowhere.* "We don't seem to be getting anywhere. We have no concrete results. Worse yet, we're more confused than we were when we started."
- *Extra Baggage.* "Why do we need organizational values? We're all good people, and we're all trying to do a good job."
- *You Can't Get There from Here.* "It's just too difficult to make the change in our culture. People are the way they are; they're going to do what they're going to do, and we should just make the best of it."
- *Long Day's Journey into Night.* "What if we, as managers, *can't* live up to these values that up until now have been words on a page? We're going to be exposed as hypocrites!"

Perhaps today's manager-leaders can take heart from the knowledge that, prior to writing the Declaration of Independence, our founding fathers spent months studying various forms of democracy, engaging in challenging conversations with one another, and wrestling with ideas so that they could finally proclaim, unequivocally, "We hold these truths to be self-evident" and pledge, in support of these truths, "our Lives, our Fortunes and our sacred Honor." The values of freedom and equality that our founding fathers bequeathed us have, indeed, endured owing largely to what Thomas J. Watson Jr., the former CEO of IBM, would describe as their "bone deep" quality (cited in Collins and Porras, 1994, p. 75).

As manager-leaders we must be willing to sign on for a formidable journey—no less than a quest—to work with others to discover values that are authentic, at the core, and to enable a mutual commitment to living them out in our work.

Takes a Systems Approach

Recognizes the interdependency of parts within the system; considers the potential impact of decisions, choices, and initiatives on what is distant in time and space as well as what is close at hand; uses the tools and methodologies of systems thinking to identify high-leverage opportunities for making significant organizational change.

We often think that when we have completed our study of one *we know all about* two, *because "two" is "one and one." We forget that we have still to make a study of "and."*
—SIR ARTHUR EDDINGTON, *THE NATURE OF THE PHYSICAL WORLD*

Say the word "systems" today and what probably comes to mind for most business people is something that has to do with the linkup of office technology—phones, faxes, PCs. Important as these systems are, they represent only a mechanical microcosm of the much larger systems that govern our universe and with which we have only recently begun to come to terms.

Russell Ackoff (1981) acknowledges the magnitude of a current shift in our thinking by claiming that we are crossing the threshold of no less than a new *age,* which he defines as a period dominated by a prevailing worldview. According to Ackoff we are moving from the Machine Age to the Systems Age. The Machine Age, which developed as a result of Newtonian physics and the philosophy of Descartes, is characterized by an *analytical* approach to reality that focuses on material (that is, quantifiable) elements and that seeks to understand the whole by reducing it to its isolated parts. This mind-set has produced a very mechanistic approach to reality and a way of organizing much of human experience by dividing things into component parts at the expense of maintaining an awareness and appreciation of the whole. Consider, for example, our educational system, which delivers knowledge by segmenting it into subjects and periods. A student has French at ten and biology at eleven, followed by music at one . . . with virtually no help in understanding how these connect as part of a larger body of knowledge. As a result, say Fred Kofman and Peter Senge, "we eventually become convinced that knowledge is accumulated bits of information and that learning has little to do with our capacity for effective action, our sense of self, and how we exist in our world" (Kofman and Senge, 1995, p. 18).

Medicine provides another graphic example. The rise of subspecialties mid-century has resulted in a view of the patient in terms of isolated parts. With all due respect, to the surgeon you're primarily a gall bladder, to the cardiologist, a heart, and to the orthopedic surgeon, a broken ankle; yet we are well aware of the array of factors, beyond a treatment or procedure, that affect healing—and the potential disaster of treating or prescribing in a vacuum. In organizations we have created what are commonly known as vertical "stovepipes" by dividing the enterprise into functional units that then become internally focused, parochial in approach, bureaucratic in their dealings, and cross-functionally competitive. We have assumed that by differentiating functions we could create the equivalent of a giant machine. The challenge was simply to engineer and maintain the machine properly—to keep it well tooled and well oiled. Obviously the vestiges of this approach are still very much with us, as the current wave of "reengineering" attests.

But what the Machine Age view fails to take into account is that the essence of any whole lies not in the isolated parts but rather in the properties that ensue from the *relationship* of the parts one to another and in combination. A prime example can be drawn from the classic high school biology lesson that values the human body at roughly ninety-six cents, when valuation is based on a breakdown of the body's chemicals, minerals, and other components. The shock value of this demonstration depends entirely on the separation of the body in its purely material aspect from the person as a system in which physical parts combine with non-physical elements to produce an individual of unique temperament and personality—and of inestimable value!

Similarly, when we carve the organization up into units, and focus on such structural elements as functions, roles, reporting relationships, and policies in isolation, we may fail to appreciate the dynamic nature of organizational relationships, the interdependency among the parts, and the potential for synergies that such interdependency affords. No organizational chart that we have yet seen, however detailed, adequately represents the flow of the organization as a human, living system that is itself part of still larger systems such as its industry, the local community within which it operates, the nation, and the world.

The dawning recognition of the value of systems thinking for organizations has brought with it powerful insights about how and why organizations can break down in the absence of such thinking. In *The Fifth Discipline*, Senge (1990a) reports the finding of a Royal Dutch/Shell survey that the average lifetime of the largest industrial enterprises is less than forty years—only about half the life expectancy of a human. Senge is convinced that this high mortality rate can be attributed in no small part to a complex of fundamental "learning disabilities" that pervade virtually all organizations but go largely undetected because of a failure to apply systems thinking.

The "I Am My Position" disability, for example, is the tendency for people to become identified with their jobs or tasks to such an extent that they lose sight of the larger purpose of the enterprise, develop a limited sense of their responsibilities, or become victims of the "system"—a force that they perceive as separate from themselves and over which they feel they have little or no control (p. 18). A by-product of "I Am My Position" is "The Enemy Is out There," whereby individuals tend to blame someone or something outside themselves when things go wrong because they do not appreciate the role their actions play in the consequences they suffer. But, as Senge points out, "'out there' and 'in here' are usually part of a single system" (p. 20): we very often collude, albeit unwittingly at times, with the very things that appear to victimize us. So, for example, we attribute our anxiety and stress to overwork and the demanding expectations of an unreasonable boss, without recognizing that in taking on more and more work we have helped create the situation we deplore. The recent imposition of fishing limits off the Gloucester, Massachusetts, coast illustrates the consequences of this disability. Although these limits represent a severe economic hardship for a community in which fishing is the major industry, they are the result of years of overfishing by Gloucester fishermen who failed to see that by focusing only on their own short-term interests they were depleting the very part of the system on which they were dependent to provide the resources for long-term survival.

What, then, does it mean to think systemically or to take a systems approach? It is beyond the scope of this book to provide a full treatment of emerging systems theory. (For a comprehensive discussion of systems thinking, see Senge, *The Fifth Discipline,* New York: Doubleday, 1990; Draper Kauffman, *Systems 1: An Introduction to Systems Thinking,* Minneapolis: S.A. Carlton Publisher, 1980; and Russell Ackoff, *Creating the Corporate Future,* New York: Wiley, 1981.) What follows, instead, is a brief overview of some fundamentals that are especially important for manager-leaders to understand.

We must first consider what a system is. Ackoff (1981, p. 15) defines a system in terms of three conditions:

1. The behavior of each element has an effect on the behavior of the whole.
2. The behavior of the elements and their effects on the whole are interdependent.
3. However subgroups of the elements are formed, each has an effect on the behavior of the whole and none has an independent effect on it.

The essence of a system, then, is that everything is connected; this interconnectedness results in predictable dynamics. For example, small actions or interventions can become amplified over time as they travel through the system. This dynamic is the famous "butterfly effect," which states that a butterfly flapping its wings in Tokyo can cause a tornado in Texas. In other words, an action or intervention that may seem small or isolated can have significant effects: the assassination of the archduke of Austria touches off a world war; a manager makes what she thinks is a simple administrative decision about parking assignments, triggering discontent among disgruntled employees, which results in subversive behavior, which undercuts trust and morale, and so on and so on. The obvious corollary is that causes and effects may be distant from each other in time and space and therefore difficult to perceive. We may thus fail to appreciate how elements of a system are linked or, as Senge (1990a) explains, the extent to which small, well-placed actions can provide leverage for bringing about significant change.

The kind of amplification illustrated by the butterfly effect is an example of a feedback process or loop that is characteristic of any system. Another type of feedback involves a balancing loop whereby a kind of self-correction occurs for the sake of maintaining a desired threshold or goal: when we get hungry, for example, we eat to maintain a sense of satisfaction; when we get too hot, we shed clothing or adjust the heat to maintain a comfortable temperature. An example of balancing processes in organizations would be stepping up marketing efforts when there is a downturn in business, or downsizing to adjust to fewer resources or less product demand.

Coupled with these feedback processes and underlying the complexity of most systems are a few generic, recurring patterns of structure known as archetypes. The "Limits to Growth" archetype (Senge, 1990a, p. 95), for example, comes into play when a reinforcing process that is gaining momentum inadvertently generates secondary effects that slow growth. For example, when a business begins to experience success and must suddenly deal with an unusually high demand for its products and services, its capability to respond may not be sufficient to keep up. As a result, customer service and satisfaction are at least temporarily diminished; the consequent leveling off of demand effectively damps growth.

A significant feature of the feedback mechanisms in any system is the delay, a phenomenon that may delude individuals into focusing only on the here and now and failing to anticipate something that simply hasn't caught up with them yet. Hence the tendency to latch onto a quick fix that provides immediate relief from a problem; we assume the fix will endure, but in fact it may ultimately exacerbate the problem. It's the "what goes around comes around" (eventually) phenomenon. Furthermore, fixing one part of the system may subsequently result in an unintended consequence in another part of the system. Thus, raising productivity levels in one unit could create a shortage in a unit that supplies to them or a backlog in a unit that must process their output.

Another systems dynamic is that of structures influencing behavior. In other words, poor performance or behavior often results not because of individuals' deficiencies but because of underlying structures or predisposing conditions within the system. Consider, for example, the organization that preaches teamwork but maintains a reward system based on individual contribution, or the school system that levies harsh punishments for absences for reasons other than illness, driving parents to fabricate excuses when they want their children released for the day to travel or to attend a special family event.

As the preceding overview and the title of Senge's book suggest, systems thinking is a discipline that comprises both concepts and skills. Although systems thinking rests on considerations as basic as seeing the parts in relation to the whole and paying attention to the interaction among the parts over time, these behaviors are not sufficient to produce the deep shifts in thinking necessary to re-create our reality and our organizations.

To be able to foster a systems approach, manager-leaders must begin by cultivating their own awareness of the larger systems—social, familial, environmental, political, and organizational—and of the ways those systems both affect and are affected by manager-leaders' actions. With a deepening understanding of the dynamics of systems, managers are then in a position to anticipate the broader implications of their actions and decisions. However, to become truly effective in shaping systems, manager-leaders will need to develop their capabilities in such areas as shared vision and collective learning, and they will need to educate themselves in the disciplines and methodologies of systems thinking. Becoming knowledgeable about feedback loops, archetypes, and the tools for analyzing these phenomena will undoubtedly represent a fairly steep learning curve for some people and will require an investment of time and effort. But these concepts and tools are the means by which managers can better understand complex problems at a more fundamental level, identify more high-leverage opportunities for bringing about desired change, and assist their staffs in applying systems thinking to daily considerations as well as to the larger questions relevant to the organization.

Manager-leaders must also be attentive to the ways in which their organizations are functioning, for it is in what goes on every day that the workings of the system play themselves out and opportunities for exercising leverage and shaping the system become manifest. Models of organization for the twenty-first century are much more fluid and dynamic than the static, highly structured models of the past. These new models focus on a moving rather than a fixed target: learning how to learn, building new capacities for the future, developing the capability to self-organize. The future is all about *process*—in the way we produce and provide products and services as well as in the way we organize to do so; for, as one senior manager commented, "We used to think it was enough to build a better mousetrap; we now know that how we deliver that mousetrap is just as important, if not more so."

Managing complexity does not depend exclusively on amassing increasing amounts of data; instead it requires that we learn to recognize and understand substrata—the relatively simple structures that underlie complexity; "it means," says Senge (1990, p. 128), "organizing complexity into a coherent story that illuminates the causes of problems and how they can be remedied in enduring ways."

Builds Community

Seeks to forge connections and strengthen personal and professional bonds among staff; stimulates the kind of esprit de corps that promotes collective learning, self-organization, and synergistic outcomes.

In every office
you hear the threads
of love and joy and fear and guilt,
the cries for celebration and reassurance,
and somehow you know that connecting those
threads
is what you are supposed to do
and business takes care of itself.

—JAMES AUTRY, *LOVE AND PROFIT*

In *Images of Organization*, social researcher Gareth Morgan (1986) investigated the various metaphors by which organizations have been understood and fashioned—from organizations as brains, machines, or organisms, to organizations as cultures, political systems, and even as psychic persons. Were he writing the same book today he would surely need to add a chapter on organizations as communities.

The word *community* evokes the interpersonal bonds developed as a result of history, shared experience, mutual interests, common purpose, proximity, and a level of familiarity at odds with our traditional notions of the workplace. In this older model of the work environment, the goal was to minimize distractions and focus attention on isolated tasks; work was structured to discourage interaction. The time and motion studies of the 1920s brought about a revolutionary outgrowth, the assembly line, the express purpose of which was to make human workers as little like people and as much like machines as possible. Similarly, the competitive model on which organizations are based, replete with hierarchical and functional structures, has segmented organizations into parts and encouraged individuals to focus on self at the expense of others. Instead of seeing self *in relation to* others, we tend to separate ourselves and view others as a means of exchange. According to Senge: "Encounters with others become transactions that can add or subtract to the possessions of the ego" (Senge and others, 1994, p. 26).

Today's organizations, pressed by the need for their members to pull together, seek to remedy that isolation by shifting to a more team-oriented approach (and, by extension, a greater sense of community as members of the organization), but the pressure on employees to become team-oriented and to pull together for the organization represent just one of the many paradoxes implicit in the new paradigm of business. First of all, the "contract" between employers and employees has become highly provisional, with no long-term guarantees. In a recent cover article on the "new deal" companies are striking with employees, *Fortune* magazine highlighted the demand for increased personal accountability coupled with the loss of job security characteristic of the new job compact and quipped: "If the old arrangement sounded like binding nuptial vows, the new one suggests a series of casual, thrilling—if often temporary—encounters"(O'Reilly, 1994, pp. 44–45). Casual encounters are hardly the stuff of which community is built.

Yet at the other end of the continuum, we hear such authors as Margaret Wheatley, M. Scott Peck, Max De Pree, Kazimierz Gozdz, and James Autry proclaiming the centrality of community to the kind of adaptive organizations required for the future. De Pree (1992, pp. 62–64) addresses community in organizations in terms that acknowledge its spiritual element. He speaks of relationships as "covenants," and he exhorts us to "derive strength from our human bonds" by becoming "submerged" in the human mix of our organizations as a way of moving "in the direction of wholeness." Part of the work of the leader, claims De Pree, is to create "a haven . . . where work becomes redemptive, where every person is included on her own terms." For De Pree the *contractual* relationship between employers and employees has only to do with terms of employment. Contractual relationships are largely legalistic—what De Pree calls the "quid pro quo of working together" (p. 58). Much more significant is the covenantal relationship that leaders make available to employees by creating organizations that are hospitable, nurturing, intimate, and inclusive—that build community.

For Wheatley, community is the means by which systems become capable of self-organization. By virtue of their ability to come together around a common purpose, develop core values, and share information, members of organizations are able to co-create, in a dynamic, bottom-up manner, activities and products that emerge with structural coherence. Speaking of organizational change programs that fail because they are imposed, Wheatley (1992) comments: "We have the capacity within ourselves to create order as needed, if certain conditions are present. Those conditions are that people need to be able to bump up against one another, to have access to many more relationships than we usually plan for, to work in an information-rich environment, and to truly understand why they are working together and what they are trying to accomplish."

Gozdz (1993), an internationally known facilitator and consultant to the Foundation for Community and Encouragement, insists that organizations that wish to become learning organizations must realize that they are *by definition* communities. He defines the organizational community as "a collective lifelong learner, responsive to change, receptive to challenge, and conscious of an increasingly complex array of alternatives" (p. 108). Because Gozdz believes community is a *process* not a *state*, he concludes that strong leadership is essential to sustain, shape, and deepen community in a way that supports self-reflection and that combines diversity with inclusiveness—like a "crisp salad" (p. 108) in which each ingredient (person) retains his or her individuality but contributes to a greater whole. Furthermore, Gozdz believes that through such leadership the organizational community functions to encourage each member to become a leader.

Autry proposes a new bumper sticker that reads, "If you're not creating community, you're not managing" (1991, p. 145). Considering such significant social changes as greater mobility and the breakdown of the traditional family structure, Autry believes that "the job is the new neighborhood. And friends and co-workers are the new extended family" (p. 143).

Jim Channon (1992), a futurist and strategic design consultant, regards contemporary business organizations as our modern-day tribes and villages. If this is true, then the organization stands to gain to the extent that it nurtures relationships that can serve to break down functional and hierarchical barriers and that—by encouraging individuals to reveal themselves more fully to their coworkers—can engender mutual understanding, the discovery of common purpose, greater trust, and more shared responsibility for outcomes. When we build community in organizations we restore a sense of wholeness that has been fractured, for many, by the requirements of maneuvering in twentieth-century (read *politicized, bureaucratized*) organizations. As Juanita Brown (1992, p. 124) observes: "Modern organizations and the promise of the 'good life' have separated us from traditional ties to the land, to our families, to the community, and perhaps most importantly, from the connection to our own spirit. In this process, millions of us have been cut off from our hearts' desire—to be a part of a larger community of endeavor that is worthy of our best effort."

Surely one of the roles of the manager-leader must be to help members of the organization recover what Annie Dillard (cited in Palmer, 1990, p. 7) calls the "unified field: our complex and inexplicable caring for each other, and for our life together here." Yet managers in modern organizations may lack experience and tools for performing this role because they have been focused, as Channon (1992, p. 54) points out, "on the fine art of making things, not the cultural art of evoking spirit."

How then do we cultivate community? Community in the workplace is nurtured whenever we enable people to feel connected. Bringing people together to commemorate personal occasions, to launch a new initiative, to celebrate individual or organizational achievements, or simply to socialize are some of the more obvious ways we can help people forge bonds that transcend job requirements. In addition, manager-leaders should consider more subtle things, for example, the role that physical space plays in encouraging communication and interaction. Are common spaces inviting or daunting? Are conference rooms formal or informal, readily accessible or remote? Do employee lounges convey a sense of caring or a sense of neglect? Steve Wynn, CEO of Mirage Resorts, attributes its consistently high rate of return to investors (22 percent a year over the last ten years) to outstanding service to guests; a norm the hotel was able to achieve in large part by treating its employees as well as it treats guests—for example, by lavishing money on the employee cafeteria and on decorating employee corridors (Reilly, 1997).

Our goal is to generate in people a sense of belonging and loyalty. We do this when we take the time to acknowledge people's personal concerns. One manager at a pharmaceutical research division found that the quality and participation at his staff meetings improved immeasurably after he began the practice of opening the meetings with a brief check-in during which each individual was encouraged to remark on something personal of note, such as an offspring's success, a meaningful experience, or a family event. We build community when we create forums for people to contribute collectively, to engage the larger questions of the organization, to participate in decision making, and to grieve the losses brought about by disruptive change.

We also build community when we leaven the workplace with fun. Herb Kelliher is famous for the spirit his high jinks have generated at Southwest Airlines. Doug Eaton, vice president of the Seaboard region for State Farm Insurance Companies, quickly discovered that the three-story atrium surrounded by balconies at the center of the new regional office would not only accommodate hundreds of people for all-staff meetings and special events but also was an excellent place to stage impromptu get-togethers: on a Friday afternoon shortly after the stressful move to the new office had been accomplished, he spontaneously announced over the intercom at 3:30 that a paper airplane flying contest would be convened at 4:00. Anyone who could hit the target would be awarded a prize. Employees showed up in great numbers and finished off a tough week with a lighter heart, thanks to a bit of frivolity in the interest of greater solidarity.

If we want the members of our organizations to work together more synergistically—as we know they must—we need to find an alternative to the competitive model that has so long prevailed and that has undercut our motivation to pull together, to take care of each other, and to pursue a shared purpose. Seeing the organization as a community and cultivating a collective sense of possibility and purpose offer such an alternative. As manager-leaders recognize mutual connectedness and build community within the organization, they will sow the seeds for extending that sense of belonging to the larger communities to which the organization belongs. Creating this sense of connection is the first step in beginning to align the values of individuals, organizations, and communities so that we can take greater responsibility for the whole, create a more sustainable world community, and allow our planet to evolve more consciously.

CHAPTER SIX

ANTICIPATING THE FUTURE

The future enters into us . . . in order to transform itself in us long before it happens.
— RAINER MARIA RILKE, *LETTERS TO A YOUNG POET*

In *Megatrends 2000,* John Naisbitt and Patricia Aburdene (1990, p. 13) look at the "overarching trends" that will have a profound effect on our personal and business lives through the 1990s into the twenty-first century. These trends—technological connectivity, global competition, customer power, telecommuting, and so on—have already brought about changes in the ways we communicate, gather and process information, relate to our workplace and colleagues, and, generally, do our jobs.

In this chapter, we look at the second aspect of the Organizational Leadership sphere: the responsibility of the manager-leader to help create an organization that is responsive to external and internal changing forces and conditions. The attributes and skills discussed in this chapter—staying current with emerging trends, inspiring pursuit of a shared vision, thinking strategically, employing dynamic planning, and enlarging capacity for change—speak to the manager-leader's new role in shaping organizational direction as someone who must sponsor change as well as achieve results.

Stays Current with Emerging Trends

Maintains awareness of social, political, economic, and technological developments that affect the business; is knowledgeable about changing directions relative to a discipline, industry, or operating environment.

Look before, or you will find yourself behind.

— BEN FRANKLIN

There was a time not so long ago when trends made themselves apparent so gradually that most of us felt little pressure to anticipate them with more than a passing interest—and with infinitely more confidence in our ability to respond to them on our own terms and in our own good time. Because the world we lived in as recently as a few decades ago was more simple, more bounded, and more stable, it was easy for managers to keep their sights set on the present, in the expectation that the future would unfold as the logical extension of the past and present.

The wake-up call that things were about to change was first sounded by *Future Shock* (Toffler, 1970) and the subsequent emergence of a new group of professionals called futurists, who dedicated themselves to discerning what lay ahead. The shock of *Future Shock* was Toffler's prediction that change would accelerate at such a rate that it would soon outstrip our ability to accommodate it. A particularly memorable metaphor was of a car hurtling down a freeway (itself a relatively new concept at the time) at such a speed that it could no longer effectively negotiate the desired exit ramp.

Just a few decades later we find ourselves on that metaphorical freeway approaching speeds that threaten to exceed even Toffler's most dire predictions and feeling very much out of control. Daryl Conner (1993), change expert and author of *Managing at the Speed of Change,* captures the exponential nature of change today by referring to our present situation as "day twenty-nine"—an allusion to the child's riddle about a large lake that on the first day has a single water lily; each day the number of lilies doubles until, by the thirtieth day, the lake is completely choked with plants. The riddle asks, "On which day was the lake half full?" The answer, of course, is day twenty-nine!

In the face of change that is at once so overwhelming and so uncertain, we run the risk of succumbing to stress, anxiety, the feeling of being victimized, and a generalized debilitation. As Conner (1993) points out, considering that our capacity for assimilation is limited at best, we have never had to cope with so many changes so fast, at so many levels—from the highly personal to the social, organizational, and global. It is tempting to resort to a kind of passivity: after all, with so much flux and uncertainty, what's the point of trying to plan? Why not just wait to see what falls out?

Although at times a wait-and-see approach may make sense, it should not be at the expense of staying in touch with what is happening in our world. For underlying the distress we feel in response to unrelenting change is nothing less than the terror of having a fundamental human need violated—that of being in control of our environment. Because control comes from being able to determine future outcomes or at least anticipate them, we feel out of control when we are surprised, and even more vulnerable when we are "surprised to be surprised" (Conner, 1993, p. 73).

A simple but profound story, on a very personal scale, may serve to illustrate. The spouse of one of the authors, a family physician (Stephen), was shocked to learn that the results of a sonogram performed on one of his obstetrical patients who was near term indicated that the fetus was anencephalic—a condition in which the brain has not developed sufficiently for the child to survive. This revelation was especially shocking because earlier tests had revealed no problems, the pregnancy had been uneventful, and the parents were anticipating the birth of a healthy child in a matter of weeks. For a caring physician, dealing with something so horrific is anguishing under any circumstances, but in this case the poignancy was compounded because the patient was a personal friend and former employee of the practice and had miscarried in her previous pregnancy.

In the two weeks that ensued between the diagnosis and the scheduled induction, Stephen, who was ordinarily able to summon a seasoned equanimity in dealing with crises after twenty years in practice, struggled to deal with his own anxieties about what might transpire in the delivery room. He tried to imagine what the baby might look like, knowing that the clinical manifestations of this condition included such gross deformities as lack of a skull, eyes, or mouth, and only the most rudimentary nose. And what if the baby wasn't stillborn (as it is possible for an anencephalic fetus to be born with a heartbeat and some respiration)? There was no way to predict exactly what would emerge into his arms—and no way to predict how he might react in his dual role as physician and friend. As the date for the delivery approached, he found, quite uncharacteristically, that he was having difficulty sleeping.

He did what he could do: researched the condition extensively, consulted with colleagues, and spent time with the parents to understand their needs and to develop mutual expectations. What should happen in the delivery room immediately after the birth? Would they want to hold the baby? How thorough an examination did they want him to perform? The parents were also preparing. Armed with the knowledge of what to expect, they began the work of coming to accept this very painful outcome. And they readied themselves for the birth event: they chose a name for their little girl, arranged for their minister to perform a baptism in the delivery room, and attended to small details—such as the selection of an heirloom bowl to catch the water. What they managed to do, despite their grief, was seek information about what to expect, accept what they could not control, and control what they could—that is, make thoughtful choices about how they would respond to their circumstances. In so doing they succeeded in transforming a potential disaster into what all present agreed could only be described as a sacred experience.

Our need, then, when we find our situation fraught with rapid, painful, or capricious change is to regain some measure of control. By expanding our capability for dealing with change and reducing the likelihood of being blindsided we increase our resilience, which Conner (1993) believes is the key. But how do we expand a capacity that is limited? How do we mitigate the surprise factor of change that is so rapid and so volatile? An obvious starting point is to recognize that we have entered a time of *discontinuous* and *ongoing* change: not only do the past and present not necessarily prepare us very well for what is to come, but change no longer occurs incrementally or in discrete events that allow us time to recover from one change before the next one is upon us.

What also becomes obvious is the need to read the environment—to actively anticipate where things are headed so that we have at least some idea of what to expect and are in a position to make some choices about how to respond. If we are aware, for example, of growing evidence that professionals' loyalties are increasingly aligned with their disciplines rather than with a particular company, then we are in a position to proactively determine what we might want to do to make our organization attractive to highly independent types or how we might offset potentially high turnover. If we are able to project that the nature of jobs will change significantly in the next several years, requiring workers to be more flexible, self-directed, and multiskilled, then we can prepare what we will need to have in place to assist us and our staffs in making the transition. Without a good understanding of the forces that are playing themselves out around us, we have no basis for developing a meaningful vision and, therein, for influencing what comes to be.

Unfortunately, staying current with emerging trends requires a commitment of time and energy at odds with the situation of most managers, who find themselves consumed with the exigencies of the here and now—who are desperately trying to keep their heads above water, never mind trying to chart what lies around the bend. Obviously, the trick is to be able to shift focus between what is close at hand and what lies farther out but has impending relevance. Amitai Etzioni's model (1968) of mixed scanning—whereby we pay attention to the detail in our immediate environment but maintain an overview of the larger environment—suggests a process for seeing both the forest and the trees.

Seeing the trees is relatively easy because they're so immediate in our experience. Seeing the forest is another matter, especially considering that our forest is a much bigger place than it used to be. In a global age during which the interconnections among all kinds of things have become more apparent than ever, it is no longer sufficient to set our sights narrowly, on only what logically pertains. Clearly one of the most fundamental trends we have observed in recent decades is a shift to a more interdisciplinary, holistic way of looking at the world—we have begun to see the value of focusing on the whole rather than the parts and of appreciating that in any system, as small as our nuclear family or as large as our universe, one thing affects another sometimes even when those things seem remote in time and space. A change in the interest rate might affect a new product launch; the development of advanced telecommunication technology is likely to influence a change in worker lifestyles and expectations.

Given the increasing discontinuities of change, we cannot hope to predict the future with certainty, but we can become more astute about our decisions, more knowledgeable in our choices, more confident in taking risks, and more able to influence outcomes—if we know where things are headed. Obviously we need to start close in by maintaining an awareness of our organization and its operating environment—as it exists today and is likely to be in the future—from as many viewpoints as possible. We need to pay attention to a variety of sources including trade journals, the business press, internal communications, professional associations, and colleagues at all levels. We need to listen to key messages in the official pipeline as well as to the more subtle signals and unstated messages. We need to notice when there is handwriting on the wall.

Then we work our attention out to the larger forces of change—major social shifts, new technologies, and the like—that are influencing future realities. At this level we need to take a broad view that enables us to make new connections, however strange certain bedfellows might appear at first blush to be. Clearly one of the most fundamental and obvious shifts in our time is toward a more interdisciplinary approach and a recognition of the value of restoring a sense of holism to a world that finds itself fractured almost beyond repair. Thus we need to read extensively in a variety of disciplines and genres. Those whose field is technical should make a point of acquainting themselves with what the arts or theology might bring to bear; conversely, those whose orientation is education, the humanities, or the social sciences might investigate new directions in the natural sciences for insights they can shed. We can pursue many other avenues as well: engage in conversations with the intent of exchanging ideas and expanding our thinking through exposure to other perspectives; avail ourselves of the many public offerings—lectures, broadcasts, interest groups—about trends, discoveries, and topics of general interest; explore electronic media to broaden our knowledge of current and future directions: get on the Internet and listen to or participate in on-line dialogues about timely issues. Finally, we need to build some opportunities for reflection into our day or week in order to make sense of our experiences—to integrate the pieces we have accumulated and to develop insights about emerging directions, opportunities, and choices.

Thinks Strategically

Draws on both hard and soft data (for example, market research, emerging trends, experience, intuition, informal learning, and interactions with others) as sources for developing strategic direction; views strategy as dynamic rather than static; discovers future opportunities in day-to-day details; involves others in contributing to the process of shaping strategy on an ongoing basis.

The big picture is painted with little strokes.
—HENRY MINTZBERG, "THE FALL AND RISE OF STRATEGIC PLANNING,"
HARVARD BUSINESS REVIEW

Anyone associated with business over the past several decades cannot help being aware of the exalted position strategic planning has commanded since its advent in the mid-sixties. In its traditional form, this corporate activity is carried out by executives or specialists who rely on analysis—both in processing market (read *quantitative*) data and in breaking down goals into steps—to produce formalized plans. Traditional strategic planning, although still a corporate priority, is clearly out of touch with the current business environment. The argument is not with planning; indeed, some degree of planning is essential to ensuring that the vision of the organization is realized. Rather, the problem is with the *way* in which strategy has been misunderstood as a planning activity and the way in which that activity has been carried out.

Start with the practice of relegating strategic planning to the executive office or professional planners. Or the supposition that strategy can be fully determined up front. Or that strategic planning is the same as strategic thinking. A hard look at these assumptions reveals an inherent bias toward hierarchical, linear, task-driven approaches that are at odds with current conditions and with the very shifts—to less hierarchical, more dynamic and inclusive processes, and to less pre-ordination and more discovery—that most would agree are imperative if we are to successfully navigate the permanent white water of high-velocity change. So, for example, the notion that a strategic plan can be mapped out in detail in advance of its implementation—what Wall and Wall (1995, p. 10) term the "Strategy Is in the Binder" myth—fails to take into account that strategy must be allowed, to a considerable degree, to *emerge* as new circumstances present themselves, especially in a volatile environment. Collins and Porras (1994) agree. Their six-year study of visionary companies exploded the myth that successful companies operate on the basis of highly planned strategy. These researchers found that what might look in retrospect like brilliant moves were actually trials, experiments, sheer opportunism, or even accidents. Visionary companies try things, and in so doing, they discover what works.

Strategy, then, is emergent as well as intentional, so there is little wisdom in trusting strategy development to any single individual, team, or function. The executive office, for example, may have the best vantage point from which to take a global view, track significant trends, and anticipate market, technological, and other kinds of changes, but consider its limitations. "Where," says Gary Hamel (1996, p. 74), "are you likely to find people with the least diversity of experience, the largest investment in the past, and the greatest reverence for industrial dogma?" Senior executives typically have little direct contact with customers as their needs evolve. In fact, as a function of the hierarchical structure of most organizations, top management is effectively *insulated* from customers and far removed from the field in which the trials and experiments that spawn new strategy occur. Hamel observes that in many companies, top executives spend so much time talking at one another, their positions crafted and rehearsed, that opportunities for new learning as a function of their interaction diminish and a kind of intellectual incest develops—they can literally finish each other's sentences. Yet ongoing learning is precisely what is required to stimulate strategic thinking that remains in synch with its environment. For, as Mintzberg (1994, p. 111) reminds us, "We think in order to act, to be sure, but we also act in order to think." Furthermore, when strategy making is confined to the executive office, managers become tacticians rather than strategic leaders. Ask the typical manager what kinds of work-related things keep him or her up at night, and you are very likely to hear answers that are focused internally and operationally rather than externally—on customers and future direction. "Unfortunately," observe Jeanne Liedtka and John Rosenblum (1996, p. 17) "a hierarchical approach to strategy making, with grand strategy envisioned by senior management alone and controlled through planning and budgeting systems, is more likely to encourage managers to crave clarity and certainty in an ambiguous world and to think narrowly and parochially within complex systems." Wall and Wall (1995) use the metaphor of theatrical improvisation to describe the shift to a more dynamic approach: whereas strategy makers in the past were like playwrights who scripted a performance that was intended to be one-way (the actors enact the plot, the audience watches), today's effective strategy makers are more like skilled improvisers who start with a given scenario but allow the plot to unfold through their interaction with one another and their environment. Mintzberg (1994, p. 111) states: "I believe that all viable strategies . . . must combine some degree of flexible learning with some degree of cerebral control."

Wall and Wall (1995, p. 6) exhort, "We need to lay aside our view of business strategy as something conceived in the mind of the brilliant general and carried out by soldiers, and learn to see it in a way that involves tapping the strategic thinking skills of leaders at all levels of the organization." As for the confusion of strategic planning with strategic thinking, we need to bear in mind, says Mintzberg (1994), that the former is about analysis—breaking down goals into formalized steps with anticipated outcomes—whereas the latter is about synthesis—creating an integrated vision for the enterprise. In the same vein, Hamel and Prahalad (1993, pp. 77–78) talk about strategy as "stretch" and "leverage," emphasizing the power of aspiration (read *vision*) for achieving competitive advantage. "Strategizing," says Hamel (1996, pp. 70, 71), "is not a rote procedure, it is a quest. . . . [S]trategy *is* revolution; everything else is tactics." Mintzberg goes so far as to claim that strategic *planning* often impedes or "spoils" strategic thinking in its focus on manipulating numbers and its trust in formal, mechanical systems at the expense of more visionary, intuitive processes. Visions, rather than plans, are the stuff of the most successful strategies, says Mintzberg—visions that arise out of the manager's willingness to immerse himself or herself in day-to-day operations with an eye to divining the larger messages lurking within the details. "Real strategists get their hands dirty digging for ideas, and real strategies are built from the occasional nuggets they uncover" (1994, p. 111).

Clearly, then, strategic planning must be informed, at every level of the organization, by strategic thinking, an activity for which managers' day-to-day experience ideally suits them. We know, for example, that managers operate in highly dynamic, unstructured ways; are tuned in to informal channels of communication; attend, primarily, to "soft" information (impressions, anecdotal reports, and gossip, as opposed to hard, analytical data); and rely on judgment rather than more systematic processes to make decisions. In short, management behavior seems to be associated with relational, holistic, discovery-oriented processes characteristic of the right hemisphere of the brain (Mintzberg, 1976). Thus managers are positioned to capitalize on spontaneous contacts, emergent phenomena, and serendipity as a means of designing strategy attuned to a dynamic environment. The recent popularization of "management by walking around" (MBWA) further encourages managers to stay close to the front lines where the action that supports strategy development takes place.

Managers who think strategically see the value of their being strategy makers, and they see the value of involving their employees in feeding the strategy-building process, for all the reasons heretofore discussed. For, say Liedtka and Rosenblum (1996, pp. 12–13), "Participation in the making of strategy . . . invites individuals into a learning process in which they come to discover a new set of possibilities that they can shape in a way that creates personal commitments worth investing in." To facilitate employee participation, manager-leaders must provide their workers with a reference point against which to gauge their day-to-day experience—customer input, competitor offerings, market developments, emerging trends, and the like—as well as the organizational structures and processes that affect their ability to deliver products and services to customers in a way that keeps them coming back. Manager-leaders must, as well, encourage their workers to exercise initiative in making experiments or taking the kind of risks from which new strategies emerge.

Managers who think strategically are clear with their staffs not only about *what* the organizational direction is but also about *why* the direction is what it is. They make a point of keeping strategic direction front-and-center, they sustain attention to that direction by making it part of an ongoing conversation in which everyone is invited to participate, and they assist their employees in translating strategy into day-to-day actions and choices. In this way managers not only serve the vision of the company but also allow their employees to see the way in which their efforts contribute to something larger and more purposeful than the task at hand or the monthly numbers.

Managers who are strategy makers are learners along with their people. According to Hamel (1996), manager-leaders

- Find ways to change their perspective and to challenge the fundamental assumptions of the industry and the organization
- Cast a broad net in seeking out facts and exploring options
- Attune their ears to those with new ideas and ensure that radical notions have a voice
- Appreciate that those outside the inner circle—the young, the geographically distant, the newcomers—are often the best source of new information and promising ideas
- Recognize that, in a time of discontinuous change, a hierarchy of imagination can be more important than a hierarchy of experience (Hamel, 1996)
- Develop a keen sensibility about where they can leverage influence, and remain mindful not to set their sights too narrowly (at their shoe tips) or too broadly (on world hunger)

In addition to these behaviors, Wall and Wall (1995) suggest that manager-leaders have four specialized roles to play. First, the manager-leader should ensure that customers' input is continuously brought into the organization; their needs and perspective can thus be taken into account in developing products and services and in designing delivery systems. For example, managers need to help their staffs recognize that although it is the staff's responsibility to represent the company to the customer, it is at least equally important that they represent the customer to the company and that they take initiative in meeting and communicating customer needs.

Second, manager-leaders should assist individuals and teams in conducting informal information-gathering activities—sometimes through off-site visits, apprenticeships, or other forms of field research—and in targeting likely sources of new information, paying attention, for example, to competitors' strategies for everything from new products to pricing and customer service; to trends and events affecting the company's current vendors and suppliers; to changes in government and regulatory agencies that could affect the industry or business; and to the emergence of new technologies.

Third, manager-leaders should cultivate an organizational mind-set whereby individuals and teams are encouraged to find synergies across functions and to work to reconcile the inevitable conflicts—in priorities, resource allocation, and so on—that arise among functions or subunits within a complex system.

Finally, manager-leaders should seek opportunities to integrate strategy by establishing linkages both horizontally, among different units and functions, and vertically, between executive leadership and the rest of the organization.

The manager-leader who thinks strategically recognizes that good strategy is the product of many types and sources of information, many minds, many perspectives, many encounters, and many experiments. He or she plays a key role in making connections among these elements and in facilitating others' ability to contribute to that process. For, as Wall and Wall (1995, p. 17) state: "[T]he more people in your company, regardless of their level, who see themselves as strategists, the more likely you are to have a strong, resilient organization that is in tune with its environment."

Inspires Pursuit of a Shared Vision

Involves others in creating a bold and compelling picture of the desired future; engages everyone in imagining and seeking to realize what could be.

A shared vision is not an idea. It is not even an important idea. . . . It is, rather, a force in people's hearts. . . . Few, if any, forces in human affairs are as powerful as shared vision.
—PETER SENGE, *THE FIFTH DISCIPLINE*

It is easy for an organization to surrender its sense of direction when the world that surrounds it is in constant flux. As members of an enterprise, we feel ourselves carried along by forces of change that are sweeping, unstoppable, and bigger than we are. We become caught up in the onslaught, buffeted about and unable to think beyond the frantic effort of getting through the present moment.

Or we begin to shut down: we try to take ourselves out of the fray, make ourselves less visible, in hopes of finding some safe haven where we can avoid dealing with realities that seem too overwhelming and we can buy some time just to maintain. Yet, ironically, there is probably no more important time to collectively sharpen our focus, look ahead, and make deliberate choices about where we want to go, precisely so that we don't forfeit our ability to influence outcomes. It's not a question of finding a direction *in spite* of the turmoil but rather *because* of the very urgency turmoil creates. Lacking a clear sense of what we want to shoot for, we find ourselves adrift, at the mercy of forces outside ourselves. The irony is that we have thus inadvertently put the organization and ourselves at greater risk of the vulnerability we had sought to avoid. On the other hand, if we can shift our perspective to see beyond the turmoil to something of lasting value, something on the other side worth pursuing, then the white water takes on a somewhat different aspect: it becomes an energizing force, a challenge to get through and rise above, not the ultimate destroyer.

The "something to shoot for" is a vision of what is possible, given the forces of change and the capability of the organization to respond. The notion of organizational vision is worth spending some time clarifying because, despite the ascendance of the term *vision* in our business vocabulary in the past decade or so, there is still considerable confusion about exactly what a vision is and how it differs from mission, values, strategic plans, and goals. One means of distinguishing these various elements is by considering what question each addresses and how each contributes to an overarching scheme.

Mission answers the most fundamental question: Why do we exist? Missions are concerned with defining the organization in terms of its products and services, its customer base, and its intended outcomes. Mission statements are straightforward, matter-of-fact, and operational from the day an organization opens its doors. Because mission statements tend to be relatively generic within an industry or segment, they are more useful for describing the scope of an enterprise than for differentiating an organization or agency within its arena. For example, large retail stores such as Lord & Taylor, Bloomingdales, John Wanamaker, and Nordstrom share a common mission—to provide a variety of high-quality merchandise for sale to the general public.

Core values, as discussed in Chapter Five, answer the next question: What do we believe in? Core values, such as innovation, stewardship, and teamwork, express the enduring qualities for which the organization wants to be known and to which the organization commits in carrying out its mission. Core values thus begin to shape the particular identity of an organization. Nordstrom, for example, has become famous for legendary customer service, the result of a deliberate choice to carry out its mission *in a particular way.*

Vision translates the core values, which are abstractions, into operational terms by answering such questions as, What do we want to create? What difference do we want to make? What do we aspire to? What legacy do we wish to leave behind? Unlike missions, visions are bold, futuristic, sensory, idealistic, and expressive. Visions paint a compelling picture of a possible dream; they appeal not so much to the intellect as to the imagination. One litmus test for a vision is, Does it pass the goosebumps test? For example, when John Wanamaker struck on the idea of making entertainment and spectacle a core value, the company began to imagine a store in which shoppers would experience not just an appealing array of merchandise but also fountains, light shows, and pipe organ concerts—and the unique vision of Wanamaker's was born.

Strategic plans offer a preliminary blueprint for realizing the vision by devising initiatives to close the gap between current reality and the desired future state. Strategic plans answer the question, How do we get there?

Goals are short-term, measurable projections relative to the vision; goals answer the question, What do we do next?

Although each of these five elements plays a role in creating the identity of an organization, a comparison of their various functions reveals vision to be the central, creative force that, when shared throughout the organization, has the power to align individual efforts, galvanize personal commitment, and impel the organization toward a future of its choosing. As Price Pritchett points out, "Martin Luther King Jr. did not say, 'I have a strategic plan.' He shouted, 'I have a dream!', and he created a crusade" (1996, p. 6).

Important and central as a shared vision is, creating a vision that is truly shared may prove to be one of the manager-leader's most formidable challenges. Evidence suggests that leaders who arbitrarily *impose* their visions, however worthy, on others cannot expect to generate thoroughgoing commitment. People may comply, for all kinds of reasons, but compliance doesn't get you to your dreams. This is not to say that the leader should not have a *personal* vision about what he or she wants to realize individually. Nor does it mean that the leader cannot be the source of a vision that becomes truly shared by virtue of its genius or its ability to tap the latent aspirations of others. When John Kennedy articulated his vision of "a man on the moon by the end of the decade" in his 1960 inaugural address, he captured the attention of the nation with a concept that, although incredibly bold and ambitious (at the time we had only a fraction of the knowledge and technology such a feat would require), was so clear and seemed so right that on July 20, 1969, Walter Cronkite would announce that we had indeed succeeded in landing on the moon. Occasionally an organizational vision comes about in this way, the result of a single individual's breakthrough idea—like Steve Jobs's concept of personal computers or cellular pioneer Craig McCaw's idea to create a celestial Internet. Sometimes an organizational vision evolves and crystallizes in the mind of a leader who is particularly tuned in to what Kouzes and Posner (1987, p. 115) refer to as "the brewing consensus," the "quiet whisperings in dark corners," the "subtle cues."

More often than not, however, in the absence of a great concept or a well-honed sense of people's hopes and dreams, the development of an organizational vision requires a more participatory process. Wheatley (Mehal and McCarey, 1993) suggests that shared vision can "emerge" through the interactions of a community of people. She makes the distinction between the conventional view of vision as something "out there," a force distant from ourselves that pulls us into a desired future, and vision as part of the *field* of organizational forces—futuristic in the aspirations it embodies, but fully present in the ideas and hopes of organizational members. Like seeds in a garden, the latent elements of a shared vision need cultivation through "thinking together, experimenting together, playing together" in order to develop deep roots and to thrive over time. In her closing keynote address to the 1996 Systems Thinker conference, Wheatley (1996) challenged those present with the notion that a primary role of organizational leaders is not to analyze, structure, design, or build the organization, but rather to *convene* the system. Creating an environment and a culture conducive to this process and a mechanism for capturing the collective thought that emerges are at the heart of the manager-leader's ability to forge a shared vision. In other words, the interactions that take place on a personal level must have some means of feeding a larger, organizational conversation about the organization's identity, opportunities, aspirations, and so on, if the organization is to realize its potential for synergy.

The spontaneous, communal exchange Wheatley (1996) describes provides a foundation for the more structured and disciplined process of arriving at a shared vision that can be articulated as an overarching frame. In such a process, members of the organization are provided with a means of assessing forces of change, identifying challenges and opportunities, and sharing their perspectives as a starting point for clarifying current reality and describing a desired future state. Any number of methodologies are available today—from conventional formats such as surveys, focus groups, and story-boarding, to more recently introduced open-systems technologies, such as future search conferences and whole-scale change events—to facilitate this inquiry across organizations. Often these methods, particularly the newer ones, can be highly effective in aligning large numbers of people and energizing their pursuit of a clear direction.

Rallying—and *sustaining*—the many and diverse members of an organization of any size around a single focus cannot be reduced to a single event or to a simple cookbook approach, however. Any number of obstacles—logistical as well as personal and organizational—are likely to present themselves. Take, for example, an organization that feels no urgency to anticipate the future and pursue a desired state: a public sector agency that is not subject to competitive pressures, an institution that has been insulated from major change, or a unit or division that has gotten by for years with doing business as usual. In these situations the manager-leader's efforts to initiate a process for creating a shared vision may be viewed (similarly to core values) as a waste of time, money, and effort that actually takes away from the "real work" of the organization or, in the case of the public sector agency, from the value that taxpayers should expect for their dollars. Prevailing paradigms and norms about work, metrics for productivity, philosophical differences, and even personal styles may also inhibit efforts to engage people in a long-term effort that does not produce immediate results. Manager-leaders may find that their best efforts at inviting a participatory process are met with resistance, are misconstrued, or otherwise backfire by dint of sheer human misunderstanding, disagreement, or perversity.

Yet however laborious or protracted the process involved in creating the vision may be, it is at that point that the hardest work—*pursuing* the vision—begins. This is also the point at which the role of the manager-leader becomes most crucial in determining whether the vision becomes a sterile document relegated to a file drawer, or a living, breathing force that governs the day-to-day actions, choices, and decisions throughout the organization. If, once the vision has been wrought, there is no sustained effort on the part of the manager-leader to keep the vision front-and-center, to consciously model behaviors and actions consistent with the vision, and to remove barriers that limit others' ability to pursue the vision, then individuals are likely to assume that they need not take the vision seriously. There is, as well, the issue of achieving shared understanding about what the articulated vision really means, as each person will interpret it according to a very personal frame of reference; although some degree of ambiguity allows for the vision to remain flexible and for individuals to realize its possibilities creatively, the vision must also be sufficiently clear and mutually understood to align individual efforts synergistically. Achieving shared understanding requires a process that is both deliberative and iterative, one that allows sufficient opportunities for people to uncover and wrestle with tough issues; to tease out semantic implications as they struggle to internalize the vision; and to come to terms with what they are committing to and with what might stand in their way. The viability of the vision depends on its immediacy, its reinforcement, and its ability to evolve—through testing, discovery, and refinement.

A final caution: a powerful organizational vision is not necessarily the same as a well-crafted vision statement. The latter is composed of words—elegant, beautiful, exciting, symbolic, even inspiring words—on a document or a coffee mug or a plaque in the reception area. The former is something that lives in the hearts of people. It derives its potency from the extent to which it becomes personalized, shared, immediate, and demonstrated in day-to-day actions that involve everyone, in ways that may be highly individual and self-expressive, in assuming ownership for the vision's continued emergence and realization.

Employs Dynamic Planning

Charts a flexible course to move the organization toward its short-term goals and long-term vision; identifies checkpoints along the way to measure progress and incorporate new learning.

There is no freeway to the future, no paved highway from here to tomorrow. There is only wilderness, only uncertain terrain. There are no roadmaps, no signposts. Instead, the explorer relies upon a compass and a dream.
—KOUZES AND POSNER, *THE LEADERSHIP CHALLENGE*

There are few cows so sacred in business as *planning.* Whether it's a business plan, a strategic plan, a financial plan, a product launch plan, or any of the other myriad plans people in organizations conceive, our being able to plot a course has always been our best defense against whatever uncertainties lay ahead. Knowing how we would proceed, step by rigorous step, gave us confidence that we knew what we were doing, that we could proceed directly from point A to point B, that we would not be deflected from our purposes, that we could achieve predictable outcomes, and that we would, by dint of sheer organization and control, prevail in the end over less savvy competitors and whatever other unknowns were out there. In a business culture that has exalted logical, analytical, action-oriented approaches, planning has obvious appeal.

The problem with traditional planning is that it starts in the past—with standardized practices and formulas developed out of what worked before—and works gradually forward from the present in a detailed fashion that establishes fixed actions and points. Characteristic of these kinds of plans is their present and past orientation, their lockstep and somewhat rigid approach, and their inability to respond to the surprises that are inevitable in a volatile environment. Because it attempts to impose structure on the unrealized future (as if the future could be assumed to function as a continuation of the past), traditional planning often lacks the flexibility necessary for accommodating unforeseen obstacles or for taking advantage of opportunities as they unfold. Even in highly structured projects for which much of the detail *must* be nailed down up front, the likelihood is that the execution will not exactly match the blueprint. Think, for example, about the last time you or someone you know undertook a major construction effort. To what extent did the actual process unfold according to the plan originally conceived? More likely you found that anticipated schedules shifted as unforeseen circumstances intervened, and design details were refined or perhaps changed altogether as new ideas, opportunities, or complications presented themselves.

As this book was being written, for example, one of the authors was in the process of converting a log smokehouse on her property into office space, including a frame addition. In the architect's original design, French doors in the addition opened onto a small, enclosed area that the architect, for both aesthetic and practical reasons, deemed the most suitable location for a door (despite the author's preference for an opening on the exposure facing an extensive meadow). Construction began, beginning with disassembling the existing structure. However, as the logs came down, a vista never before seen revealed itself, including a view of a nearby mountain off the meadow side. It was obvious at that point to anyone who actually stood in the space that the French doors should, indeed, open out onto the meadow. Nevertheless, the architect, who had not yet visited the site, continued to resist the change—until he stood in the space.

Better forecasting is not the answer. Although we talked in the last section about the value of staying current with emerging trends, few things (much less *sequences* of things) more specific than trends can be predicted in a highly complex environment. There are just too many variables, and there are too many possible outcomes when those multitudinous variables interact. Referring to the previously mentioned butterfly effect ("a butterfly flapping its wings in Tokyo can create a tornado in Texas"), one senior manager recently commented, "the butterfly's wings are flapping"; his implication was, clearly: "and who knows *how* things will come out down the road!"

Nor is the answer to forgo all planning and simply "go with the flow" indefinitely in hopes that we will end up in the right place. Yes, occasionally it may make sense for short periods to allow oneself to be carried along or to indulge spontaneous side trips with abandon, but these approaches lack focus, and if employed indefinitely they may limit one's ability to pursue a desired end. For example, many years ago the parents of one of the authors decided to take their young family on a virtually unplanned summer vacation. No destination was determined in advance, no reservations were made—in fact, which way they would turn at the end of the driveway remained an open question until all nine of them were piled into the station wagon and backing out. And so the trip continued, with each turn at a junction determined entirely by whim. The vision was clear: to end up *somewhere* appealing by late afternoon, to stop at a motel with a pool and let us kids splash to our hearts' content. Then splurge on dinner at a family-style restaurant and a drive-in movie where we kids could pad the back of the station wagon with pillows and curl up in our pajamas. Unfortunately, our whimsical choices at critical junctures led us further and further into remote, rural areas with few motels of any description. It became increasingly clear as we drove on and on that a motel with a pool was out of the question. The car was hot, the trip was long, and we kids were bored and restless—we weren't having any fun yet, and it didn't look like we were going to any time soon. Out of desperation we finally stopped at the next place we came to. The details of that evening have been forgotten, although "modest" would be a stretch for both the lodgings and the meal. Frustrated and defeated, we aborted our (mis)adventure the following day by driving home and trying to salvage the outing with a smorgasbord dinner in our hometown. We tried for a drive-in movie, too, but there was no family fare on the playbill, so we gave up and went home to bed. So much for serendipity.

What are the alternatives to traditional planning or no planning? One possibility is a more dynamic kind of planning that finds its starting point in the future and allows for learning along the way. Driven by a vision rather than by prescriptive routines, dynamic planning works backward from the desired state to identify landmarks and checkpoints along the way. Dynamic planning incorporates exploration and acknowledges the possibility of more than one route to the intended destination. Relying on key markers and checkpoints rather than tedious detail, dynamic planning provides direction but at the same time encourages flexibility. Whereas a highly wrought plan can constrain responsiveness, a dynamic plan is a guide within which adaptation and creativity become possible. W. Bricker, CEO of Diamond Shamrock, likens this kind of planning to a compass; he suggests that when one is lost on a highway a detailed map can be very useful, but when one is lost in terrain that is constantly changing, as in a swamp, a road map is of little use; a compass, on the other hand—which indicates general direction but allows for ingenuity in forging a path—is much more valuable (in Kouzes and Posner, 1987).

In dynamic planning, checkpoints, or what some refer to as "mileposts," are determined not by dates on a calendar but by significant stages or events. These checkpoints provide opportunities for reflective learning and reassessment, so that new factors or knowledge acquired as the effort progresses is made available for subsequent decisions and replanning. Rather than "blunder along" as Zenas Block and Ian MacMillan (1985, p. 196) describe it, "adhering to a fixed plan that out of ignorance they have based on faulty projections," managers and employees can use checkpoints to test their assumptions and adjust their course—to slow down, speed up, try something new, change scale, redirect, postpone, or resequence certain activities. If, for example, we had used checkpoints on our family vacation, we might have determined relatively early on that we had made a wrong assumption about the ready availability of motels in other locations and that the direction we were going was taking us away from metropolitan areas (which in the

1950s were the only places you *might* find motels with swimming pools); we could then have decided to consult a map and route ourselves to a city of some size rather than continuing on our random odyssey. Checkpoints are also valuable for breaking sustained initiatives into "doable" stages that breed interim successes—the "small wins" that help to mitigate resistance to change, build confidence in the project, and provide opportunities to celebrate ongoing efforts.

Dynamic planning allows for what Kouzes and Posner (1987, p. 237) term "guided autonomy": a dynamic plan that serves as a framework within which we and our employees can entertain choices, make decisions, and assume responsibility. By building in flexibility, dynamic planning enables us to respond to changing conditions and to make experiments, to take some risks and innovate as we go—to accommodate a certain amount of chaos without losing sight of our vision. It is both critical and empowering to realize that no matter how well we have prepared, success will depend on our ability to "read the surface of the water" in real time as a means of discovering precisely, or maybe not so precisely, what steps to take next.

Enlarges Capacity for Change

Works to shape an adaptive organization that responds to emerging imperatives; challenges the status quo and encourages others to do the same; champions new initiatives; allows for the discovery of order out of chaos.

Excuse us while we remove yesterday and prepare for tomorrow.
—NEWARK AIRPORT TERMINAL CONSTRUCTION NOTICE

So far throughout this book we have been talking about change as an external force or combination of forces that we find ourselves pitted against and struggling to overcome. It's the modern-day version of a classic conflict: man (and woman) *against* nature. In this last section of the book, however, we believe that in the spirit of systems thinking, it is fitting to reframe the phenomenon of change and our response to it so that instead of *reacting* to change we *participate in* and *influence* change in meaningful directions.

Although there are those who contend that change has always been with us and that what we are currently experiencing is really no different from what occurred at the time of, for example, the Industrial Revolution, most would agree that contemporary change differs in some very fundamental ways from anything we have known before. It is faster, more encompassing, and more complex; it is volatile, discontinuous, and global; its effects are exponential. In an earlier time we could anticipate change and plan for it. Now we find ourselves caught up in its tumultuous wake. The obvious corollary is that surviving—and thriving on—this new kind of change necessitates a significant shift in the way we respond to change.

How do we accomplish such a shift? First of all, we need to change the way we *think about* change. When we view change as an enemy or threat we limit our ability to work *with* it. If, however, instead of seeing change as adversarial we recognize it as a context that both surrounds and affects us, we can begin to envision ways of capitalizing on its energy. Second, we can change the way we *respond to* change. If, instead of clinging to safety and security, we allow ourselves to enter into and move with change, we increase our ability to influence its direction and affect outcomes. Third, we can *be proactive* in developing a clear sense of direction in the midst of change. If, instead of allowing the flow of change to dictate our fate, we determine what is important to us and where we want to head, we are in a position to take advantage of the momentum of change in guiding our movements toward the desired end. For, as Pritchett (1994, p. iv) notes, "change always comes bearing gifts."

Change expert Daryl Conner (1993) believes that resilience is the key to handling high-velocity change successfully. By *resilience* he means the ability to bounce back from a setback, to create new paradigms in the face of ambiguity, to reframe the uncertainty and mystery of change into a manageable process that incorporates an understanding of the human dynamics which are a predictable part of change efforts. Consider the play in the word *resilience* and in the way Conner uses it: what resilience implies is not a static, detached view of change as a thing "out there" that we can anticipate, plan for, and bring into submission, but rather is an interactive, ongoing experience of change that we are connected to and engage with dynamically, allowing the energy and momentum of change to influence us as much as we seek to influence it.

Resilience is critical for manager-leaders at a very personal level, but it is critical for organizations as well. For in the same way that individuals must be able to "ride the waves," organizations must be able to develop sufficient flexibility and agility to adapt to new markets, incorporate new technologies, respond to competitors' strategies, and position themselves for whatever the next wave brings. Trying to build these qualities into organizations has been aptly described as teaching elephants to dance (Belasco, 1990). The challenge of building resilience into organizations is formidable, because they have been structured for stability, not flexibility. Faced with the potentially ambiguous or "messy" complexities of an organization, we like to impose order, so we spend countless hours devising organizational charts, writing policies and job descriptions, and compiling rules for everything from business ethics to dress code. In an organization of any size, the product of this effort can be at least one and maybe several tome-like manuals that are more daunting than useful. (For example, one of the authors was hired by a Fortune 500 company to write an abbreviated version of the human resources manual to serve as a desk reference for managers, who had all but given up using the original because it had become so weighty and cumbersome.) In addition to the prescribed structures and roles and rules there are any number of unwritten norms that take on the weight of rules and have the effect of governing behavior. It may not be stated anywhere, for example, that those who want to get ahead need to stay late, show up at the office on weekends, or be willing to uproot their families every few years for the sake of the next assignment, but once these patterns become established they might as well be added to the section on promotion in the human resources manual. What makes these structures, policies, and rules—both written and unwritten—so dangerous is the conformity they encourage, the hierarchy they reflect, the intractability they take on, and the way in which all of these factors limit individuals' ability to respond creatively, in real time, to the exigencies of the moment. What we may like most about structure and rules—the sense of order and control they allow—is the very thing that may make us most vulnerable in an environment of high-velocity change. When we establish rigid structures we are encouraging people to operate within a set framework that may work for the time and circumstances in which it was developed but is likely to become increasingly irrelevant as circumstances change. When we prescribe an abundance of rules we are encouraging people to obey rather than to think: the easiest, most secure thing in the world is to be able to hide behind the dictates of some higher authority; if I can quote chapter and verse from the policy manual, I can absolve myself of responsibility for exercising judgment or taking a risk. Clearly, an organization that focuses its efforts on creating stable structures and prescribing behavior at a time of high-velocity change, intensified competition, and customization, limits its ability to respond proactively to the demands—and the opportunities—of this brave new business world.

An organization that builds in flexibility enhances its capacity for making the most of change and for discovering new, more natural kinds of order. There is evidence in the physical universe, for example, that order can emerge out of chaos or unfold from within an organism rather than being imposed from without. Many living systems have now been found to be self-organizing; that is, they are able to coordinate collective efforts without external structures or direction. Birds flock, ants colonize, and certain species of termites build complex towers—all without organizational charts or hierarchical management structures. A growing number of organizational theorists and practitioners have come to believe that human systems have this same capability and that human models already exist. Consider the unpredictable action of the most well executed basketball game, the "groove" of a jazz ensemble that is jamming, or the highly improvisational performances of the Grateful Dead.

As part of its tribute to Jerry Garcia on the night of his death in August 1995, National Public Radio featured an interview with one of Garcia's biographers. Reflecting on the quality of the Dead's music, he observed that attending a Dead concert was a lot like going on a journey where you weren't in the driver's seat: you could recognize the song the band was playing, but you had no way of knowing where they were going with it. The biographer went on to say that Garcia's approach to a concert was not a bad approach to life: that is, if we didn't have to prearrange the universe and have everything nailed down in advance, we could allow for discovery and "spontaneous collaboration." This is not to endorse anarchy but rather to appreciate the possibilities inherent in the creative tension that exists when some elements are stable and others are highly dynamic. At any point in a Dead concert, for example, the *what* (the song being performed) was not in question, which allowed the *how* to become a creative, self-expressive, dynamic act in which each player participated. Anchored in the piece, the musicians were free to respond in real time—to each other, to the audience, to the musical possibilities as they presented themselves. Although the process was not predictable, it was nonetheless ordered; that is, it ultimately produced a thing of beauty, complexity, integrity, and *shape*. It evolved *as* design but not *by* design.

We have surely all been parts of self-organizing systems at one time or another. Times of crisis, for example, when nothing is as we think it should be, have a way of pulling people together and galvanizing their energies to produce very purposeful efforts despite a lack of external structure. On a June afternoon in 1996, Chicago O'Hare, the busiest airport in the world, ground to a halt as severe weather in the areas surrounding the airport prevented or delayed virtually all departures and arrivals. When one of the authors, on her way home from a conference, unwittingly entered the terminal to check in for her flight, she was stunned to see a mob scene. Passengers were everywhere. Some stood in serpentine lines that doubled back on themselves interminably and appeared not to be moving. Some milled about looking dazed and confused. Some stood in front of arrival and departure boards trying to comprehend that one flight after another, to every destination, was listed as canceled or delayed. Chaos prevailed as thousands of stranded travelers tried to figure out what to do next in the absence, initially, of any useful information.

Then a rather amazing thing happened: out of this randomness, order and a contagious sense of community began to emerge as individuals, drawn together by mutual need, turned to one another for information and support. A chic businesswoman, for example, offered to share her large luggage cart with the person behind her in line who was struggling to manage several bags—who in turn befriended a distressed young woman, an au pair returning to the United States to visit her host family, who spoke very little English and had been dealing with delays and bumped flights for over twenty-four hours. People offered to hold others' places in line so that they could make a phone call or use the rest room. Individuals who would ordinarily not have taken their eyes off their luggage entrusted it to the care of someone they had never met so that they could navigate among concourses in the hopes of finding alternate flights. Virtual communities formed and re-formed as people clustered around schedule boards trading whatever information they had, or assisted one another in moving all their gear (passengers had been advised *not* to check luggage due to the unsettled status of flights), in some cases the length of a concourse, to accommodate last-minute gate changes. At least one person assumed a role, in keeping with her skills, that was of benefit not just to herself but to others as well: she would disappear periodically from the line we were standing in (still uncertain whether or not it was the *right* line) and return with bits of information—about what was happening at the front of the line, about how the agents were handling reticketing, about rental car and hotel accommodations. (We later found out that she was a research librarian.)

Many wearing hours later, after hopes for rescheduled flights were repeatedly disappointed and standby lists had become ridiculously long, the sense of pulling together to deal with the predicament nevertheless persisted. When it was announced at one gate that only a fraction of the standby list stood any chance of getting on a plane that might finally depart at midnight, a cluster of people began to compare their standby numbers and tell their stories. When the person with the lowest number (and an urgent need to get to her destination) was finally called, the others, most of whom would surely be left behind, cheered, and that was only one example of selflessness. The woman who befriended the au pair gave the young traveler her standby seat on the last flight out and was rewarded by another woman in the group, who offered to share a room she had access to in the city.

This experience testifies to the inherent ability of people who are bound together by a common purpose to respond to changing circumstances with a high degree of trust, flexibility, community, and effectiveness. It also speaks to the possibility of living in organizations at "the edge of chaos" (Wheatley, 1994), a place that represents the creative tension between a core of relatively stable elements that ground members of the organization and provide focus, and other elements that can then afford to be highly dynamic and responsive. In other words, if instead of emphasizing structures and rules and hierarchy we could work to ensure that members of the organization shared a clear sense of mission, core values, and vision, we could free people to determine what the right things to do are—and to do them. We could share information—which many scientists believe is *the* fundamental organizing principle—more freely, assume more flexible roles and behaviors, and allow for more risk taking and creativity, confident that the shape we are looking to produce will, indeed, emerge (Wheatley, in Mehal and McCarey, 1993).

Living at the edge of chaos means leaving the realm of structures and entering into the realm of processes, says author and consultant Langdon Morris (1995). In the realm of processes, information fuels interaction as the basis for self-organization. Structures evolve as a function of process and are only temporarily stabilized in the same way that a caterpillar and a butterfly, for example, are temporarily stabilized manifestations of an organism that is coherently evolving, constantly *becoming* (Jantsch, cited in Morris, 1995).

Not all organisms undergo as dramatic a transformation in their normal life cycle as the butterfly does, but all organisms must evolve relative to their environment if they are not to become extinct. The same holds true for organizations, according to Gilbert Amelio (Sneider, 1996), former head of National Semiconductor who became CEO of Apple Computer: "Every company that endures has to in effect reinvent itself every generation. Successful companies, [sic] go through a period—I call it waves of change. There's this nice smooth period . . . and then all of a sudden there's this unbelievable chaos and out of that emerges a new order. . . . Some companies don't survive that transition. They're not able to remake themselves in a way that's relevant" (p. 9). Fortunately, the price of adapting does not have to be the organism's identity; in fact, the opposite is true: organisms that adapt most successfully are those that maintain their core identity but modify their nonessential parts to effectively accommodate change (a process known as autopoiesis).

Clearly, we can no longer afford rigid structures and procedures and order to be the essence of our organizations. Bridges (1994), claims that jobs themselves are quickly becoming social artifacts because of shifts in the very nature of work: as a result of automation, outsourcing, and other such things, the historical conditions that led to the creation of jobs are disappearing. And the staggering number of reorganizations in most companies today is testimony to the short shelf life of anything constructed in the midst of the current sea change.

In light of these shifts, manager-leaders must take on new and daunting challenges. One of these is learning to work *with* rather than against chaos and to see its critical potential for revitalizing the organization; as Zaleznik observes (1992, p. 5), "If you don't have order, you have infinite possibilities." Analyzing these possibilities, of course, is not without its price. The popular adage "to make an omelette you have to break some eggs" says it all: major change involves a certain amount of chaos, and chaos is disruptive to the status quo. Manager-leaders need to help others view chaos not with fear but with optimism and openness; they must nurture in others a sense of hope and confidence in the possibilities chaos offers. By way of empowerment, Morgan Jamsky (cited in Stewart, 1996) of 3M testifies to the way that highly successful company operates: "One of the imponderables of 3M is the multiplicity of interaction—it's not explainable and it's not orderly."

A second challenge for manager-leaders is to refocus the attention of others to the really essential aspects of the organization's identity: its aspirations and struggles, its opportunities and liabilities, its successes and failures, its strengths and deficiencies, its capabilities and potential, its connection to its members and to the larger systems of which it is a part. In so doing, manager-leaders must seek to shift the locus of control from the artifice of fragile structures to something much more genuine and sustainable—from mechanisms externally imposed to commitments internally motivated. In these ways managers can truly lead their organizations into a future as filled with promise as it is with uncertainty.

PART TWO

THE LEADERSHIP ODYSSEY ATTRIBUTES AND SKILLS ASSESSMENT KIT

HOW TO USE THE KIT

Part Two contains the assessment kit you will use to gather personal feedback on the Self-Leadership, People Leadership, and Organizational Leadership attributes and skills described in Part One. The kit contains forms for assessing yourself and gathering feedback from others; there is also a guide for summarizing feedback data, interpreting messages and themes, and identifying developmental targets.

Guidelines for Using the Assessment Form

The following are important steps to consider in collecting and processing your feedback data.

Select Respondents with Care

As much as we like to think that we know our strengths and weaknesses, it is virtually impossible for us to see ourselves as others see us. Yet others' perceptions of who and how we are influence their behavior toward us and, as a result, our behavior toward them. When selecting people to give you feedback, choose respondents who are central to your work and whose perceptions—positive or negative—can have an impact on your career. Choose people who know you, who can be candid and honest with you, and, most important, whose judgment you respect.

Understand Your Work Environment

Does your organization actively encourage its employees to gather and use feedback as a vehicle for developmental growth? If so, you should be able to select the appropriate respondents and administer the assessment with little difficulty. A brief discussion with prospective respondents (or a cover note attached to the assessment) explaining the purpose of the assessment and asking for their support of your self-development efforts should suffice. If, on the other hand, giving and receiving developmental feedback is not part of your organization's culture, you may need to lay some groundwork. For example, you may have to spend more time explaining the process and responding to such questions as:

"Why have you selected me to give you feedback?"

"Why have some people been asked to give feedback while others have not?"

"How will you use my feedback?"

"Will you know which feedback comes from me?"

Allow Respondents the Option of Anonymity

Although it can be helpful to know who has provided you with which feedback for purposes of seeking clarification or additional information, many respondents will feel uncomfortable giving candid feedback if they are required to identify themselves on the assessment form. In addition to allowing these respondents to remain anonymous, be sure that you provide them with a mechanism for returning the completed form to you anonymously. Remember to request that those who choose to remain anonymous indicate their work relationship to you by marking the appropriate box (manager, peer, direct report) on the assessment form. Being able to sort feedback by respondent group will assist you in analyzing discrepancies in your behavior.

Collect Adequate Feedback

Even in the most supportive environments, people become too busy, get called away on business, or just forget to do what they promised. Although feedback from one person has value, his or her message becomes clearer when a significant number of other people are—or are not—saying the same thing. To ensure that you have an adequate amount of data, be sure to follow up with respondents. This will allow you to deal with questions and concerns proactively, select alternate respondents if it becomes necessary, remind the forgetful, and let people know that you genuinely want to hear what they think.

Reuse the Assessment Kit As Needed

Consider repeating any or all of the assessment kit intermittently as a means of gauging progress toward your developmental goals.

Responding to Feedback

As difficult as receiving feedback on our personal behaviors or style can be, constructive feedback is a gift and should be received as such. We offer the following guidelines to assist you in responding to feedback.

Allow for a Cycle of Reactions to Negative Feedback

Should you receive negative feedback that you are not expecting, you are likely to experience a predictable cycle of reactions, easily remembered as "SARA":

S	= Shock	(What?!!!!)
A	= Anger	(How dare they!)
R	= Rationalization	(What do *they* know?) (I can explain this . . .)
A	= Acceptance	(Maybe there's some truth in what they're saying . . .)

Keep in mind that until you reach the acceptance stage, you are not in a good frame of mind to act on your feedback. For example, if you feel you need to go back to your respondent(s) to get clarification about your data, wait until you can listen with an open mind.

Seek Clarification of the Feedback Where Needed

Although this assessment tool encourages respondents to support their numerical ratings with specific examples and observations, you may need further explanation to understand how various items apply in your situation. There are numerous ways to go about getting clarification, including the following:

• *Individual meetings.* One approach is to meet individually with each of the respondents—boss, peers, direct reports—to discuss the specific areas in which you would like clarification and support. If you use this approach, be sure to avoid putting the individual on the spot or leading the conversation in a way that might violate anonymity.

• *Staff or peer meeting.* If you are very comfortable with your staff or peer group and have a high-trust, open relationship, you might consider meeting with each group separately to review their feedback. To raise their comfort level, you could list on a flipchart a few key areas you would like to focus on, and then leave the room to give them some time to develop and record thoughts or suggestions for general discussion when you return.

• *One-on-one consultation.* A third alternative is to seek out a trusted peer or direct report who can offer perspective. Be sure that you choose someone whose judgment you trust, who will feel free to be candid, and who has enough experience observing you to offer valuable insights.

Regardless of the method you choose, the following guidelines will help to ensure that you have a constructive exchange.

• *Thank respondents for their efforts.* Regardless of how pleased or displeased you might be with your feedback, the fact is that your respondents took the time to accommodate your request. Be sure to let them know that you appreciate their effort and value their input.

• *Focus the conversation.* Create safe boundaries for you and the respondent(s) by limiting the scope of the exchange to a few critical areas and by addressing specific behaviors or instances. For example, ask the respondent(s) to describe specifically what they would like to see you do more of or do differently.

• *Listen actively and openly.* Avoid defensive behaviors—discounting the respondent's point of view, rationalizing your behavior, and so on. Instead, concentrate on truly hearing and acknowledging what respondent(s) have to say regardless of whether or not you agree. Test your understanding frequently to ensure that you have heard the message as it was intended.

• *If appropriate, summarize any agreements or conclusions.* Ensure that there is clear, mutual understanding of any actions to be taken or roles to be played in following up decisions or commitments as a result of this session.

◆ ◆ ◆

When you have reviewed the preceding guidelines and feel prepared to start gathering your feedback, proceed with distributing the assessment form. Remember to do the following:

• Complete an assessment form about yourself.
• Distribute the assessment forms to your boss and to a minimum of three peers and three direct reports.
• Provide respondents with information regarding how and by what date they should return their completed forms.
• Provide a courtesy follow-up call to each respondent. Avoid creating the impression that you have singled anyone out because you are aware that they have not yet responded, especially if anonymity is a consideration.

LEADERSHIP ODYSSEY ATTRIBUTES AND SKILLS ASSESSMENT FORM

A Word to Respondents

Allow up to ninety minutes to complete this assessment of the thirty-seven leadership attributes and skills. Your evaluation will give the person who requested the feedback an overall impression of how he or she demonstrates these attributes and skills at work, and will help focus his or her development efforts. Because your ratings will *not* be used by anyone else to evaluate this person's performance, you can be most helpful by responding thoughtfully and candidly. Please review the following directions and examples before beginning your assessment.

Directions and Examples

Review the thirty-seven attributes and skills and their descriptions; think about to what extent *generally* and in a *work setting* each attribute describes the person you are rating. Make your ratings on the basis of your own interactions with this person or your personal observations of his or her interactions with others.

Scan the assessment form to identify those attributes and skills that you cannot legitimately evaluate because you have no experience or observations upon which to base a rating. For these attributes and skills, check the box labeled "Unable to Assess." *Note: If you find that you need to use this option frequently, inform the person who requested the feedback that he or she might want to select another respondent who has had more opportunity to observe his or her behavior.*

Rate the remaining attributes and skills by circling the number (7 = highest; 1 = lowest) that best reflects your assessment based on specific instances or observations. Record these instances in the space marked "Observations." You may find that starting with attributes and skills you can easily rate as high or low will help you sort out ratings that are not as clear-cut.

Review your ratings and select up to four (4) attributes and skills that you would like to see this person develop. Check the "Target for Development" box located to the right of the rating scale.

Return your completed assessment form to the person who requested your feedback or to a designated collection point.

Examples

SELF-LEADERSHIP ATTRIBUTES AND SKILLS	Rating Scale	Target for Development	Unable to Assess
Vision: possesses a vivid, compelling view of the future or is capable of imagining what the future could be; subscribes to the belief that one can influence the future by pursuing a desired end.	1 2 3 4 5 6 7 (circled 2)	☑	☐

Observations: Seems too focused on the here and now and not enough on tomorrow. Uncomfortable with discussions about ideas for approaching things differently.

Balance: integrates and harmonizes career, family, personal, and community responsibilities.	1 2 3 4 5 6 7 (circled 6)	☐	☐

Observations: Encourages us to use all our vacation time. Does not insist on unreasonable amounts of overtime.

Tolerates Ambiguity and Paradox: functions effectively in "messy" situations where information, goals, values, or direction is uncertain or apparently conflicting, or where processes cannot be tightly structured; is able to live with questions that allow for discovery; resists premature closure and pat answers.	1 2 3 4 5 6 7	☐	☑

Observations:

Name (optional): _CG_____

Relationship (check one):   Manager ☐   Peer ☒   Direct Report ☒

SELF-LEADERSHIP ATTRIBUTES AND SKILLS	Rating Scale	Target for Development	Unable to Assess
Vision: possesses a vivid, compelling view of the future or is capable of imagining what the future could be; subscribes to the belief that one can influence the future by pursuing a desired end.	1 2 3 4 5 ⑥ 7	☐	☐

Observations:

Integrity: adheres to high ethical standards; has internalized a system of values and beliefs; exemplifies moral soundness.	1 2 3 4 5 6 ⑦	☐	☐

Observations:

SELF-LEADERSHIP ATTRIBUTES AND SKILLS	Rating Scale	Target for Development	Unable to Assess

Passion and Courage: is compelled by what he or she deems important; is willing to accept the personal consequences of difficult choices and decisions; can be relied on to stand up for what's right.

								☐	☐
1	2	3	4	5	⑥	7			

Observations:

Optimism and Self-Confidence: maintains a positive outlook based on a belief in his or her capabilities and the essential goodness of things; sees the glass as half-full rather than half-empty; views challenges as opportunities.

								☐	☐
1	2	3	4	5	⑥	7			

Observations:

SELF-LEADERSHIP ATTRIBUTES AND SKILLS	Rating Scale	Target for Development	Unable to Assess
Focus and Discipline: sets appropriate priorities in the face of multiple, competing demands; sticks with the task at hand in spite of difficulties or distractions.	1 2 3 4 5 ⑥ 7	☐	☐

Observations:

Flexibility: is able to adapt to different people, situations, and approaches; revises plans and objectives as circumstances warrant.	1 2 3 4 5 ⑥ 7	☐	☐

Observations:

SELF-LEADERSHIP ATTRIBUTES AND SKILLS	Rating Scale	Target for Development	Unable to Assess

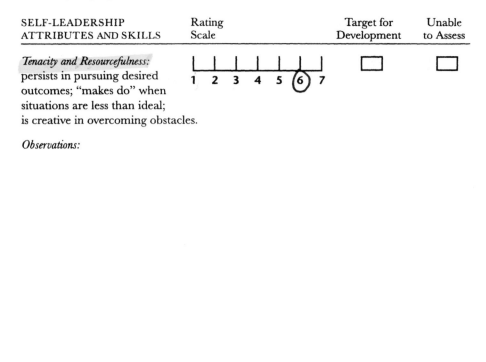

Tenacity and Resourcefulness: persists in pursuing desired outcomes; "makes do" when situations are less than ideal; is creative in overcoming obstacles.

1 2 3 4 5 ⑥ 7

Observations:

Humanity: genuinely cares about, values, and responds to others; believes in human potential; is sensitive to individual differences.

1 2 3 4 5 6 ⑦

Observations:

SELF-LEADERSHIP ATTRIBUTES AND SKILLS	Rating Scale	Target for Development	Unable to Assess
Self-Renewal: takes time to develop, improve, and nurture self in the interest of achieving a sense of wholeness and well-being; discovers opportunities for ongoing learning; reflects on experience for what it can teach.	1 2 3 ④ 5 6 7	☒	☐
Observations:			

Balance: integrates and harmonizes career, family, personal, and community responsibilities.	1 2 3 4 5 ⑥ 7	☐	☐
Observations:			

SELF-LEADERSHIP ATTRIBUTES AND SKILLS	Rating Scale	Target for Development	Unable to Assess

Embraces Change: seeks new ideas and approaches; regards change as a source of vitality and opportunity; uses the energy and momentum of change to best advantage; goes *with* change rather than *against* it.

1 2 3 4 5 (6) 7

☐ ☐

Observations:

Tests Assumptions: uncovers and examines underlying premises and encourages others to do the same.

1 2 3 4 (5) 6 7

☐ ☐

Observations:

SELF-LEADERSHIP ATTRIBUTES AND SKILLS	Rating Scale	Target for Development	Unable to Assess

Shifts Paradigms: is open to new ways of viewing things; adapts own thinking to accommodate emerging ideas, recent discoveries, new insights; avoids undue reliance on the way things have been done in the past.

1 2 3 4 5 (6) 7   ☐   ☐

Observations:

Thinks Holistically: sees the "big picture"; uses an interdisciplinary approach; appreciates how the parts affect the whole.

1 2 3 4 5 6 (7)   ☐   ☐

Observations:

SELF-LEADERSHIP ATTRIBUTES AND SKILLS	Rating Scale	Target for Development	Unable to Assess

Tolerates Ambiguity and Paradox: functions effectively in "messy" situations where information, direction, goals, or values are uncertain or apparently conflicting, or where processes cannot be tightly structured; is able to live with questions that allow for discovery; resists premature closure and pat answers.

1 2 3 4 5 6 (7)

☐ ☐

Observations:

Trusts Intuition: relies on informed judgment and well-developed instincts in lieu of conclusive proof in making decisions; balances need for data with confidence in personal knowledge and experience.

1 2 3 4 5 6 (7)

☐ ☐

Observations:

SELF-LEADERSHIP ATTRIBUTES AND SKILLS	Rating Scale	Target for Development	Unable to Assess
Takes Risks: tries things even when the possibility of failure exists; makes experiments in the interest of discovering new opportunities and solutions.	1 2 3 4 ⑤ 6 7	☐	☐

Observations:

Seeks Synergies: encourages and practices collaboration; works with others to achieve breakthrough outcomes.

1 2 3 4 5 ⑥ 7   ☐   ☐

Observations:

SELF-LEADERSHIP ATTRIBUTES AND SKILLS	Rating Scale	Target for Development	Unable to Assess
✳ *Models Values:* communicates values and acts accordingly; demonstrates personal convictions; "walks the talk."	1 2 3 4 5 ⑥ 7	☐	☐

Observations:

PEOPLE LEADERSHIP ATTRIBUTES AND SKILLS	Rating Scale	Target for Development	Unable to Assess

Sets Parameters: assists employees and teams in developing a clear understanding of both desired performance outcomes and the boundaries and conditions within which they are free to make choices about how they achieve those outcomes.

Rating Scale: 1 2 3 4 (5) 6 7

Observations:

Re-Presents the Organization: actively conveys the organization's and work unit's history, culture, missions, values, and visions; ensures that employees and teams understand how their efforts contribute to the larger purposes of the organization.

Rating Scale: 1 2 3 4 5 (6) 7

Observations:

PEOPLE LEADERSHIP ATTRIBUTES AND SKILLS	Rating Scale	Target for Development	Unable to Assess

Expands Access to Information and New Knowledge: establishes an information-rich environment in which employees and teams are encouraged to understand relevant business factors, make connections, develop insights, share learning, and respond dynamically to rapidly changing conditions.

Rating Scale: 1 2 3 4 5 ⑥ 7   Target for Development: ☐   Unable to Assess: ☐

Observations:

Cultivates Diverse Resources: views individual differences as potential strengths and seeks to understand, appreciate, and tap the unique capabilities of each person.

Rating Scale: 1 2 3 4 5 6 ⑦   Target for Development: ☐   Unable to Assess: ☐

Observations:

PEOPLE LEADERSHIP ATTRIBUTES AND SKILLS	Rating Scale	Target for Development	Unable to Assess

Promotes Continuous Learning: actively encourages employees and teams to pursue new ideas, new ways of thinking, and appropriate behavior changes in a variety of ways (for example, formal training, on-the-job development, mentoring, reading, feedback, and reflection); creates an environment that fosters experimentation and learning from experience collectively as well as individually.

1 2 3 4 5 ⑥ 7

☐   ☐

Observations:

Facilitates Contribution: expands capability of employees and teams to contribute to the organization in a variety of ways, ranging from providing input on decisions to owning and developing their work; provides management direction and support appropriate to what individual employees and teams require in order to continuously improve performance.

1 2 3 4 5 ⑥ 7

☐   ☐

Observations:

PEOPLE LEADERSHIP ATTRIBUTES AND SKILLS	Rating Scale	Target for Development	Unable to Assess

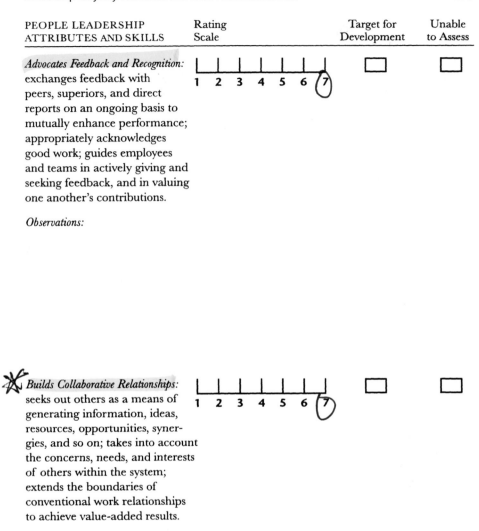

Advocates Feedback and Recognition: exchanges feedback with peers, superiors, and direct reports on an ongoing basis to mutually enhance performance; appropriately acknowledges good work; guides employees and teams in actively giving and seeking feedback, and in valuing one another's contributions.

1 2 3 4 5 6 7

Observations:

Builds Collaborative Relationships: seeks out others as a means of generating information, ideas, resources, opportunities, synergies, and so on; takes into account the concerns, needs, and interests of others within the system; extends the boundaries of conventional work relationships to achieve value-added results.

1 2 3 4 5 6 7

Observations:

PEOPLE LEADERSHIP ATTRIBUTES AND SKILLS	Rating Scale	Target for Development	Unable to Assess

Engages in Dialogue: initiates exploratory conversations as a means of examining assumptions, beliefs, "what ifs," and so on; willing to suspend the need to know, the need to win a point, the need to judge or decide, in the interest of allowing greater understanding to emerge through shared inquiry.

Rating: 1 2 3 4 5 ⑥ 7 — Target for Development: ☐ — Unable to Assess: ☐

Observations:

Achieves Integrative Agreements: works to produce win-win solutions—outcomes that reconcile differences and mutually satisfy the needs and values of self and others.

Rating: 1 2 3 4 5 ⑥ 7 — Target for Development: ☐ — Unable to Assess: ☐

Observations:

ORGANIZATIONAL LEADERSHIP ATTRIBUTES AND SKILLS	Rating Scale	Target for Development	Unable to Assess

Develops Core Values: facilitates consensus around a set of shared beliefs about what the organization or work unit stands for; works to ensure that these beliefs are reflected in the systems, structures, choices, and decisions of the organization as a means of shaping its organizational culture.

1 2 3 4 5 6 ⑦   ☐   ☐

Observations:

Takes a Systems Approach: recognizes the interdependency of parts within the system; considers the potential impact of decisions, choices, and initiatives on what is distant in time and space as well as what is close at hand; uses the tools and methodologies of systems thinking to identify high-leverage opportunities for making significant organizational change.

1 2 3 ④ 5 6 7   ☒   ☐

Observations:

ORGANIZATIONAL LEADERSHIP ATTRIBUTES AND SKILLS	Rating Scale	Target for Development	Unable to Assess

Builds Community: seeks to forge connections and strengthen personal and professional bonds among staff; stimulates the kind of esprit de corps that promotes collective learning, self-organization, and synergistic outcomes.

1   2   3   4   5   6   (7)   ☐   ☐

Observations:

Stays Current with Emerging Trends: maintains awareness of social, political, economic, and technological developments that affect the business; is knowledgeable about changing directions relative to a discipline, industry, or operating environment.

1   2   3   4   5   6   (7)   ☐   ☐

Observations:

ORGANIZATIONAL LEADERSHIP ATTRIBUTES AND SKILLS	Rating Scale	Target for Development	Unable to Assess

Thinks Strategically: draws on both hard and soft data (for example, market research, emerging trends, experience, intuition, informal learning, and interactions with others) as sources for developing strategic direction; views strategy as dynamic rather than static; discovers future opportunities in day-to-day details; involves others in contributing to the process of shaping strategy on an ongoing basis.

Rating Scale: 1 2 3 4 (5) 6 7 — Target for Development: ☒ — Unable to Assess: ☐

Observations:

Inspires Pursuit of a Shared Vision: involves others in creating a bold and compelling picture of the desired future; engages everyone in imagining and seeking to realize what could be.

Rating Scale: 1 2 3 4 5 6 (7) — Target for Development: ☐ — Unable to Assess: ☐

Observations:

ORGANIZATIONAL LEADERSHIP ATTRIBUTES AND SKILLS	Rating Scale	Target for Development	Unable to Assess

Employs Dynamic Planning: charts a flexible course to move the organization toward its short-term goals and long-term vision; identifies checkpoints along the way to measure progress and incorporate new learning.

1 2 3 4 5 ⑥ 7 ☐ ☐

Observations:

Enlarges Capacity for Change: works to fashion an adaptive organization that responds to emerging imperatives; challenges the status quo and encourages others to do the same; champions new initiatives; allows for the discovery of order out of chaos.

1 2 3 4 5 6 ⑦ ☐ ☐

Observations:

FEEDBACK ANALYSIS

The process of analyzing the feedback you have collected includes the following steps: recording your data, sorting your data, and clarifying messages. The directions for each step are accompanied by a sample for you to review before working with your own data. Take the time to review both the directions and examples before proceeding.

Step One: Recording Your Data

Refer to Example Report A when working on Step One.

- Starting with the assessment you filled out about yourself, transfer your ratings for each attribute or skill to the appropriate boxes under the "Self" column on the report form. Insert an asterisk (*) next to those ratings for which you checked the box "TD" (Target for Development).
- Using the same process, transfer your manager's ratings, including an asterisk for ratings he or she targeted for development, under the "Mgr" column. If "Unable to Assess" has been checked for any of the attributes, record U/A in the appropriate box.
- To record data from the remaining respondents, first group them by category—peers and direct reports—then enter each name with the appropriate category

in the boxes at the top of the report form, starting with the box in the third column. For purposes of recording anonymous feedback, assign each unidentified respondent a number. Continue transferring ratings, including asterisks, until all data have been recorded. Make additional copies of the report forms as needed.

- Total the number of asterisks for each attribute, including your own, and record that total in the Target for Development column, labeled "TD."

EXAMPLE REPORT A

SELF-LEADERSHIP ATTRIBUTES AND SKILLS	Self	Mgr	P	P	P	DR	DR	DR	TD	Messages
Vision: possesses a vivid, compelling view of the future or is capable of imagining what the future could be; subscribes to the belief that one can influence the future by pursuing a desired end.	2*	3*	2	3*	3	2*	4	4	4	
Optimism and Self-Confidence: maintains a positive outlook based on a belief in his or her capabilities and the essential goodness of things; sees the glass as half-full rather than half-empty; views challenges as opportunities.	7	6	3	3	2*	U/A	5	4	1	
Flexibility: is able to adapt to different people, situations, and approaches; revises plans and objectives as circumstances warrant.	5	3	6	7	5	2	3	2	0	

Step Two: Sorting Your Data

Refer to Example Report B when working on this step. On your report form:

- Circle any ratings from respondents that are three points higher or lower than your rating.

- Circle any totals in the "TD" (Target for Development) column that represent a minimum of 50 percent of the number of respondents (including yourself). In Example Report B, four (4) out of eight (8) respondents (50 percent) targeted Vision for development, as indicated by the asterisks.

- Circle any other ratings that you think deserve special attention. In Example Report B, although the manager's rating for Flexibility differs from yours by only two points, it is considered important enough to circle.

EXAMPLE REPORT B

SELF-LEADERSHIP ATTRIBUTES AND SKILLS	Self	Mgr	P	P	P	DR	DR	DR	TD	Messages
Vision: possesses a vivid, compelling view of the future or is capable of imagining what the future could be; subscribes to the belief that one can influence the future by pursuing a desired end.	2*	3*	2	3*	3	2*	4	4	(4)	
Optimism and Self-Confidence: maintains a positive outlook based on a belief in his or her capabilities and the essential goodness of things; sees the glass as half-full rather than half-empty; views challenges as opportunities.	7	6	(3)	(3)	(2*)	U/A	5	(4)	1	

SELF-LEADERSHIP ATTRIBUTES AND SKILLS	Self	Mgr	P	*i*	P	DR	DR	DR	TD	Messages
Flexibility: is able to adapt to different people, situations, and approaches; revises plans and objectives as circumstances warrant.	5	③	6	7	5	②	3	②	0	

In sorting your feedback data make some initial observations:

- Do you think people were honest with you? Why or why not? Do you think their ratings are valid? Why or why not?
- Are there any obvious discrepancies in ratings between yourself and other individuals? If so, can you account for why they might differ?
- Are there any obvious discrepancies in ratings among feedback groups—your peers versus your direct reports, your manager versus your peers? If so, can you account for why they might differ?

Step Three: Clarifying Key Messages

The power of feedback is not in "crunching" the numbers but in understanding what the numbers mean. In this step you will go back to the data you sorted to discover key messages. To assist you in identifying those messages, consider the following questions:

- Do the respondents agree on which attributes you need to target for development? Do you agree with them? Why or why not?
- Do the ratings indicate that you have a blind spot—that you rated yourself consistently higher or lower than respondents rated you?
- Are there any ratings or observations for which you need to seek clarification from respondents?
- Did you receive any conflicting ratings or observations—between you and others or among the respondents themselves? If so, how can you account for them?
- What patterns or relationships do you see among the ratings you received? Would changes in your behavior in one area be likely to help in other areas as well?

- What specific messages can you infer from the feedback you have received?
- As a result of this assessment process, can you iden fy areas that you want to target for development?

Now enter the messages implied by your data in the far right column of your report form (see Example Report C).

EXAMPLE REPORT C

SELF-LEADERSHIP ATTRIBUTES AND SKILLS	Self	Mgr	P	P	P	DR	DR	DR	TD	Messages
Vision: possesses a vivid, compelling view of the future or is capable of imagining what the future could be; subscribes to the belief that one can influence the future by pursuing a desired end.	2*	3*	2	3*	3	2*	4	4	④	*This is clearly a high priority for development*
Optimism and Self-Confidence: maintains a positive outlook based on a belief in his or her capabilities and the essential goodness of things; sees the glass as half-full rather than half-empty; views challenges as opportunities.	7	6	③	③	②*	U/A	5	④	1	*Appear to be relating differently to my peers than to my boss and direct reports*
Flexibility: is able to adapt to different people, situations, and approaches; revises plans and objectives as circumstances warrant.	5	③	6	7	5	②	3	②	0	*Need to get more in-depth feedback on this rating from the boss and from direct reports.*

Feedback Analysis Form

SELF-LEADERSHIP ATTRIBUTES AND SKILLS	Self	Mgr	P	P	P	DR	DR	DR	TD	Messages
Vision: possesses a vivid, compelling view of the future or is capable of imagining what the future could be; subscribes to the belief that one can influence the future by pursuing a desired end.										
Integrity: adheres to high ethical standards; has internalized a system of values and beliefs; exemplifies moral soundness.										

SELF-LEADERSHIP ATTRIBUTES AND SKILLS	Self	Mgr	P	P	P	DR	DR	DR	TD	Messages
Passion and Courage: is compelled by what he or she deems important; is willing to accept the personal consequences of difficult choices and decisions; can be relied on to stand up for what's right.										
Optimism and Self-Confidence: maintains a positive outlook based on a belief in his or her capabilities and the essential goodness of things; sees the glass as half-full rather than half-empty; views challenges as opportunities.										

SELF-LEADERSHIP ATTRIBUTES AND SKILLS	Self	Mgr	P	P	P	DR	DR	DR	TD	Messages
Focus and Discipline: sets appropriate priorities in the face of multiple, competing demands; sticks with the task at hand in spite of difficulties or distractions.										
Flexibility: is able to adapt to different people, situations, and approaches; revises plans and objectives as circumstances warrant.										

SELF-LEADERSHIP ATTRIBUTES AND SKILLS	Self	Mgr	P	P	P	DR	DR	DR	TD	Messages
Tenacity and Resourcefulness: persists in pursuing desired outcomes; "makes do" when situations are less than ideal; is creative in overcoming obstacles.										
Humanity: genuinely cares about, values, and responds to others; believes in human potential; is sensitive to individual differences.										

SELF-LEADERSHIP ATTRIBUTES AND SKILLS	Self	Mgr	P	P	P	DR	DR	DR	TD	Messages
Self-Renewal: takes time to develop, improve, and nurture self in the interest of achieving a sense of wholeness and well-being; discovers opportunities for ongoing learning; reflects on experience for what it can teach.										
Balance: integrates and harmonizes career, family, personal, and community responsibilities.										

SELF-LEADERSHIP ATTRIBUTES AND SKILLS	Self	Mgr	P	P	P	DR	DR	DR	TD	Messages
Embraces Change: Seeks new ideas and approaches; regards change as a source of vitality and opportunity; uses the energy and momentum of change to best advantage; goes *with* change rather than *against* it.										
Tests Assumptions: uncovers and examines underlying premises and encourages others to do the same.										

SELF-LEADERSHIP ATTRIBUTES AND SKILLS	Self	Mgr	P	P	P	DR	DR	DR	TD	Messages
Shifts Paradigms: is open to new ways of viewing things; adapts own thinking to accommodate emerging ideas, recent discoveries, new insights; avoids undue reliance on the way things have been done in the past.										
Thinks Holistically: sees the "big picture"; uses an interdisciplinary approach; appreciates how the parts affect the whole.										

SELF-LEADERSHIP ATTRIBUTES AND SKILLS	Self	Mgr	P	P	P	DR	DR	DR	TD	Messages
Tolerates Ambiguity and Paradox: functions effectively in "messy" situations where information, goals, values, or direction is uncertain or conflicting, or where processes cannot be tightly structured; is able to live with questions that allow for discovery; resists premature closure and pat answers.										
Trusts Intuition: relies on informed judgment and well-developed instincts in lieu of conclusive proof in making decisions; balances need for data with confidence in personal knowledge and experience.										

SELF-LEADERSHIP ATTRIBUTES AND SKILLS	Self	Mgr	P	P	P	DR	DR	DR	TD	Messages
Takes Risks: tries things even when the possibility of failure exists; makes experiments in the interest of discovering new opportunities and solutions.										
Seeks Synergies: encourages and practices collaboration; works with others to achieve breakthrough outcomes.										

SELF-LEADERSHIP ATTRIBUTES AND SKILLS	Self	Mgr	P	P	P	DR	DR	DR	TD	Messages
Models Values: communicates values and acts accordingly; demonstrates personal convictions; "walks the talk."										

PEOPLE-LEADERSHIP ATTRIBUTES AND SKILLS	Self	Mgr	P	P	P	DR	DR	DR	TD	Messages
Sets Parameters: assists employees and teams in developing a clear understanding of both desired performance outcomes and the boundaries and conditions within which they are free to make choices about how they achieve those outcomes.										
Re-Presents the Organization: actively conveys the organization's and work unit's history, culture, missions, values, and visions; ensures that employees and teams understand how their efforts contribute to the larger purposes of the organization.										

PEOPLE-LEADERSHIP ATTRIBUTES AND SKILLS	Self	Mgr	P	P	P	DR	DR	DR	TD	Messages
Expands Access to Information and New Knowledge: establishes an information-rich environment in which employees and teams are encouraged to understand relevant business factors, make connections, develop insights, share learning, and respond dynamically to rapidly changing conditions.										
Cultivates Diverse Resources: views individual differences as potential strengths and seeks to understand, appreciate, and tap the unique capabilities of each person.										

PEOPLE-LEADERSHIP ATTRIBUTES AND SKILLS	Self	Mgr	P	P	P	DR	DR	DR	TD	Messages
Promotes Continuous Learning: actively encourages employees and teams to pursue new ideas, new ways of thinking, and appropriate behavior changes in a variety of ways (for example, formal training, on-the-job development, mentoring, reading, feedback, and reflection); creates an environment that fosters experimentation and learning from experience collectively as well as individually.										
Facilitates Contribution: expands capability of employees and teams to contribute to the organization in a variety of ways, ranging from providing input on decisions to owning and developing their work; provides management direction and support appropriate to what individual employees and teams require in order to continuously improve performance.										

PEOPLE-LEADERSHIP ATTRIBUTES AND SKILLS	Self	Mgr	P	P	P	DR	DR	DR	TD	Messages
Advocates Feedback and Recognition: exchanges feedback with peers, superiors, and direct reports on an ongoing basis to mutually enhance performance; appropriately acknowledges good work; guides employees and teams in actively giving and seeking feedback, and in valuing one another's contributions.										
Builds Collaborative Relationships: Seeks out others as a means of generating information, ideas, resources, opportunities, synergies, and so on; takes into account the concerns, needs, and interests of others within the system; extends the boundaries of conventional work relationships to achieve value-added results.										

PEOPLE-LEADERSHIP ATTRIBUTES AND SKILLS	Self	Mgr	P	P	P	DR	DR	DR	TD	Messages
Engages in Dialogue: initiates exploratory conversations as a means of examining assumptions, beliefs, "what ifs," and so on; willing to suspend the need to know, the need to win a point, the need to judge or decide, in the interest of allowing greater understanding to emerge through shared inquiry.										
Achieves Integrative Agreements: works to produce win-win solutions—outcomes that reconcile differ-ences and mutually satisfy the needs and values of self and others.										

ORGANIZATIONAL LEADERSHIP ATTRIBUTES AND SKILLS	Self	Mgr	P	P	P	DR	DR	DR	TD	Messages
Develops Core Values: facilitates consensus around a set of shared beliefs about what the organization or work unit stands for; works to ensure that these beliefs are reflected in the systems, structures, choices, and decisions of the organization as a means of shaping its organizational culture.										
Takes a Systems Approach: recognizes the interdependency of parts within the system; considers the potential impact of decisions, choices, and initiatives on what is distant in time and space as well as what is close at hand; uses the tools and methodologies of systems thinking to identify high-leverage opportunities for making significant organizational change.										

ORGANIZATIONAL LEADERSHIP ATTRIBUTES AND SKILLS	Self	Mgr	P	P	P	DR	DR	DR	TD	Messages
Builds Community: seeks to forge connections and strengthen personal and professional bonds among staff; stimulates the kind of esprit de corps that promotes collective learning, self-organization, and synergistic outcomes.										
Stays Current with Emerging Trends: maintains awareness of social, political, economic, and technological developments that affect the business; is knowledgeable about changing directions relative to a discipline, industry, or operating environment.										

ORGANIZATIONAL LEADERSHIP ATTRIBUTES AND SKILLS	Self	Mgr	P	P	P	DR	DR	DR	TD	Messages
Thinks Strategically: Draws on both hard and soft data (for example, market research, emerging trends, experience, intuition, informal learning, and interactions with others) as sources for developing strategic direction; views strategy as dynamic rather than static; discovers future opportunities in day-to-day details; involves others in contributing to the process of shaping strategy on an ongoing basis.										
Inspires Pursuit of a Shared Vision: involves others in creating a bold and compelling picture of the desired future; engages everyone in imagining and seeking to realize what could be.										

ORGANIZATIONAL LEADERSHIP ATTRIBUTES AND SKILLS	Self	Mgr	P	P	P	DR	DR	DR	TD	Messages
Employs Dynamic Planning: charts a flexible course to move the organization toward its short-term goals and long-term vision; identifies checkpoints along the way to measure progress and incorporate new learning.										
Enlarges Capacity for Change: works to fashion an adaptive organization that responds to emerging imperatives; challenges the status quo and encourages others to do the same; champions new initiatives; allows for the discovery of order out of chaos.										

PART THREE

THE LEADERSHIP ODYSSEY SELF-DEVELOPMENT EXERCISES

LEARNING TO LEARN

Learning is not attained by chance; it must be sought for with ardor and attended to with diligence.

—ABIGAIL ADAMS, *LETTER TO JOHN QUINCY ADAMS*, MAY 8, 1780

No matter how many talents or credentials we brought to our careers in the beginning, for us to remain successful in an organization today requires an increasing array and refinement of skills, many of which are not entirely known or understood at this point. Accelerating change necessitates that we find ways to quickly become knowledgeable about everything from technologies that are revolutionized overnight to new paradigms for managing and leading. We must seek opportunities to learn, recognize the learning implicit in our day-to-day experiences, and develop a reflective habit of mind that enables us to take charge of our own learning. Waiting until learning is packaged for us may mean missing the boat.

Education Versus Learning

Becoming a self-directed learner will not necessarily be easy, for although most of us have put in many years as *students* we may have only limited capabilities as *learners* in the truest sense of that word. The idea of self-directed learning pre-dates schools; self-education was central to the ideals and personal development of the Greek philosophers. Socrates, for example, described himself as a self-learner who capitalized on opportunities to learn from those around him. Plato believed that the ultimate goal of education for the young should be to develop an ability to function as a self-learner in adulthood. Aristotle emphasized self-realization—"a potential wisdom that can be developed either with or without the guidance of a teacher" (Brockett and Hiemstra, 1991, p. 7).

The educational systems through which most of us gained our formal education typically do little to engender self-direction. The traditional approaches to learning that characterize mass educational systems focus on a teacher-centered style and a reactive posture. The result is what some have called "maintenance learning"—the acquisition of prescribed tasks for dealing with predictable (that is, known) situations (Botkin, Elmadjra, and Malitza, 1979, p. 22). Alvin Toffler (cited in Long, 1990) asserts that the curricula of industrial societies are remarkably similar in terms of three "hidden" agendas—punctuality, obedience, and rote, repetitive work. These agendas encourage standardization rather than innovation, and deference to the norms of those in authority. E. L. Boyer (1987) adds to Toffler's charges by concluding that what today's colleges teach most successfully is competence in meeting the demands associated with the educational system and, by extension, the traditional workplace—getting grades, acquiring credits, meeting schedules, mastering information—and in dealing with discrete problems.

Clearly these are not the kinds of realities—nor the kinds of skills—that the present and the future are all about. So we must start with the problem of learning how to learn differently, for, in T. S. Eliot's words, "We had the experience but missed the meaning" (1970, p. 194). Add to that what might be called the learning dilemma of managers and executives.

Managers and Learning

An instructor stood before a class of high-level managers, all participants in a week-long leadership development program. In what was later revealed to be the opening gambit of an exercise on learning to learn, he announced that the managers had been asked to participate in a charity track meet. After listing three events—pole-vaulting, distance running, or walking—he asked each, in turn, to choose one. In a subsequent round, the instructor queried each person about why he or she chose a particular event. With few exceptions, the participants' choices had something to do with their comfort level and confidence—confidence that they would be able to perform successfully and avoid appearing the fool.

To the extent that these managers were reluctant to engage in activities that challenged their competence, they betray a tendency to avoid an opportunity to learn in the interest of playing safe. On the one hand, it is ironic that those whom we might expect to be role models of learning in organizations are often, in a *sense,* the most learning disabled by virtue of a mind-set that limits what they are willing to try. On the other hand, we can easily understand the obstacles to managerial or executive learning. First, managers are plagued with the same limitations as any other adult. We have all spent a lifetime internalizing the rules of parents, teachers, religious institutions, and the like, in a world where it is assumed that by the time you become an adult you have the answers. Second, all of us are what ambiguity expert Michael McCaskey (1982, p. 25) calls "inference machines": we cannot resist rendering the reality we see (however limited our vantage point) into mental models to which we then cling in such a way that we mistake the map for the territory.

These generic obstacles are compounded by factors inherent to the manager's or executive's position: intense time pressures, urgent short-term demands, and the need to make decisions—to be in charge and in the know. Furthermore, managers typically are successful people who have limited experience with failure and have a vested interest in avoiding the kind of vulnerability, embarrassment, or outright pain that often accompanies the most profound kinds of learning.

Organizations often exacerbate managers' learning dilemmas by fostering hierarchy, rewarding authoritarianism, and discouraging risk taking and experimentation. Well-intended practices associated with feedback and promotions frequently obstruct potential learning opportunities. For example, new assignments are often made on the basis of a manager's demonstrated strengths rather than as developmental opportunities; vertical promotions foster a highly parochial perspective; individuals are moved out of jobs before their mistakes surface; strengths turn into career liabilities through excess or misdirection because feedback is focused on results at the expense of process, and learning is equated with training. Even when organizations introduce an initiative such as TQM with the ostensible purpose of promoting learning, the program's learning potential can become so subverted in the implementation that instead of spawning new insights and approaches, it breeds pervasive skepticism.

Learning As Competitive Advantage

The good news is that we have begun to recognize learning as the critical technology (Carnevale, 1992): because learning stimulates innovation, the capacity to learn represents a true and sustainable competitive advantage. Such companies as Skandia Group, Dow Chemical, and Hughes Aircraft, for example, are actually managing their intellectual capability as a business asset and have created such positions as Director of Intellectual Capital (Stewart, 1994). And significant attention is being paid these days to the prospect of building learning organizations, a concept that may lead us not only to new ways of learning *collectively* but to new ways for *individuals* to learn and to think about learning.

As we discussed earlier, there is no doubt that the realities emerging today require new skills and new ways of acquiring them. Instead of relying exclusively on maintenance learning, with its emphasis on mastering fixed models and methods for coping with predictable phenomena, we also will need to embrace innovative or generative learning—a more proactive, creative way of gleaning the significance and direction of changing events. For only by equipping ourselves, on an ongoing basis, to anticipate and respond to accelerating complexity and change can we hope to capitalize on change. The alternative is to be victimized by circumstances and events: events that fly in the face of what we have sought in vain to establish.

A Model for Self-Managed Learning

The shift to innovative learning invites not just new ways of thinking but also new ways of engaging in ongoing learning through a learner-centered, self-directed process that combines experience with reflection. We all know people (maybe even ourselves in certain instances) who repeat ineffective behavior again and again: the person with a string of failed relationships; the person with chronic "bad luck"; the person who can't seem to hold down a job; the person whose life is inordinately complicated, troubled, or stressful; the person who never follows through on goals but blames a host of other things for his or her lack of success. These people appear to be unaware that with a better understanding of the situation and their own role in its dynamics, they could bring about a different outcome.

Often the problem involves experience without learning—treating life as if it happens *to* us and not as if our choices affect outcomes. This is like putting all our hopes on winning the lottery in lieu of figuring out how to make the best use of the resources that are clearly within our reach. The efficacious person, on the other hand, is able to learn continuously from experience in ways that allow him or her to modify behavior, build skills, and, in so doing, acquire competence in the variety of situations that life presents. This is the process we are talking about when we use such terms as *learner centered* and *self-directed*.

Self-directed learning differs from other types of learning in the responsibility it puts on us, the learner, to structure the learning opportunity. For much of the learning we do, we must rely on others. As children we learn most of what we know about the world from our parents or from teachers in the classroom. As adults, much of what we learn—skiing, driving a car, operating a computer, and so on—involves manual maneuvers or cognitive processes; the resources for learning these skills are external to us, and, once the skills are learned, are available for recall.

Other kinds of learning, however—learning how to manage conflict in inter-personal relationships, learning how to function as a member of a team, or learn-ing how to deal with highly ambiguous situations—are not as simple and straightforward. Although certain tangible skills may be involved, these more com-plex situations lend themselves to a kind of learning that is not primarily physical or intellectual; it requires a process of reflection in which we draw on the inter-nal resources of our previous experiences to gain a very personal understanding of a current event or experience. Unlike learning to ski or memorizing math tables, mastery of complex situations is generally not acquired quickly or predictably but over time as subsequent experiences build what is more aptly termed *wisdom* than simply skill. It makes sense that our learning needs to become more self-directed and reflective in response to the increasing complexity of our adult lives, espe-cially as the environment around us grows more volatile and ambiguous. Allen Tough (1982), author of *Intentional Changes,* states that less than 30 percent of what adults learn occurs through formal classes, professional educators, counselors, friends, bosses, and so on. As much as 70 percent of what adults learn results from events they experience, and is therefore within their own control.

Unfortunately, because our experiences are typically unanticipated and our responses to them unstructured, this learning often occurs subliminally, as a cop-ing response. The learning value of these experiences can thus be subverted, and the wrong things get reinforced: learning *not* to contribute at meetings because people argue down your ideas or ignore them altogether; learning to be overly cautious in making decisions because mistakes are viewed in your organization as failures; learning to suppress problems because your organization "shoots the messenger"; learning to put bottom-line results before people because results lead to the rewards.

The reflective learning cycle describes a process for ensuring that we gain the right lessons from experience as a means of sustaining personal and professional growth. As the graphic features of the cycle suggest, reflective learning is a con-scious "time-out" from ongoing experience in which actions and events are con-sidered in a conscious, deliberative way, so as to yield up insights that can inform future actions and behavior. The cycle, represented by a loop, involves a process, triggered by an experience, that begins with reflection and moves the self in an inward direction through discovery and planning. Equipped with new learning, the self then emerges to re-engage with experience in the experiment phase.

Experience. At the starting point for learning, the learner is a participant in an occurrence, event, interaction, or activity that serves as a focus for reflection and represents a learning opportunity.

Reflect. The learner consciously considers the experience, alone or in consulta-tion with others, as a way of allowing the significance of the experience to emerge.

THE REFLECTIVE LEARNING CYCLE.

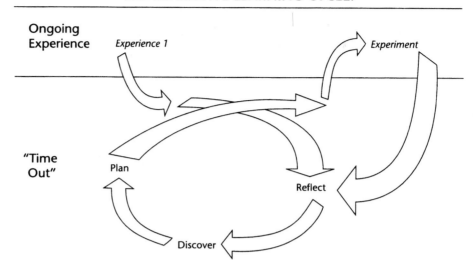

Discover. As a function of reflecting on the experience, the learner seeks to derive insights about its significance that can inform future actions and behavior.

Plan. Based on insights that have emerged through the reflection and discovery phases, the learner develops appropriate strategies, adaptations, behavior modifications, applications, perspectives, and so on.

Experiment. The learner tries out the new strategies, and applications, in a subsequent experience, which in turn serves to initiate the next iteration of the reflective learning cycle.

Several additional features of the cycle are noteworthy:

- It is experiential. The learner *participates* in a way that links cognition with action in real time.
- It is iterative. Each significant experience and experiment represents an opportunity for entering into the reflective cycle so that learning is continuous. Shakespeare claims that "all the world's a stage"; it is potentially a classroom as well.
- It is learner centered. The learner takes responsibility for learning: the learner initiates the process, intentionally seeks the lessons implicit in his or her experiences, and acts to integrate learning in his or her response to subsequent experiences.
- It is self-directed. The learner takes responsibility for managing his or her own learning process.

GUIDELINES FOR USING
THE DEVELOPMENTAL EXERCISES

The exercises in the next section are designed to be used in conjunction with the reflective learning model and to provide experiences for developing or enhancing the Self-Leadership, People Leadership, and Organizational Leadership attributes and skills discussed in Part One. Developmental exercises vary in their level of ambitiousness—from those that are simple and can be completed independently in a very short period of time, to those that represent a longer-term commitment and may require the involvement and support of others. Activities span the four key aspects of most professionals' lives—family, self, community, and career—in the interest of encouraging a developmental approach that is balanced and integrative. Consider these activity lists as thought-starters—combine, adapt, or add to them as suits your needs.

Understand Your Level of Commitment

Before selecting experiential exercises, determine how much time you have or are willing to commit for the development of a targeted attribute or skill. Recognize that skill development is a process that generally takes time and repeated practice. A single activity or a single iteration of an activity is unlikely to change behavior or to produce competency in a new skill.

213

Select a Series of Activities

You may want to choose a series of related exercises to assist you in moving through the learning curve. Think about starting with a relatively simple activity and progressing to more ambitious ones when you feel you are ready. Or think about choosing a number of related exercises that apply in a variety of settings—home, work, and community, for example—as a way of reinforcing a targeted behavior or skill.

Practice Targeted Behaviors and Track Progress

Once you have completed an activity, find opportunities to continue practicing the targeted attribute or skill and to monitor your progress in successfully demonstrating the associated behaviors. This will enable you to adjust learning goals appropriately and to continue to build strength over time by repeating exercises or selecting new ones. Remember to challenge yourself, but be realistic about what you can feasibly take on.

Enhance Strengths and Address Deficiencies

Consider choosing some exercises for the purpose of refining or extending what you already do well. Or use the exercises as a means of learning to learn—look for new applications in specific situations, make connections among seemingly unconnected things, think outside the box. For example, think about ways you can transfer a strength that you use outside of work to your job.

Apply the Reflective Learning Cycle

Integrate the steps of the reflective learning cycle—experience, reflect, discover, plan, experiment—into all the exercises.

Construct a Learning Plan

Although you can learn in a variety of ways, the best means of insuring that your efforts result in the desired outcome is to plan learning experiences so that they are systematic and integrated. The following steps will assist you in maximizing your learning.

1. *Develop clear objectives.* Decide what it is you want to get out of the learning experience, both short- and long-term. Determining objectives in advance

will increase the likelihood that you will make progress in acquiring the desired skill.

2. *Select appropriate exercises.* Choose exercises that are suited to the objectives you have developed as well as to the time and energy you are willing and able to commit.

3. *Identify available resources.* Determine what support you will need in order to reach your objective(s), including people (manager, peers, friends, spouse), institutions (libraries, local colleges, community centers), and materials (readings, audio- and videotapes, classes, specific supplies).

4. *Establish accountability.* Enlist the support of the people you will need and ensure that their roles, responsibilities, and expectations are clear.

5. *Identify costs.* Assess what will be required of you in terms of time, energy, money, and lifestyle changes, relative to the anticipated benefits.

6. *Identify obstacles.* Determine what could interfere with progress toward your objective(s).

7. *Establish measurements.* Build in qualitative as well as quantitative ways of assessing your progress as you work toward your objective(s).

8. *Anticipate rewards.* Identify ways to celebrate progress ("small wins") toward your objective(s).

One final tip: you will note that many of the exercises involve keeping a journal as a means of monitoring events, interactions, progress, and other details related to the development of a particular attribute or skill. Beyond the specialized use of a journal for isolated developmental exercises, we encourage you to consider keeping a journal on an ongoing basis. We know of no better way to build reflective learning into days that are otherwise overloaded with competing demands.

Keeping a journal need not be a complicated or time-consuming project. There is no prescribed format for keeping a journal. Simply make a point of spending a few minutes every day or once a week (or whatever time frame works best for you) considering your experiences and jotting down your observations. Give yourself quiet, uninterrupted time to reflect on a regular basis, and be sure to capture what comes to mind—reactions, questions, issues, and insights. You will find that the mere act of converting thoughts into words for the sake of making journal entries will help you clarify and shape your thoughts in ways that make their meaning and value more accessible. Although the time required to keep a journal is relatively short, the benefits are many. A brief time-out allows us to step back from our busy-ness, to consider what we're doing, how we're doing, and what we can learn, and it creates one of the most invaluable resources we have for dealing with the future: lessons of experience.

DEVELOPMENTAL EXERCISES

Self-Leadership: Qualities of Being

Vision

Possesses a vivid, compelling view of the future or is capable of imagining what the future could be; subscribes to the belief that one can influence the future by pursuing a desired end.

1. Engage in corporate daydreaming at odd moments (while in the shower, stuck in traffic, working out, and so on). Fantasize about future possibilities as if you were experiencing them; keep a journal of what you discover.
2. Read and study the ideas, thoughts, and beliefs of experts in your field and related fields as sources of inspiration. For example, read the writings of a leading economist, historian, futurist, or scientist as a way of making the connections between what you already know and an unrealized possibility. Use your findings to help formulate a vision.
3. Use mental imagery to create a vision for your personal and professional growth. Based on your vision, establish short-term goals focused on closing the gap between where you are and where you want to be.
4. Establish formal and informal communication channels to gain access to new and different ideas and approaches to the future (for example, take part in

professional associations or networking groups). Seek out people both within and outside your field. Ask lots of questions, listen, understand, and imagine.

5. Convene a family session in which all members brainstorm about their dream vacations. Have them describe in detail where they are, what they're doing, how they are feeling, what the weather is, what is going on around them, and so on. Use these ideas as the basis for identifying shared interests and planning your next family vacation.

6. Find some quiet time to be reflective (take a walk, meditate, listen to classical music); take a step back from your current situation—view it from the outside in. Use this new, broader perspective to help shape goals and plans.

7. Write a eulogy for yourself. Think about what you want to be remembered for—what difference(s) you've made to family, community, church, your organization, society. Identify what you would need to do to make this an accurate description of yourself.

8. Picture yourself ten years from now as you'd like to be. What do you look like? What are you doing at work, at home, socially? What interests and hobbies do you have? Identify the steps you would need to take to make this picture a reality.

Integrity

Adheres to high ethical standards; has internalized a system of values and beliefs; exemplifies moral soundness.

1. Practice the following principles in your dealings with others:
   • When you make a mistake, admit it.
   • When questioned or challenged, answer honestly; don't be afraid to say "I don't know."
   • Practice the Golden Rule.
   • Give credit where credit is due.
   • Keep the promises you make; don't make promises you can't keep.

2. Ensure that everyone in your work group has access to your company's ethics policy. Allot time at your next staff meeting to discuss the policy and its implications for your work. Reinforce awareness by continuing to encourage open discussions about the impact of ethics violations on business decisions.

3. Sit down with family members and discuss values as they relate to family, work, and community.
   • What values do individual members have in common? Why?
   • What values are different? Why?
   • How does each person prioritize his or her values? Why?

- How can an understanding of each other's value systems exert a positive influence on family dynamics? Decision making? Problem solving? Mutual support?

4. Choose a value that is important to you personally. List some specific ways you currently demonstrate this value in your day-to-day behavior. Identify additional things you could do to live out this value.

5. Act on your beliefs: take pains to recycle; discourage offensive jokes; avoid using products that are destructive to the environment; actively protest discriminatory practices; and so on.

Passion and Courage

Is compelled by what he or she deems important; is willing to accept the personal consequences of difficult choices and decisions; can be relied on to stand up for what's right.

1. Take on the assignment of communicating a difficult or unpopular decision to your staff or peers. In delivering the message, provide enough information so that those affected can understand the rationale behind the decision.
   - Allow enough time for people to process the message and express their feelings.
   - Take ownership of the decision without becoming defensive or angry in the face of negative reactions (state your position; show that you are listening and understanding).
2. Be an advocate for your people. Do not be afraid to
   - Support their decisions when appropriate, despite opposition.
   - Allow them to take risks, make mistakes, and learn—protect them from undue pressure to always be right.
   - Provide them with timely, ongoing feedback about performance problems and issues.
3. Identify a risk you are afraid to take (for example, speaking up at a meeting, taking an unpopular position, refusing to back down on an ethical issue). List the potential benefits and negative consequences of taking the risk. Determine what you would do if the worst-case scenario occurred. Determine what you could do to reduce the risk and to influence a positive outcome.
4. Develop a list of your most deeply held beliefs. Ask yourself the following questions:
   - What values, beliefs, and principles are most important to me?
   - On which of these will I never compromise? Why?
   - For which of these am I willing to fight? Why?

5. Learn from others: find out how others approach making difficult decisions and how they handle the "aftereffects." Talk with them about what does and does not work. Incorporate their best ideas into your approach.

6. Become actively involved in a national or local organization. Take a public stand, contributing your time and effort to move the position of the association forward (for example, go door-to-door to gather signatures, make speeches to local associations).

7. Develop a philosophy of leadership that you are committed to. Articulate your philosophy to others. Involve them in periodically evaluating to what extent you are living up to your beliefs.

8. Flex your "courage muscle" by taking advantage of opportunities to operate outside your comfort level—make a speech, perform a solo, chair a high-visibility committee, and so on.

Optimism and Self-Confidence

Maintains a positive outlook based on a belief in his or her capabilities and the essential goodness of things; sees the glass as half-full rather than half-empty; views challenges as opportunities.

1. Mark the successful completion of intermediate stages in a complex or difficult project you are currently involved in: celebrate "small wins." Establish self-rewards that will give you a pat on the back and provide an incentive to move forward.

2. Be alert to negative or self-defeating thoughts in conversations with yourself. Replace them with positive inner dialogues.

3. Work to develop the following characteristics:
   • Ability to recognize your strengths and compensate for your weaknesses—avoiding the extremes of complacency or defeatism
   • Ability to develop your capabilities and talents through focused efforts
   • Ability to assess the fit between your strengths and weaknesses and the organization's needs—determining how you can best contribute

4. Examine the possible barriers to maintaining an optimistic and self-confident outlook.
   • Make a list of what gets you down.
   • Identify causes (for example, fear of failure, lack of knowledge or skill, wrong job or career).
   • Identify steps you can take to remove or minimize barriers.

5. Reflect on a recent mistake or failure you have experienced as a way of gaining self-confidence. Examine the following points:

- What went right
- What went wrong
- How you can use what you've learned to become strong

6. Identify a relationship that is not entirely satisfactory. Look at what you like and what you dislike about the relationship. Identify actions you can take that will build on the strengths.

7. Use the half-full versus half-empty approach. Each week, list all the things that are going right about a difficult or complex situation in which you are involved. Think about ways to enhance the positive.

Focus and Discipline

Sets appropriate priorities in the face of multiple, competing demands; sticks with the task at hand in spite of difficulties or distractions.

1. Consistently use tools that focus activity and encourage accountability:
   - Keep a monthly or weekly planner, or a daily "To Do" list; review on a regular basis to assess your progress.
   - Set goals to improve the degree to which you routinely accomplish what you set out to do.
   - Use a "tickler file" to prompt yourself about important things you need to stay alert to.

2. "Eat the crust first": plan your day so that you do the most difficult or unpleasant tasks before going on to those that are easier or more enjoyable.

3. Learn from others: identify role models both inside and outside the company. Find out how they manage multiple tasks; talk with them about what has worked, what hasn't worked, and why. Incorporate the best of their ideas into your work routine.

4. Analyze your work routine.
   - For one to two weeks, keep a log of how you spend your time.
   - Periodically during each day, record your tasks and the time involved.
   - At the end of the time allotted assess the log, comparing what tasks you actually spent time on as opposed to high-priority tasks for which you have responsibility. Is the proportion of time devoted to high-priority tasks appropriate?
   - Use this analysis to align time and attention with job priorities.
   - Repeat this process periodically to ensure that desirable habits are reinforced.

5. Spend ten minutes a day meditating in a quiet place on a single idea, topic, or thought. Work at eliminating distractions and achieving greater depth of thought and concentration.

6. Set deadlines for yourself on high-priority tasks:
   - Post deadlines where they are visible to you and others.
   - Use contrasting colors and symbols to check off those deadlines you made and those you missed.
   - Reward yourself for each deadline you meet.
7. Break difficult tasks into small, "doable" steps. Reinforce behavior change by rewarding yourself with a "small win" as each step is completed.

Flexibility

Is able to adapt to different people, situations, and approaches; revises plans and objectives as circumstances warrant.

1. Ask a trusted co-worker to observe you during business meetings or other group events in order to identify instances of rigidity or intolerance. Arrange a feedback session to discuss his or her findings.
2. Schedule time (ten to fifteen minutes) for personal reflection following meetings you attend. Use this time to look for instances when you dismissed new ideas or solutions because "they aren't the way we've always done it" or "they weren't invented here." Set goals for yourself to practice flexibility:
   - Make a conscious effort to gather ideas from a variety of sources, including some that you would not consider "conventional."
   - Strive to use the best parts of these ideas to build something better.
   - Practice continuous improvement, looking for ways to make an ongoing practice or procedure better.
3. Attend a social event (such as a party, sporting event, club gathering, or lecture) that you would not typically attend. Set relevant goals for yourself:
   - Learn enough about the event to be able to hold an in-depth discussion with someone else.
   - Learn enough about the topic to determine whether you want to pursue it as an interest.
   - At a party or social gathering, meet and talk with three new people.
4. Volunteer to chair a community service or school committee with which you are unfamiliar (in terms of its subject, the people involved, or both). Depend on the committee members to educate you, guide you, and show you new or alternative approaches.
5. Examine attitudes, family values, "commandments," "rules of the road"—any baggage you carry with you—that may influence your reaction to new ideas, situations, and people.
6. Try varying a routine: the way you drive to work in the morning, the way you execute familiar tasks, where and with whom you have lunch, and so on.

7. Vary the routines in your life. Investigate
   - A new route to work
   - A new trend in music
   - A new work process
   - A new type of cuisine
   - A new style of clothing

Tenacity and Resourcefulness

Persists in pursuing desired outcomes; "makes do" when situations are less than ideal;
is creative in overcoming obstacles.

1. When faced with an obstacle, solicit potential solutions from people outside
   your discipline and department. They can help you view the problem from a
   new and different perspective. Listen and understand—look for ways to apply
   their ideas.
2. Put yourself and your family on a strict budget for a period of time. Together,
   look for ways to
   - Lower your food cost while maintaining a healthy diet and appealing menu.
   - Entertain yourself and each other at little or no cost.
   - Save money on incidentals and stay within the budget.
3. Volunteer through a community organization to do financial counseling with
   people who have economic difficulties. Work with them to pay off bills and
   improve their credit rating.
4. Whenever possible, involve your staff or other people in a round of "what-
   iffing." Before launching a project or program, create a variety of scenarios
   that encompass what might go wrong. Look for viable alternative solutions or
   approaches.
5. Expand your understanding of resources by taking a common implement like
   a coat hanger and thinking of all the ways it could be used in addition to its
   designated purpose. For example, list how it can be used in relation to food (as
   a skewer), sound (as a drum stick), or flight (as a boomerang).
6. Expect the unexpected: imagine what kinds of things could affect a current
   plan or project, a long-term goal, and so on.
7. Take note of the obvious: what possibilities are right at your fingertips that
   you may be overlooking?

improvisation

Humanity

Genuinely cares about, values, and responds to others; believes in human potential;
is sensitive to individual differences.

1. Identify a specific situation in which you have felt valued and cared about by another. Think about what interactions took place that made you feel that way. List as many specific behaviors as you can. Identify situations where you can apply these behaviors.

2. Understand your paradigms about the people you work with.
   - Complete as many of the following statements as possible:

     "With regard to my direct reports, I act as if . . ."

     "With regard to my peers, I act as if . . ."

     "With regard to my boss, I act as if . . ."

     "With regard to my customers, I act as if . . ."

   - Ask a trusted colleague to complete the same exercise about you using the following stems:

     "With regard to your direct reports, you act as if . . ."

     "With regard to your peers, you act as if . . ."

     "With regard to your boss, you act as if . . ."

     "With regard to your customers, you act as if . . ."

   - Compare lists and discuss any implications.

3. Set a goal for developing relationships across levels and functions; at lunch, sit with people you don't normally spend time with (such as members of another department or the clerical staff).

4. Keep a journal tracking your personal interactions with significant others (family members, colleagues, friends) over the course of a week. At the end of each day take time to review your journal entries and reflect on opportunities you capitalized on and opportunities you missed to enhance those relationships.

5. When you encounter people, make eye contact and extend a greeting; when you are introduced to someone new, make a point of remembering his or her name.

6. Set a goal to deepen your knowledge and understanding of your employees and their knowledge and understanding of you. Put in place some practical steps to accomplish this. For example:
   - Set frequent (monthly, weekly) one-on-one meetings, allotting time for getting to know employees' interests and capabilities.
   - Identify the unique contributions and capabilities of each of your employees; give each appropriate recognition.
   - Gather concerns and reactions from your employees about a problem you are trying to solve or a decision you must make.
   - Establish your own open-door policy by setting aside regular blocks of time when employees can come in to discuss their concerns; focus on actively listening to the employee during these visits.

- Devise and implement a system for systematically gathering feedback on your behavior.
- Keep track of and acknowledge important dates in your employees' lives: work anniversaries, birthdays, personal or community achievements, and the like.
- Invite an employee to lunch with no agenda other than getting to know that person better.

7. Explore the paradigms you have about family and friends.
   - Complete as many of the following statements as possible:

     "With regard to my spouse, I act as if . . ."

     "With regard to my children, I act as if . . ."

     "With regard to my friends, I act as if . . ."

   - Ask a family member or friend to complete the same exercise about you using the following stems:

     "With regard to your spouse, you act as if . . ."

     "With regard to your children, you act as if . . ."

     "With regard to your friends, you act as if . . ."

   - Compare lists and discuss implications.

Self-Renewal

Takes time to develop, improve, and nurture self in the interest of achieving a sense of wholeness and well-being; discovers opportunities for ongoing learning; reflects on experience for what it can teach.

1. Devise and implement a system for periodically gathering specific behavioral feedback from colleagues, employees, and family members on your progress.
2. Practice meditation or yoga as a means of developing your capacity for conscious reflection.
3. Set aside time to practice reflective learning.
   - Choose a behavior you would like to assess or change. Take a long walk in the woods, on a beach; reflect, and listen for insights and awarenesses.
   - Take yourself on a private retreat; get in touch with who you are: your values, beliefs, goals, preferences, and interests. Keep a daily journal of your findings; use this as a basis for periodic reflection and continuous self-learning.
   - Let your thoughts wander while doing routine tasks—mowing the lawn, jogging, washing dishes, stacking firewood, gardening—and explore them. Jot down insights and observations you would like to remember.

4. Keep a daily journal of personal lessons learned—what you handled well and why; what you could have handled differently and why. Periodically review and assess behaviors you've strengthened and behaviors you've changed.

5. Take a course at the local college or community center on a subject that you know nothing about as a way of expanding your mental horizons.

6. Arrange for structured self-development on a regular basis:
   - Attend an assessment-based management or leadership program.
   - Attend a professional conference.
   - Read a thought-provoking book.
   - Participate in a self-help workshop.

7. Try something you've never done before. Reflect on the experiences and outcomes. Record your observations in a journal.

8. Conduct a "postmortem" on a recent project with other project members. Analyze the successes, the failures, the lessons learned.

9. Review recent performance appraisals and other feedback you have received; identify developmental needs and build an action plan.

10. Ask a role model for assistance in developing a specific skill or competency.

11. Routinely ask coworkers or customers about what they would like to see you keep doing and what they would like to see you do differently.

12. Look at a process or procedure that you use daily. Examine each of the steps separately. What can you do to improve them—eliminate, modify, add to them? Track how your changes affect the process.

13. Meet with your manager to review your career goals and developmental needs and to build an action plan.

14. Listen to educational audiocassettes.

15. Ask a co-worker, friend, mentor, or manager to share stories about difficult lessons he or she has learned. Share your own.

16. Dedicate a percentage of your commuting time to listening to a program that will enhance your knowledge or skills in a selected area.

See also: Vision, no. 4; Shifts Paradigms, no. 1.

Balance

Integrates and harmonizes career, family, personal, and community responsibilities.

1. The pie chart shows an example of how the 168 hours in a week might be divided. Using this as a model, complete two circles: one showing how you currently use your 168 hours and another showing how you would like to use your time. Compare both circles and identify changes (in activities, behaviors,

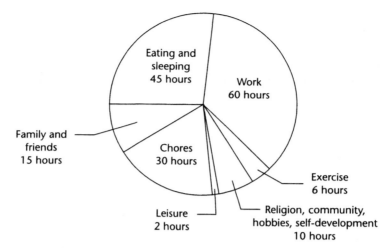

priorities, and so on) you need to make to move closer to your desired state. Consider the following categories in constructing your circles: work, family, exercise, community, hobbies-interests, eating-sleeping, leisure, chores, friend-ships-relationships, personal development, religion.

2. Hold a family discussion about what *balance* means for each person and how individual needs can be balanced with family needs. Together develop a real-istic plan that includes the following:
   - How responsibilities will be carried out within the family
   - What can be hired out

3. Create a life log. Record your activities and the time spent over the course of two weeks. Review and describe changes you will need to make to achieve the balance you would like.

4. Participate in a sponsored or self-styled retreat with your spouse or significant other for the purpose of evaluating and reaffirming mutual values and prior-ities in your relationship.

5. Sponsor a cross-organizational project group for purposes of identifying the high-priority work and family concerns of employees, and of making improve-ment recommendations for company action.

6. Hold a company contest to generate ideas for how employees can achieve a better balance between work life and family life while maintaining high cus-tomer satisfaction and productivity. Form an employee-management group to build a work and family life plan based on the best suggestions. Hold a meet-ing to launch the plan and to give public recognition to the employees who made major contributions. Follow up to measure effectiveness and make nec-essary improvements.

Self-Leadership: Habits of Mind

Embraces Change

Seeks new ideas and approaches; regards change as a source of vitality and opportunity; uses the energy and momentum of change to best advantage; goes *with* change rather than *against* it.

1. Make change a regular discussion topic on your staff meeting agendas. Use the time with your employees to
   - Review impending business changes and examine the implications for your customers and your work.
   - Explore opportunities for change.
2. Make a presentation on a new trend or technique; include a potential application that you have devised.
3. Think of an innovation or approach that you initially resisted but have come to accept.
   - First, identify the specific ways that the innovation or approach has benefited you.
   - Second, look at what form your resistance took and how you overcame it. For example: Did you finally just try it? Did you wait until you saw other people use it? Were you pressured into using it?
   - Third, determine what you could have done to lessen your resistance and make the change less painful.
   - Fourth, use your findings to develop and implement a plan to facilitate learning an innovation or approach that you are currently being asked to adopt.
4. Use brainstorming to generate original ideas when making decisions or solving problems.
5. Invite a teenager to explain the following to you:
   - How they view a current world or local situation
   - How they would handle that situation
   - Why they would approach something differently from you
   - How to do something they know about and you don't
6. Sponsor an employee recognition program for contributions of innovative ideas. Make it broad based or have a rotating theme (for example, improving customer satisfaction, balancing work and family life, improving return on assets).
7. Identify specific situations in which you could bend a rule or make an exception to it, adapt an approach, or revise a policy in response to changing conditions or extenuating circumstances. Implement the change.

See also: Flexibility, no. 7.

Tests Assumptions

Uncovers and examines underlying premises and encourages others to do the same.

1. Devote the first fifteen minutes of your next staff meeting to testing assumptions with others. Invite each participant to express something they assume (for example, about the company in general, about the reason for the meeting, about the topic at hand). Allow time for discussion and clarification.

2. Examine a problem that you are having difficulty solving. List your assumptions as they relate to the problem's cause, its effect, and your solutions. Review your assumption list with people who can provide other perspectives. Test out the reality of some of your assumptions.

3. What follows are three scenarios accompanied by problem statements. For each problem statement, list the implied assumptions.
   - Scenario one: The director of career counseling and placement at a small liberal arts college is concerned about the relatively small percentage of students who go on to graduate school or secure a job in their chosen field immediately upon graduation. He laments that the vast majority do other things (travel, volunteer abroad, coach, bar-tend in Wyoming, take a year off, and so on). He states the problem in this way: "How can we raise the percentage of students who either go on to graduate school or find employment in their chosen field immediately upon graduation?"
   - Scenario two: In response to pressure to show a greater financial return, the senior management team deals with how to increase bottom-line profits. They state the problem in this way: "How can we cut costs?"
   - Scenario three: A manager, aware of efforts to unionize, is fearful of the consequences should a union be established. She states the problem in this way: "How can I prevent a union from coming in?"

4. Complete each of the items that follow by comparing what appears in the stem with something familiar and concrete that you feel gets at its essence (for example, Life is like . . . a bowl of cherries).
   - Life is like . . .
   - Being a manager in the nineties is like . . .
   - My company is like . . .
   - My boss is like . . .
   - An unproductive employee is like . . .

   For each of the items you just completed, identify your underlying assumptions. The assumptions for the "Life is like a bowl of cherries" example might be that life is something to be happy about, that the good far outweighs the bad, or that life is basically a pleasurable experience.

See also: Engages in Dialogue, no. 2.

Shifts Paradigms

Is open to new ways of viewing things; adapts own thinking to accommodate emerging ideas, recent discoveries, new insights; avoids undue reliance on the way things have been done in the past.

1. Establish mechanisms for keeping your knowledge "cutting edge":
   - Talk regularly with your customers and suppliers—stay aware of changing requirements and specifications.
   - Become involved in industry or professional associations—attend their seminars, read their publications, serve on their committees.
   - Subscribe to key publications in your field.
2. Over the course of the last several decades, we have witnessed vast paradigm shifts in such areas as
   - Attitudes toward the rights of minorities
   - The value of something "made in Japan"
   - What the family stands for and what a day in the life of a typical family is like
   - Women's roles
   - The relationship between the United States and Russia

   Choose one of these areas and describe how it used to be versus how it is now. Examine in what ways the shift represents progress, more enlightened thinking, expanded opportunities, and so on. Now use the same process to examine a paradigm shift that has recently occurred in your life.
3. Assemble a group of people (new employees, professionals from other disciplines, and so on) who have not been steeped in "the way it has always been done" to find solutions for some of your ongoing business problems. Allow them the freedom and time to look at the problem with fresh eyes and to experiment, to take risks, and to fail with potential solutions.
4. Invite new employees to look at company policies, processes, and procedures and suggest how they might make them better.
5. Practice listening "outside the boxes" of your own paradigms. Avoid using such phases as the following:
   - "That's not the way it's done around here."
   - "I wish it were that easy."
   - "You know management will never buy that."
   - "When you've been here longer, you'll understand how things really work."
   - "We've already tried that."
6. Use the "paradigm shift" question from Joel Barker's *Paradigms* (1992), "What is impossible to do in your business (field, discipline, department, division, technology, etc.), but if it could be done, would fundamentally change things?" to initiate discussions that explore new directions, initiatives, and so on.

Ask the question at all levels of the company. Ask it often. Listen to the answers. Don't reject any answer as impossible; instead, consider any indicators that suggest it might be possible.

7. Look for sacred cows.
   - Ask friends and family to help you identify paradigms that are no longer appropriate but that you are still using.
   - Ask your employees to look for work policies, programs, processes, and so on that are no longer appropriate but are still being used.
8. Examine your own management paradigm. Are your definitions of what constitute good management practices consistent with today's management paradigm of fostering empowerment, collaboration, and continuous learning in employees?

See also: Humanity, nos. 1 and 8.

Thinks Holistically

Sees the "big picture"; uses an interdisciplinary approach; appreciates how the parts affect the whole.

1. Invite several colleagues or counterparts from other functions to sit down with you and exchange their visions, purposes, and goals. Discuss to what extent these are compatible with yours. How can you support one another in the realization of these?
2. Bring others (senior managers, employees, peer managers) into problem-solving meetings to expand the group's thinking beyond parochial interests.
3. Label a blank sheet of paper "Connections." Use it as a decision-making tool by jotting down any links that you see between one thing and another as you analyze various data (such as thoughts and activities, products and services, interactions and events, and so on).
4. Compare notes with a colleague or counterpart in another function to identify mutual, superordinate goals.
5. Create a tree, diagraming how your work unit's vision, mission, goals, and objectives cascade down from company or link to goals and objectives.
6. Think about a major decision you recently implemented (such as a new or amended policy, procedure, or process). Starting with you, the decision maker, make a diagram that shows the flow of whom the decision has affected (both inside and outside the company). If you get stuck, ask people how they were affected and who else they would include. When you have completed the diagram, think about

- What far-reaching impacts the decision had
- Questions you would want to ask yourself and others prior to making major decisions in the future

Ask yourself how specific items relate to overall objectives.

Tolerates Ambiguity and Paradox

Functions effectively in "messy" situations where information, goals, values, or direction is uncertain or apparently conflicting, or where processes cannot be tightly structured; is able to live with questions that allow for discovery; resists premature closure and pat answers.

1. Seek opportunities to perform in situations where you have no experience or that are unstructured; keep a journal on your reactions; gather feedback on how you could be more effective.
2. Force yourself to move periodically from details to concepts.
3. Learn from others: identify role models both inside and outside of the company. Find out how they handle ambiguous and paradoxical situations. Talk with them about what has worked, what hasn't, and why.
4. Take a drive with no planned destination. Allow your route and activities to take shape as you go.
5. Identify an area of life—an interest, project, or initiative—in which you can choose to operate without a focused goal and set plans.
   - Start with a broad perception of what you want to do.
   - Identify a direction based on internal preferences.
   - Plan as you go.
   - Integrate new information.
   - Take advantage of opportunities as they present themselves.
   - Tolerate redundancy, false leads, and side trips.

See also: Flexibility, no. 4; Focus and Discipline, no. 5.

Trusts Intuition

Relies on informed judgment and well-developed instincts in lieu of conclusive proof in making decisions; balances need for data with confidence in personal knowledge and experience.

1. Heighten your awareness of the less obvious elements of a situation by practicing the following exercises:
   - Place yourself in a setting of your choice (a quiet place where you won't be interrupted), then experience your surroundings as fully as you can by

focusing on only one sense at a time for extended periods (for example, close your eyes and just listen). Record the details you experience for each sense.

- Write for as long as you can about something small and incidental—one side of a coin, the back of your thumb, a bottle cap. Look closely to discover details you may never have noticed before.

2. Keep a daily journal of random observations.
3. Write down any thoughts that come to you about a problem or situation while you are sleeping, shaving, showering, working out, or performing any other mundane task.
4. Immediately verbalize your "hunches" whenever possible; keep a track record of how they played out.
5. Make a list of some of the things you "know" from experience. Ask yourself
   - How well these "truths" have served you
   - If they still hold true
6. Describe at least one instance when you or someone you know was right about something that they had no empirical proof of in advance.

Takes Risks

Tries things even when the possibility of failure exists; makes experiments in the interest of discovering new opportunities and solutions.

1. Learn from others: identify role models both inside and outside the company. Find out how they go about assessing whether or not to take a risk. Talk to them about what has worked, what hasn't, and why. Try some of their approaches to stretch your "risk comfort" level.
2. Identify the factors holding you back from taking appropriate risks. Consider the following: a need to gather excessive data; lack of knowledge of true risk level; discomfort about consequences of failure; discomfort about unknown risk factors; discomfort about specific areas of endeavor (for example, capital expenditures, marketing campaigns). Use the following techniques to increase your risk-taking ability.
   - Set limits: determine up front how much detail, documentation, research, supporting evidence, and so on are necessary for the task or decision you are about to undertake.
   - Put risks in perspective by developing a worst-case scenario and considering its long-term impact on you and the organization.
   - Develop a risk-benefit analysis for a prospective commitment. Try to identify more benefits than risks.

- Get in the habit of publicly committing to small efforts as a way of overcoming fear and minimizing risks; develop a mechanism for ensuring that you follow through.

3. Try something socially you haven't done before or that you know you're uncomfortable with.
   - Take a whitewater rafting trip or a wilderness survival course.
   - Travel without an itinerary.
   - Take a trip by yourself.
   - Go to a social function or party by yourself and find a way to enter in.
   - Try a new recipe when you are entertaining.

See also: Courage, nos. 1, 3, and 8.

Seeks Synergies

Encourages and practices collaboration; works with others to achieve breakthrough outcomes.

1. Use consensus decision making to develop a plan for a family outing. As a group:
   - Brainstorm to identify a range of options.

     Encourage everyone to say whatever idea comes to mind.

     Record all responses and do not evaluate.

     Encourage individuals to expand on each other's idea.

     After all ideas have been recorded, review the list to make sure everyone clearly understands each idea.
   - Reduce the list—combine similar ideas and eliminate duplicates.
   - Use selected criteria (such as when you will go, length of time outing will last, specific amount of money that can be spent) to evaluate ideas.

2. Practice using open-ended or indirect probing questions to encourage people to develop and expand on their contributions in problem-solving or decision-making situations. Effective probing questions usually begin with such words as *what, why, how, to what extent, in what way, explain, describe,* and *compare.* Avoid leading and closed questions—those that suggest a desired response or that can be answered by a simple yes or no. Leading and closed questions usually begin with such words as: *is, have, do, will, would, when, how much, who, where,* and *which.*

3. Identify a key decision you must make in the coming weeks. Brainstorm a list of people from whom you can solicit information, potential solutions,

approaches, and so on. Be sure to include at least two people whom you would not ordinarily include—individuals who are not experts on the subject or with whose opinions you typically disagree. Discuss the decision with these people and record their input without labeling whose idea is which. Put your notes aside for a period of time before reviewing them. What ideas, approaches, and solutions can you use? How can you combine the ideas? What new ideas have others provided that strengthen your solution?

4. Examine your support systems and determine how the synergy in these relationships has produced a greater effect than you could have achieved alone. (An example of a support system is the relationship built by a couple to help their children grow happy, healthy, and productive.) Look at the support systems you have with
   - Your spouse or significant other
   - Friends
   - Work colleagues
   - Your children or other family members

5. Ensure that your vision, mission, and objectives not only tie to company goals but also are not in conflict with those of other work groups your staff must collaborate with.

6. Prior to launching an initiative in your organization, list all the people involved, both internal and external. Meet with them throughout the planning and implementation phases in order to
   - Determine their requirements
   - Explore synergistic approaches
   - Review progress
   - Uncover potential problems and opportunities

Models Values

Communicates values and acts accordingly; demonstrates personal convictions; "walks the talk."

1. Take a periodic audit of yourself, asking:
   - "How am I doing?"
   - "Where am I going?"
   - "Is this the way I want to be?"
   - "What should I be doing differently?"

2. Seek opportunities for publicly owning your beliefs, your decisions, and your reactions, even when they differ from those of other people. In preparation, write down a belief, a decision, a reaction. Below it, list as many ways as you can think of to demonstrate your conviction.

3. Develop personal visions—one for work, one for family, one for community, and one for yourself. For each vision describe in detail the desired state and the unique contributions and strengths you will be using to reach that end state. Take your time and be as specific as possible. Compare the visions. Where are there overlaps in contributions and strengths? Where are there differences? Are there strengths and contributions from one vision that you can use in another?

4. Periodically ask yourself, "Am I doing the right thing?" If the answer is yes, then proceed to do it. If the answer is no, reconsider your actions.

See also: Integrity, nos. 5 and 6; Courage, nos. 4, 6, and 7.

People Leadership: Enabling Individual and Team Performance

Sets Parameters

Assists employees and teams in developing a clear understanding of both desired performance outcomes and the boundaries and conditions within which they are free to make choices about how they achieve those outcomes.

1. At the beginning of a project, meet with your team to ensure that they clearly understand the project's desired outcome(s) and parameters (that is, objectives, scope of project, criteria for success, decision-making authority, budget, timelines, constraints). Ask that the team's status reports reflect progress toward the desired outcome(s), obstacles they've encountered, changes in direction, emerging issues, and any contingency plans they've developed or implemented.

2. Consider a privilege your teenager has recently requested (for example, staying up later on school nights or changing a weekend curfew). Work with him or her to determine a mutually acceptable agreement (such as a later time with which you both are satisfied) and the specific parameters of the privilege (for example, having a trial period, completing homework or chores by a certain time, deciding what the extra time is used for). Meet subsequently to discuss whether you both continue to be satisfied. Negotiate modifications when necessary.

3. Ask an employee to prioritize his or her top five performance objectives. Independently, develop your own list of the employee's top objectives and priorities. Meet to compare the lists and discuss the following:
   - What factors (assumptions, relationship to department goals and directions, interests, abilities, developmental needs, impending organizational changes) did each of you use to select the performance objectives?

- What factors did each of you use to prioritize the objectives?

   Work together to reconcile differences and to gain a clearer understanding of the employee's job and his or her potential in that job.

4. Ask your direct reports to analyze their own and others' roles in achieving specific performance objectives using the following questions for each objective:
   - Where does the direct reports' responsibility start and end?
   - Whom must they depend on to achieve the objectives? (Encourage them to look up, down, and across the organization in answering this question.)
   - Who, ultimately, benefits from the outcome of the objective?
   - What is the organizational goal or vision the objective contributes to?

   Meet with each employee to discuss responses, mutually correct any misconceptions, and ensure that they understand the parameters of their job.

5. Call a meeting to establish performance objectives for your team. Start by ensuring that the team has a clear understanding of the organization's direction and strategy and of the work unit's focus. Break the team into small groups and have each group brainstorm performance priorities for the team. Bring the team together to compare answers, combine the lists, and gain consensus on the team's top performance objectives. Next, ask each of the groups to select one of these objectives and answer the following questions:
   - Is the objective an end in itself or does it contribute to a larger project? If so, who owns the project?
   - What are the specific output(s) the team needs to achieve, and who will receive them?
   - What are the major steps the team needs to accomplish to meet this objective?
   - Who are the people (stakeholders) who have a vested interest in the success of the project? In what way and how often does the team need to keep them informed of its progress?
   - Who needs to give input before and during work on the objective to ensure the team's success?
   - What criteria will the team use to measure both its process and outcome(s)?

   Bring the team together to discuss each group's findings and to reach agreement on the critical success factors for each objective.

6. Assist a nonbusiness (community, school, religious) group you are involved with to move ahead on a project by using the following process to help them define critical success factors for the project.
   - Break the group into subgroups and have each develop a statement they think describes the overall outcome of the project. Include the goal of the project and the long-and short-term benefits to the group, the recipients of the project, and the community as a whole.

- Bring the subgroups together to compare statements, combine them, and gain consensus on an overall description of the goal(s) of the project.
- Next, ask each subgroup to use that statement to answer the following questions:

    What are the specific output(s) of the project that the group needs to achieve? Who will receive these output(s)?

    What are the major steps involved in achieving each output?

    Who, outside of the group, has a major interest in the project and needs to be kept informed? In what way and how often will this be accomplished?

    Who, from inside and outside the group, needs to give input about the project both before and during its implementation?

    What criteria will the group use to measure its success while the project is being implemented and at its completion?
- Bring the group together to review each subgroup's findings and to reach agreement on the project's critical success factors.

7. Involve your school-age children in planning a family vacation or outing. Provide them with information about the length of time and amount of funds available for the trip, and work with them to brainstorm possibilities, research lodgings, plan activities, budget costs, and so on.

8. Develop a regimen for your personal fitness and well-being by setting parameters within which you can make a variety of choices. For example:
   - Determine how much time per week you will spend working out.
   - Determine approximately how often you will allow yourself such dietary indulgences as alcohol and desserts.
   - Determine how much time per week you will devote to quiet reflection, journal keeping, or a special project, interest, hobby, or self-improvement activity.

See also: Tenacity and Resourcefulness, no. 3.

Re-Presents the Organization

Actively conveys the organization's and work unit's history, culture, missions, values, and visions; ensures that employees and teams understand how their efforts contribute to the larger purposes of the organization.

1. Share with your direct reports information about your performance objectives; upper management's objectives; the company's strategic direction, vision, and mission; and the goals of your specific organization. Have them refer to

this information as a context for developing their own performance objectives. Meet as a group to share and discuss the work of the team and the goals of the company, focusing on making connections among each individual's work.

2. As preparation for your next staff meeting, ask your direct reports to identify the overarching values they see reflected in current company communications (such as the company vision and mission statements, annual and interim reports, current business priorities, and articles or speeches by the president and upper management). At the meeting discuss the following:
   - How the values of the work group connect to or conflict with the company values
   - To what extent apparent conflicts can be resolved
   - What additional steps the group can take to enhance their contribution

3. Ask your direct reports or team to create a tree diagram that shows the connections between the work unit's vision, mission, goals, and objectives and the company's vision, mission, and goals.

4. Develop ways to keep company vision, mission, priorities, and values front-and-center with employees. For example:
   - Imprint T-shirts, coffee cups, posters, pocket cards.
   - Provide special recognition to employees who have made outstanding efforts in support of the company vision, mission, priorities, or values.
   - Use the company magazine or newsletter to publish success stories of employees and teams who have moved the company closer to realizing its vision.

5. Work with your spouse and children to develop a family tree. Research genealogy. Discover and take turns telling the stories of your ancestors.

6. As a part of the orientation for new employees, incorporate stories that highlight the history, legends, and heroes of the organization.

7. As a family activity, read Alex Haley's *Roots* aloud (or listen to the audiotape). Discuss how our history influences our identity.

8. Celebrate family ethnic origins by observing specific holidays with retellings or reenactments of events the day is based on, literature and music of the country, and traditional foods.

9. Make a practice of telling the children in your family stories about memorable experiences in your own growing up as a way of helping them develop a sense of family history and continuity.

10. Keep a journal in which you tell your own story; track turning points, successes, low points, memorable experiences, and so on.

See also: Vision, no. 2.

Expands Access to Information and New Knowledge

Establishes an information-rich environment in which employees and teams are encouraged to understand relevant business factors, make connections, develop insights, share learning, and respond dynamically to rapidly changing conditions.

1. Identify information that you have not typically shared with your direct reports (for example, budget, strategic direction, new products or services, and policy changes). Set aside time at staff meetings to share in-depth information about one of these areas. Include such information as business rationales, long-term plans, and pending changes. Encourage people to ask questions and discuss how this new information might facilitate their work or create obstacles. Help them look for ways to minimize obstacles and capitalize on opportunities.

2. Join with other managers to sponsor brown-bag lunch programs for employees. Encourage employees to suggest topics and take an active role in sponsoring activities or in leading discussions. Use these events to
   - Present new information.
   - Share success stories.
   - Engage in dialogue about a company issue or problem.
   - Conduct roundtable discussions on current topics.

3. Look for additional ways to help your direct reports gain easy access to information.
   - Subscribe to an on-line service.
   - Subscribe to a books-on-tape club.
   - Circulate trade magazines and other relevant materials.
   - Create a resource library.
   - Hold "video lunches," during which the staff previews and discusses films on a variety of issues.

4. Use memos, voice mail, quick meetings, and e-mail to keep your direct reports up-to-date on internal information (such as new directives, changing priorities, market data, and interim results).

5. Set an expectation that all members of the work group (yourself included) will share their learning from conferences and training programs. Set aside specific time for this activity on the staff meeting agenda.

6. Begin a family tradition that encourages each member of the family to share at dinner something new that they learned that day.

7. Create opportunities for your direct reports to gain knowledge and broaden their work perspective by taking part in
   - Professional associations
   - Networking groups

- Cross-organizational exchanges
- Multi-organization task forces

8. Plan regular family experiences designed to expand members' knowledge:
   - Take trips to museums and libraries.
   - Explore cyberspace resources.
   - Pick a topic of shared interest and research it in the encyclopedia.
   - Take field trips to study natural phenomena: mountains, ponds, rivers, swamps, and so on.
9. Dedicate some time each week to investigating an area outside your field. Look for connections or insights that could enhance some aspect of your work.
10. Create a "parking lot" board in a prominent place in the office. Encourage employees to post issues, questions, concerns, rumors. Review and discuss postings at staff meetings.

Cultivates Diverse Resources

Views individual differences as potential strengths and seeks to understand, appreciate, and tap the unique capabilities of each person.

1. Arrange a diversity training workshop for your group. Work with the facilitator to ensure that the program content achieves some depth. Build in exercises or group discussions that use the key learnings and concepts from the training as the basis for identifying the following:
   - Relevant group issues about diversity
   - The group's strengths in fostering diversity
   - Areas for development related to diversity
   - Action steps to address identified needs

   Continue to revisit and follow up on these action steps.
2. Establish group practices that highlight the unique contributions of each member of the group:
   - Initiate a program that allows employees to recognize each other through peer awards: dinner-out certificates, wall plaques, gift certificates, and the like.
   - Save ten minutes at the end of your next staff meeting for each person to recognize others in the group.
   - At your next staff meeting, take time to focus on how each person's strengths, attributes, and contributions make the group stronger and more productive; focus on what is distinctive about each member of the group.

   Note: You may want to make this exercise visual by posting an enlargement of the "Core Values" graphic shown here, and encouraging each group mem-

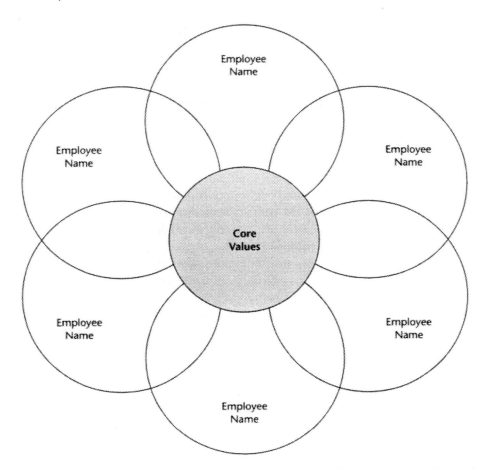

ber to fill in their own and other members' unique gifts, talents, strengths, and qualities as a starting point to developing the shared purpose, core values, and vision represented by the overlap.

3. Work to develop both work and social relationships with people whose backgrounds and experiences are different from yours. Keep a journal that captures the new things you have learned from these relationships (such as new knowledge, different perspectives, and new approaches).

4. Become a mentor to a high-potential employee who differs from you in gender, age, ethnic background, race, or values. In providing guidance and information to the employee, be sure that you have clearly distinguished between

   • Those legitimate behavior standards that are expected by the company (for example, completing staff work, keeping up-to-date on new products and services, having a sense of urgency when responding to customer issues).

- Those behaviors that are your personal success criteria derived from your unique strengths (for example, being a good storyteller, having a high degree of patience) or that are unwritten company codes based on excessive stereotyping (such as being highly competitive or adhering rigidly to a preferred dress code).

  Assist the employee in developing criteria for successful self-expression, building on his or her unique strengths and capabilities.

5. Make an effort at the next party or social gathering you attend to meet and talk with two or three new people who differ from you in gender, age, ethnic background, or race.

6. Look for ways to involve your family in learning about diversity:
   - Host an exchange student for the school year.
   - Invite an inner-city child to your home for the summer.
   - As a family, volunteer to help inner-city youth, the elderly, the homeless, AIDS patients, new immigrants, or another group.
   - Encourage your children to apply for studies abroad.
   - Make a family project of learning another language.
   - Take a family study trip with the express purpose of experiencing another culture.

7. Make a point of investigating experiences that are not just like your own. For example:
   - Attend a religious service of a different faith.
   - Listen to TV and radio programs that represent viewpoints different from your own.
   - Participate in community programs that focus on learning about different people and cultures.

8. Look for ways to represent diversity in your work surroundings. For example:
   - Display artwork that represents diverse cultures or styles.
   - Circulate reading materials that reflect a variety of viewpoints.
   - Encourage employees to display personal items in their office (such as photos, children's drawings, a favorite plant).

9. Gather input from a wide variety of people when faced with an issue you need to deal with. Look for ways to incorporate their different points of view and approaches to broaden your own perspective.

10. Broaden the diversity of your hiring pool by
    - Advertising in niche magazines
    - Seeking recommendations from employees
    - Working with ethnic clubs or groups in your community

- Being available for exploratory interviews with a variety of types of employees

See also: Humanity, nos. 1, 2, 5, 7, and 8.

Promotes Continuous Learning

Actively encourages employees and teams to pursue new ideas, new ways of thinking, and appropriate behavior changes in a variety of ways (for example, formal training, on-the-job development, mentoring, reading, feedback, and reflection); creates an environment that fosters experimentation and learning from experience collectively as well as individually.

1. Have direct reports develop two learning objectives (preferably related to identified developmental needs) in addition to their annual performance objectives. Each objective should include action steps (for example, an experiential activity or formal training) and measurement criteria. Meet with your employees at least once a quarter to review progress.
2. Encourage employees to keep a daily journal of "lessons learned" while working on a team project. The journal should record their thoughts about the successes and failures they encounter as well as what they learn. Throughout the project, encourage the team to share the learnings that they think would contribute to the team's effectiveness and productivity.
3. Create an environment where mistakes are viewed as learning opportunities, not the "end of my job."
   - Conduct "postmortems" for projects. Analyze the successes, the failures, and the lessons learned.
   - Give a "Failure of the Year" award for the person (or team) who learned the most from a failed effort. Make the presentation of the award a positive event, focusing on what was learned and how that learning benefited the organization.
   - Help employees learn from mistakes. In discussing the mistake, analyze what went wrong, use problem solving to explore alternative approaches, and, if necessary, develop an action plan detailing corrective steps.
4. Take time during staff meetings for reflection. During a discussion that has multiple elements or nuances, take five minutes for people to jot down their thoughts and feelings about the topic. Continue the discussion, allowing the statements, questions, and feelings that arise from the reflective period to enhance the discussion.

5. Structure experiences that will help your direct reports to learn from others:
   - Encourage employees to discuss problems and issues with peers.
   - Help employees meet others, both internally and externally, who can add to their knowledge base.
   - Sponsor employees at professional conferences and meetings on a regular basis.
6. During status updates in staff meetings, have people give their information anecdotally (by telling a story) rather by reporting facts or data. Notice whether interest and retention of information increase.
7. Join with your direct reports to create a vision of a learning organization. Use the following questions as a guide:
   - What policies, events, or aspects of behavior in this new organization help it thrive and succeed?
   - How do people behave inside the organization? How do they interact with the outside world?
   - What are some of the differences between this ideal organization and the organization for which you work now?
   - What are some the steps you can take now to begin closing the gap?

See also: Learns Continuously, no. 2; Assumptions, no. 2; Creates Access to Information and New Knowledge, nos. 2, 5, 6, 7, 8, and 9.

Facilitates Contribution

Expands capability of employees and teams to contribute to the organization in a variety of ways, ranging from providing input on decisions to owning and developing their work; provides management direction and support appropriate to what individual employees and teams require in order to continuously improve performance.

1. Assess each of your children in terms of his or her confidence and ability to take on more responsibility and act more autonomously. Determine the areas in which you can lower your level of supervision or the child can assume new or different challenges, and what continued or additional support he or she will need to make success more likely. Evaluate each child's progress periodically by
   - Revisiting your assessment
   - Discussing with the child how he or she feels about the changes
   - Implementing modifications, as needed
2. Mark the successful completion of intermediate stages in a complex or difficult project as times to involve your team in celebrating "small wins." Establish these mini-rewards as a way of reviewing progress and planning next steps.

3. Foster "communities of practice" (Wenger and Lave, 1991) around major projects in your organization. Each project team should include diverse representation and should provide team members with the following:
   - Opportunities to use expertise, assume the lead, and teach others
   - Opportunities to broaden their experience and knowledge, and to contribute a new perspective

   For each project ensure that
   - Outcomes and performance standards have been clearly articulated.
   - Teams have the necessary resources and authority (for example, information, training, tools, decision-making capacity).
   - Interim and final measurement standards have been established.

4. Resist telling another person (co-worker, family member, friend) how to handle a problem he or she has encountered. Ask questions to help the person explore alternatives and determine consequences. Even if it is what you consider to be a wrong decision, take the time to recognize the person's initiative in making an independent choice. Talk through the outcomes of the decision to identify what went right and what could have been handled differently.

5. Find opportunities to showcase individuals and teams; encourage presentations at staff meetings and to other parts of the organization as appropriate.

6. Encourage each family member to take turns initiating a topic for a family dinner conversation.

See also: Embraces Change, no. 6; Seeks Synergies, no. 2; Resourcefulness, no. 5; Shifts Paradigms, no. 3.

Advocates Feedback and Recognition

Exchanges feedback with peers, superiors, and direct reports on an ongoing basis to mutually enhance performance; appropriately acknowledges good work; guides employees and teams in actively giving and seeking feedback, and in valuing one another's contributions.

1. Ask each person in your organization to put up a bulletin board in his or her office that is easily accessible to others. Each board should be labeled "I can help you do your job better by . . ." and "I have helped to do a better job by . . ." Encourage everyone to use the boards as a way of providing pertinent, ongoing feedback on everyday activities.

2. Ask your direct reports to design a reward and recognition program that can be used for recognizing each other and people outside the immediate organization. The design should include criteria for recognition, levels of recognition, and processes for selection, approval, and presentation.

3. Establish Monday morning team meetings to assess team progress toward major goals and objectives. The following are some of the topics team members should review and discuss:
   - The quality of the process and product
   - The status of deliverables
   - Progress toward deadlines
   - Meeting customer requirements
   - Communication to or collaboration with others
   - New information or lessons learned

4. Frame feedback sessions with your employees using answers to the following questions:
   - Questions from employee to manager:
     What do I do that helps you do your job?
     What do I do that hampers you or makes life difficult for you?
   - Questions from manager to employees:
     What can I do to help you?
     What could I stop doing that would help you?

5. Institute an Employee of the Month program that provides recognition for desired behavior. When announcing the award, be very specific about how the employee's effort or behavior brought value to the organization. (For example: John went out of his way to solve a customer problem, even using his own time to make sure the problem got solved in a timely manner.) Encourage employees to suggest nominees.

6. Invite customers and other organizations with which you work closely to attend your staff meetings. Ask them to share feedback on how your group helps and hinders their performance.

See also: Humanity no. 7; Promotes Continuous Learning, no. 3.

People Leadership: Managing Relationships Across Boundaries

Builds Collaborative Relationships

Seeks out others as a means of generating information, ideas, resources, opportunities, synergies, and so on; takes into account the concerns, needs, and interests of others within the system; extends the boundaries of conventional work relationships to achieve value-added results.

1. Look for nontraditional opportunities to work with other managers as a way to build relationships. Gather other managers together to

- Work on a community project (for example, meet on a Saturday to paint or make repairs to the home of a needy family).
- Sponsor a group barbecue for your staff, for which the managers do all the preparation and cooking.
- Arrange an experiential team-building event.

2. Schedule lunch on a regular basis with people from other parts of the organization to exchange ideas and explore opportunities.
3. Actively seek out people in the organization who are championing an innovation (such as a new product, service, application, approach). Look for ways for people in your organization to partner with or support them.
4. Initiate a monthly breakfast roundtable with people from across the organization to discuss current issues, trends, innovations, and ways to work together.
5. As a way of building relationships, take advantage of each opportunity as it presents itself (in the hallway, at lunch, during meeting breaks) to engage in conversations with others and show an interest in their activities.
6. Be attuned to personal and professional events taking place in the lives of the people you work with (for example, service anniversaries, a child's winning a scholarship, birthdays, deaths or illness in a family, winning the 10K). Write a note to the person, expressing your personal sentiments.
7. Plan ways you can strengthen your relationship with new or distant members of your extended family—special, personalized activities that will help increase trust, companionship, and love.
8. Review chapter 5 of *The Empowered Manager* (Block, 1987). Use Block's matrix on trust and agreement to identify the approaches you need to use to influence

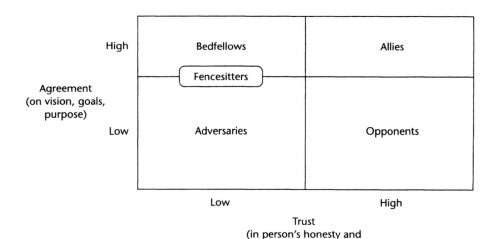

those people (boss, peers, customers, vendors, direct reports, and so on) who are critical to the success of a project or innovation you want to implement. Once you have identified where people are on the matrix, use the appropriate influencing approaches in chapter 5 to

- Discuss with the other person what you are trying to accomplish.
- Affirm your agreement or negotiate a new agreement.
- Affirm your trust, or negotiate what you both want to get out of a joint venture as a way of building trust.

See also: Thinks Holistically, nos. 1, 2, and 4; Humanity, no. 4.

Engages in Dialogue

Initiates exploratory conversations as a means of examining assumptions, beliefs, "what ifs," and so on; willing to suspend the need to know, the need to win a point, the need to judge or decide, in the interest of allowing greater understanding to emerge through shared inquiry.

1. Read Peter Senge on dialogue and the difference between dialogue and discussion in *The Fifth Discipline* (1990a, pp. 243–248).
2. To foster a more open and revealing dialogue in your next problem-solving meeting, adopt Senge's (1990a, p. 243) rule of "suspending all assumptions." Use the following group guidelines:
   - All participants must be able to treat each other as peers (no matter what the hierarchical structure).
   - All participants must be willing to "suspend their assumptions":
     Recognize the assumptions they are making
     Be willing to express their assumptions but not spend time defending them
     Be willing to leave their assumptions open to questioning and observation
     Stay away from non-negotiable, rigid opinions
   - Appoint a group facilitator who will
     Carry out meeting processes
     Ensure that hidden assumptions do not inhibit the flow and thoroughness of the group's conversation
     Ensure that all aspects of a subject have been explored
3. Start a problem-solving meeting with a dialogue on relevant issues. Explore the issues in an open, speculative manner, using "what if" questions and not pushing to arrive at answers or reach conclusions. Focus this time on entertaining the question rather than on finding answers and making points.
4. Work with a friend to practice suspending assumptions during a dialogue. Choose a topic that has high relevance and interest to both of you. Write

down several statements that reflect your thoughts on this topic. Review each statement to uncover its underlying assumptions. Now engage in a dialogue with one another on this topic. Monitor yourselves, making sure that these and other assumptions do not hinder your ability to explore the topic thoroughly.

5. With your spouse or significant other, engage in a dialogue. Choose a topic of mutual interest to both of you. Avoid letting the conversation become a debate. Instead allow yourselves to think out loud, looking at the topic from all sides and exploring new avenues of thought.

6. Listen to your listening: make a point of monitoring your internal voice as you are participating in conversations and meetings. How do you process ideas? What specific factors influence the judgments you make about what you hear? To what extent do you enhance or inhibit the evolution of new connections, meanings, possibilities, or knowledge?

Achieves Integrative Agreements

Works to produce win-win solutions—outcomes that reconcile differences and mutually satisfy the needs and values of self and others.

1. Practice giving yourself time to get used to new ideas by letting them "stick around" for awhile instead of instantly rejecting them. Provide the same time to others by not pressing for a quick reaction when presenting them with new ideas.

2. Distance yourself from instantly reacting during tense negotiations. Before responding give yourself sufficient time to
   - Look at what has taken place between you and the other party (for example, conflict, disagreement, or attack).
   - Understand your own feelings (for example, anger or intimidation).
   - Re-identify those items that are "must haves" (a car) and those items that are "nice to haves" (a particular color or model) that you desire from this negotiation.

3. Use the following techniques to begin to uncover what the other party in a negotiation is thinking and feeling—what they want to achieve, what they hope to achieve, what they are concerned about (adapted from Ury, 1991, p. 13):
   - Look for their point of view. You don't necessarily need to agree with it, but you do need to understand how strong and legitimate they think their view is. Help them understand your point of view by discussing it openly and frankly.
   - Stay in touch with your own and the other side's feelings about the issues being discussed (fears, concerns, frustrations). Do not deny that these emotions exist: encourage that they be aired openly to explore their validity.

- Listen actively to the other side and indicate that you have heard them and understand their point of view by maintaining good eye contact, verifying your understanding of what they have said, and summarizing key points they have made.

4. Before beginning a negotiation, look for established processes, precedents, practices, and standards to use in resolving sticking points and arriving at fair decisions.

5. Test yourself on the differences between principled negotiating and soft and hard bargaining as discussed in *Getting to Yes: Negotiating Agreement Without Giving In* (Fisher and Ury, 1981). Use page thirteen of the book, covering up the third column. After reviewing the soft and hard bargaining approaches outlined in columns 1 and 2, determine what the appropriate principled style would be for each approach. Check your responses against column 3. Determine how you would use each of these principled negotiating approaches in a current situation.

Organizational Leadership: Creating a Culture

Develops Core Values

Facilitates consensus around a set of shared beliefs about what the organization or work unit stands for; works to ensure that these beliefs are reflected in the systems, structures, choices, and decisions of the organization as a means of shaping its organizational culture.

1. Institute an annual retreat with your senior management staff to revisit the organization's core values. Explore the values in relation to the organization's culture and direction. Revise as appropriate. Build plans for disseminating the values throughout the organization and integrating them into the organization's systems and structures.

2. Bring your management team members together on an annual basis to rededicate themselves to the organization's values and to share their plans for modeling those values and making them a living part of the organization.

3. Organize a management discussion around gaining a clearer understanding of the organization's values. Use the discussion to achieve agreement on the behaviors and measurements implied for each value. For example the group might want to discuss: What constitutes "best practices"? How do we measure "fair and equitable treatment" of employees? What does an "empowered" employee or team look like? Publish and distribute a list of the values and their corresponding behaviors and measurements to all employees. Incorporate

these behaviors and measurements as part of the performance standards for appraisals and reward and recognition programs.

4. In *The Leadership Challenge,* Kouzes and Posner (1987, pp. 195–197) describe three qualities of values that highly successful companies have in common:

   • Clarity: employees understand what their organization stands for.

   • Consensus: employees understand, share, and agree with the organization's values.

   • Intensity: employees have made the organization's values their own and act on them.

   Use these definitions to measure your organization's effectiveness with regard to the clarity, consensus, and intensity of its values.

5. Take a periodic survey of your organization to uncover employees' thoughts and feelings about the effectiveness of the organization's values:

   • Do employees know and understand the values?

   • Do they see the values reflected in company policies and practices?

   • Do the organization's current direction and structure accurately reflect the values?

   • Is there congruence between management's actions and the organization's values?

   Use the information gathered from the survey to reinforce what is working well and to develop new strategies for ensuring that the values and the organizational direction, structures, and practices are aligned.

6. Spend some time around the family dinner table finding out what kinds of things each member most values about your family life. Use this as a starting point for exploring and making explicit your family's core values. Brainstorm some ways that these values can be consistently lived out and mutually supported day-to-day. Plan a family activity that reinforces one of the core values you have identified.

7. Margaret Wheatley, author of *Leadership and the New Science* (1992) claims that core values should *emerge* in an organization through the interactions of its members, specifically through their "good thinking" and "good hearts." To understand how this process might work on a much smaller scale, complete the following exercise.

   • Identify a personal relationship that is (or has been) *particularly important to you* and *highly satisfying* (for example, your spouse or significant other, a close friend, a favorite relative, a co-worker or colleague).

   • Describe what, specifically, makes the relationship so satisfying. What, for example, do you share in a unique or special way? What constitutes the common ground of the relationship?

- Based on what you described, what three or four values would you say best characterize the relationship (for example, intimacy, mutual support, common purpose, affection, creativity, partnership, caring, achievement)? To what extent do you believe the other person in the relationship would arrive at similar answers?
- By what specific means have these values *emerged* or become apparent in the relationship?
- Considering the discoveries you have made exploring the phenomenon of emergent core values at the personal level, what would it take to foster the emergence of core values within an organization?

See also: Integrity, nos. 3, 4, and 5; Models Values, nos. 1 and 2; Re-Presents the Organization, no. 2.

Takes a Systems Approach

Recognizes the interdependency of parts within the system; considers the potential impact of decisions, choices, and initiatives on what is distant in time and space as well as what is close at hand; uses the tools and methodologies of systems thinking to identify high-leverage opportunities for making significant organizational change.

1. Build an ecosystem with your family (an ant farm, a fish tank, a terrarium or vivarium).
   - Diagram the system to depict how the individual parts work together to create the whole system.
   - Watch what happens over time to the individual parts of the system and the system as a whole. Determine if the system is in balance, with all its parts working together, or if it is out of balance. Look for the cause(s) of any imbalance and make corrections to the system.
   - Remove part of the system or add a new element. Watch what changes occur to the individual parts of the system and to the system as a whole. Determine the cause(s) of those changes.
2. Choose an event in history to research with your family (such as Edward VIII of England's abdication of the throne, Rosa Parks's bus ride, the first walk on the moon). Map out all the events—personal, national, and global—that you think the original event influenced in some way. Predict how you think it will continue to influence events to come.
3. Choose an event (a policy decision, a new program, a company acquisition) that has occurred in your organization during the last two years. Map out all

the ways—positive and negative—that you think this event has influenced company direction, employee attitudes, work culture, and organizational values. Interview other managers and employees to gather their thoughts. Once your research is completed, use your list to predict how this event will continue to affect the future. Determine what interventions you can make to reinforce positive effects and mitigate negative effects.

4. When doing a routine task (mowing the lawn, riding a bike, washing windows), mentally outline how all the parts of the "system" work together and what part each plays toward the completion of the task.

5. Use the following reading list to increase your knowledge of systems theory, concepts, and skills:
   - Peter Senge, *The Fifth Discipline: The Art and Practice of the Learning Organization.* (New York: Doubleday, 1990).
   - Draper Kauffman, *Systems 1: An Introduction to Systems Thinking* (Minneapolis: S. A. Carlton, 1980).
   - Russell Ackoff, *Creating the Corporate Future: Plan or Be Planned For* (New York: Wiley, 1981).
   - Barry Oshry, *Seeing Systems: Unlocking the Mysteries of Organizational* Life (San Francisco: Berrett-Koehler, 1996).
   - Margaret Wheatley, *Leadership and the New Science* (San Francisco: Berrett-Koehler, 1992).
   - Pegasus Communications, *Systems Thinker* newsletter, One Moody Street, Waltham, MA 02154.

6. From your own experience, identify examples of the following systems "rules of thumb":
   - Everything is connected to everything else.
   - You can never do just one thing.
   - There is no free lunch.
   - Nature knows best.
   - "Obvious solutions" do more harm than good.
   - Look for high-leverage points.
   - Nothing grows forever.
   - It isn't what you don't know that hurts you; it's what you *do* know that isn't so.
   - Don't fight positive feedback; support negative feedback instead.
   - A butterfly flapping its wings in Tokyo can create a tornado in Texas.
   - Don't try to control the players; instead change the rules.
   - Don't make rules that can't be enforced.
   - There are no simple solutions.
   - Good intentions are not enough.

- High morality depends on accurate prophecy.
- If you can't make people self-sufficient, your aid does more harm than good.
- Every solution creates new problems.
- Loose systems are often better than tight, precise systems.
- Competition is often cooperation in disguise.
- There are no final answers.

See also: Thinks Holistically, nos. 3 and 6; Seeks Synergies, no. 4.

Builds Community

Seeks to forge connections and strengthen personal and professional bonds among staff; stimulates the kind of esprit de corps that promotes collective learning, self-organization, and synergistic outcomes.

1. Look for ways to enrich your work environment, both physically and emotionally. For example:
   - Pay attention to colors, room arrangements, lighting, equipment and furniture, and noise.
   - Introduce reward and recognition programs, flex-time, child-and elder-care programs, the ability to work from home, education and training opportunities.
   - Consider how space can best be arranged to encourage interaction and collaboration.
2. Using Autry's description of "Special Treatment"(1991, pp. 23–25), determine how you can provide special treatment for each of your employees, your peers, your manager, and your family. Special Treatment is "treating people as individuals with differing needs; using common sense to get best results; accepting and working with differences; acknowledging differences and using that information to support productivity and improved performance."
3. Expand your reward and recognition program (or create one) to include excellence awards for
   - The people who go the extra mile to get the job done
   - The people who are willing to try new things in the pursuit of making the job or product better
   - The people who use personal time and effort to ensure that a customer is kept satisfied
   - The people who best support their coworkers personally and professionally
4. Schedule special events to coincide with staff meetings. For example:
   - Conduct your staff meeting at a local park, combining business with a picnic.

- Bring in featured speakers on both business and personal topics.
- At the end of a meeting, take everyone to a fun, unusual event (for example, bowling or a boat ride).
- Celebrate special events (for example, birthdays, anniversaries).

5. Hold monthly "let's have pizza" or "bring a surprise dish" lunches where everyone can relax and talk together.

See also: Vision, nos. 2 and 10; Integrity, no. 3; Humanity, no. 7; Balance, no. 5; Embraces Change, no. 6; Creates Access to Information and New Knowledge, nos. 2, 5, and 10; Cultivates Diverse Resources, nos. 2, 3, 8, and 10; Promotes Continuous Learning, nos. 1, 2, 3, and 7; Urges Contribution, nos. 2 and 5; Encourages Feedback, nos. 1, 2, and 5; Builds Collaborative Alliances, nos. 1, 6, and 7.

Organizational Leadership: Anticipating the Future

Stays Current with Emerging Trends

Maintains awareness of social, political, economic, and technological developments that affect the business; is knowledgeable about changing directions relative to a discipline, industry, or operating environment.

1. Read and study the ideas, thoughts, and beliefs of experts in your field and related fields as sources of knowledge about current and future trends. For example, read the writings of a leading economist, historian, futurist, or scientist as way of anticipating change in the business environment.
2. Look for ways to stay abreast of emerging trends and developments in your business field:
   - Become involved in an industry or professional association—attend their seminars, read their publications, serve on their committees.
   - Talk regularly with customers and suppliers to stay aware of how the changes in their industries will have an impact on yours.
   - Subscribe to key publications in your field.
3. Select a current world event or development (economic, political, or societal) that is being written about or being discussed in the media. After reading the article or listening to the discussion, analyze the impact that event may have on your business.
4. Make a list of six current innovations in technology, business, and society (such as fiber optics, the virtual office, or olestra). For each innovation list new prod-

ucts or services, new industries, and any new trends that have resulted from the change.

5. Spend time studying the future.

- Read the leading futurists (for example, John Naisbitt, Joel Barker, and Alvin Toffler).
- Subscribe to reports from futurist research organizations (for example, the University of Southern California's Center for Futures Research, the Conference Board in New York City, or the World Futures Society in Washington, D.C.) on events relevant to business.

6. Set up a futures research committee in your organization to study social, political, economic, and technological developments as well as potential changes that might affect your business.

Thinks Strategically

Draws on both hard and soft data (for example, market research, emerging trends, experience, intuition, informal learning, and interactions with others) as sources for developing strategic direction; views strategy as dynamic rather than static; discovers future opportunities in day-to-day details; involves others in contributing to the process of shaping strategy on an ongoing basis.

1. In his article "The Fall and Rise of Strategic Planning," Mintzberg (1994, p. 107) states that strategy can be deliberate and also emergent—that is, it can "develop inadvertently without the conscious intention of senior management, often through a process of learning." To better understand how this process works, think of a time when a strategy you were involved in implementing evolved as circumstances changed. Identify what caused circumstances to change (for example, people, resources, rules and regulations, competition, other strategies) and how those changes affected the strategy. Consider what would have happened if the original strategy had been implemented without adaptation.

2. Try to find out as much as you can about a new phenomenon (for example, an emerging technology such as the Internet or a growing social issue such as Workforce 2000) and its implications for your organization. Use traditional avenues, such as market research, customer surveys, financial records, opinion polls, and so on, in addition to nontraditional sources: talk with people to find out what they've heard; ask how they think it will affect them professionally and personally; review popular magazines (*Psychology Today, Good Housekeeping*) for relevant articles, and send for tapes of talk shows that have discussed the issue.

3. Identify those people in your organization who have direct access to your customers (salespeople, receptionists, clerks, telephone operators, and service representatives). Ensure that these employees have a means of communicating their customer knowledge to others in the organization:
   - What customers like and don't like about your products, services, advertising, and so on
   - What problems are occurring
   - What additional features or enhancements customers would like to have
   - New customer opportunities

   Also ensure that your organization has a system in place to synthesize and use the information.

4. Learn from others: seek out people in your organization or community who are highly skilled in strategic thinking. Explore with them how they identify and address strategic issues.
   - What types of information do they seek out?
   - What types of information sources do they use (for example, people, hard and soft data)?

5. Work with your team to identify processes or habits that restrict its ability to approach problems and opportunities more strategically. Implement a process to minimize these barriers.

6. In identifying a strategic issue:
   - Identify everyone who is involved—the issue owner, stakeholders, customers, implementers, and information- or data-givers.
   - Talk with them to understand how they would define the issue.
   - Integrate their viewpoints to gain a broader perspective on the issue.

7. According to Mintzberg (1994), strategic planning is not the same as strategic thinking. Whereas strategic planning deals with analyzing and elaborating on existing strategies, strategic thinking involves using intuition and creativity in looking for innovative ideas. To practice this aspect of strategic thinking, select a personal project (vacation, construction project, major purchase) and ask family and friends to brainstorm what the perfect project would look like, refining it as explicitly as possible (for example, what should a newly built addition look like, how should it be used, what conveniences should it have, what amount of light should it contain, how should traffic flow through it, where should doorways be located). Use these ideas to build your plan.

8. Mapping your current skills and knowledge with the company's vision, values, and strategic direction, determine how you can increase the value you add to your company by developing your contribution.

9. Sponsor a monthly contest in your organization that gives recognition to the employee who contributes the most radical (revolutionary) new idea to take the business forward.

10. Make it a part of your monthly staff meetings to look for new opportunities to take the business forward.

11. Establish a centrally located bulletin board labeled "Voice of the Customer." Encourage all employees to post external and internal customer comments (advice, ideas, issues, concerns, complaints, questions). Process the comments at staff meetings, establishing action items as appropriate. Continue to follow up to ensure closure.

12. Keep a daily journal of work events. At the end of the week, review the journal and continue to review it until you've found one new application that will influence your work in a positive way.

13. Use the following exercise to uncover emerging trends and identify strategic implications. Draw a small circle and inside it write the issue or opportunity statement you want to explore. Around that circle draw a series of concentric circles that maps the issue or opportunity from its local impact to it global impact. Starting at the local level, brainstorm the trends you see emerging from the issue or opportunity.

See also: Vision, no. 4; Flexibility, nos. 4 and 5; Tenacity and Resourcefulness, nos. 2 and 5; Tests Assumptions, no. 2; Shifts Paradigms, nos. 1, 3, and 6; Thinks Holistically, nos. 2 and 3; Creates Access to Information and New Knowledge, nos. 3, 5, 6, 7, 8, and 9; Builds Collaborative Alliances, nos. 3 and 4; Takes a Systems Approach, no. 3.

Inspires Pursuit of a Shared Vision

Involves others in creating a bold and compelling picture of the desired future; engages everyone in imagining and seeking to realize what could be.

1. Work with others in your unit or organization (direct reports or peers) to imagine a possible dream for the future of your organization.
   - What are some of the future forces or conditions (in the next five to ten years) that will affect the way you do business: think about your customers' expectations, your employees' expectations, your competition, your suppliers, new technologies, the environment, and the economy.
   - Using the answers to the preceding questions, look at what you should be doing to meet these new expectations and changes:
     What services or products should you be providing, and in what way?
     What should your group look like, and how should it function?

What are the definable gaps (such as needed skills, organizational culture shifts, or structure changes) between where you would like to be and where you are today?

Will filling those gaps (realizing the vision) result in an organization that is better for your customers, for your suppliers, and for you personally and professionally?

2. Coach a children's sport team based on such goals as learning, involvement, and fun. Before each game have team members describe how they will reach these goals, and discuss how well they did after the event. Work with them to develop interim goals as needed.

3. With your staff, develop a vision for your organization or unit (for example, a new product or innovation, a higher level of service). Involve each employee in identifying how his or her needs and wants will be met by working toward this vision.

4. Identify the opportunities (expressed as values) inherent in a vision you hold (business or personal). Use the following list to get started, and add to it. How will working toward this vision provide people with the opportunity to

   - Learn new things?
   - Develop new skills?
   - Accomplish something worthwhile?
   - Change things for the better?
   - Be a part of something new and different?

5. Practice communicating your vision to a group of trusted colleagues. Use a rating scale of 5 to 1 (5 = excellent, 3 = average, and 1 = poor) to have them rate your effectiveness and provide feedback in the following areas (adapted from Kouzes and Posner, 1987):

   - You used a lot of images and word pictures.
   - I could relate to the examples you used.
   - Your references were credible.
   - You referred to common values and beliefs.
   - You knew your audience.
   - You included everyone, across the organization.
   - You were positive and talked about hope for the future.
   - You shifted from talking about my vision to talking about our vision.
   - You spoke with an emotion and passion that showed you are personally committed to the vision.

6. According to Kouzes and Posner (1987), being able to communicate a vision effectively has been proven to have a positive impact on the level of people's

   - Satisfaction with their jobs
   - Commitment and loyalty to the organization

- Feeling a part of the business
- Understanding the organization's values
- Productivity

Ask colleagues to listen for and provide feedback on evidence that you have communicated a vision effectively relative to these criteria.

Employs Dynamic Planning

Charts a flexible course to move the organization toward its short-term goals and long-term vision; identifies checkpoints along the way to measure progress and incorporate new learning.

1. Develop progress mileposts so that planning is divided into manageable pieces. Make progress toward these mileposts very visible to the organization. For example, post storyboards, publish progress articles in the company newspaper, or sponsor events that showcase progress to date.

2. Practice dynamic planning by holding a picnic in which children plan what to take. Set parameters for the decisions the children will make about the picnic (for example, all four food groups must be represented, only so much money can be spent, each person can take only one game or toy). Let the children make up the shopping list, do the shopping, and pack for the picnic. During these activities, have them recheck their decisions to confirm whether they need to amend their plan.

3. Ask your planning team to do a mental walk-through of how the plan will be implemented. Have them think through and share their findings on the communication processes, milepost objectives and measurements, tasks and activities that lead toward mileposts, and people's reactions from throughout the organization.

4. Involve the implementers, stakeholders, end users, and internal customers in the planning process for an initiative and during its implementation.

5. Use dynamic planning on a hobby or interest. For example, maximize your vegetable garden's yield. Develop a list of assumptions around such factors as amount of expected rainfall, average temperatures during the growing season, seeds or seedlings, use of chemicals, and so on. Use these assumptions to develop your initial plan as well as contingency plans should your assumptions not hold true.

6. During implementation of a plan, create reflective learning opportunities for your team that allow for changing course, exploring new directions, and exploding old paradigms.

7. To explore alternative implementation possibilities, ask your planning team to identify the underlying assumptions the plan is based on and to build implementation scenarios:
   - Divide the team into two or more groups and ask each group to develop their list of assumptions.
   - Come together to share and synthesize the lists into one list of primary assumptions.
   - Use the list of assumptions to build a variety of implementation scenarios. For example, have the team build one scenario based on all the assumptions being true; then have them build several other scenarios using various groupings of the assumptions.
   - Use these scenarios to develop the implementation plan and contingencies.
   - Revisit the assumptions and scenarios at mileposts to reaffirm the validity of plans.
8. Use dynamic planning in organizing an outing with a group of friends. To assist your planning decisions, take along such things as a walking map and road map of the area, a current newspaper, a set amount of money, a compass, binoculars, a snack, a guidebook, a camera, and a change of clothing. Preplan only the first stop, and then let the rest of the day evolve based on personal interests, encounters with people you meet, and discoveries along the way.

Enlarges Capacity for Change

Works to fashion an adaptive organization that responds to emerging imperatives; challenges the status quo and encourages others to do the same; champions new initiatives; allows for the discovery of order out of chaos.

1. Involve your staff in developing the long-term business strategy for your organization or work unit. Actively engage them in planning for change and implementing the new direction collectively by
   - Exploring the opportunities for change (for example, new business opportunities or directions)
   - Building a vision around the change strategy
   - Allowing people to discuss the possible positive and negative effects of the desired change on themselves, both professionally and personally
   - Determining who else needs to be involved, consulted, or informed to ensure successful implementation of the strategy
   - Building a transition plan by establishing the long-term and interim objectives for achieving the desired change and by defining the time frames and responsibilities

- Establishing a process for learning from the successes and failures you encounter along the way

2. Learn from others: find out how others have successfully championed change in their organizations. Talk with them about what does and does not work. Incorporate their best ideas into your approach.

3. With your team, look for routines and practices within your organization that are hindering creativity and change. Develop lists of the individual and team routines and practices in which you are involved. Ask which are critical to the success and growth of the organization. Retain those routines that are essential and eliminate the others.

4. Look for ways of allowing people to express their concerns, openly ask questions, and discuss the process of change they are experiencing:
   - Set time aside in staff meetings for people to share their personal experiences with the change.
   - Institute an employee suggestion program that deals exclusively with the change. Openly respond to all input.
   - Meet frequently, one-on-one, with your staff to provide individualized support.

5. Before introducing a change to your team, look for ways to bridge from the old to the new. Ask yourself:
   - What tasks, activities, or practices will remain the same? If they will change, to what degree?
   - What new tasks, activities, or practices will be required?
   - What competencies (skills and knowledge) will carry over?
   - What new competencies will be required?

   Use your analysis to help the team look at the change as a transition.

6. Reflect on changes, large and small, that have occurred in your life. Think about how you reacted to those changes. For example, think about your degree of resistance, your willingness to learn new skills, your emotional state (fear or excitement), and the length of time it took you to become comfortable with a change. Discuss your findings with friends and family to broaden your perspective. Apply the learnings from your personal experiences to help others become more comfortable with changes they face.

7. Plan changes incrementally to allow people to take "baby steps" toward the final destination. Make recognition of desired behavior very visible to the organization.

See also: Embraces Change, nos. 1, 2, 3, 4, 5, 6, and 7; Flexibility, nos. 6 and 7.

POSTSCRIPT

"Permanent white water" has served as a governing metaphor throughout this book. It is a useful device for helping us think about the unrelenting turbulence of the times and the implications of such an environment for those charged with steering organizations through the rapids into a viable future.

What the white water metaphor does *not* fully express, however, is the depth and magnitude of forces underlying the turbulence. For we are experiencing not just surface disturbance; we are experiencing no less than a sea change. And our healthy respect for something so sweeping and potentially overpowering may cause us to retreat or to become immobilized—or to want to fully prepare ourselves before we venture forth.

The fact is, we don't have the time or the luxury for any of these approaches. Nor should we delude ourselves into believing that we ever could be fully prepared. For if conditions around us are in constant flux, then we, too, must expect to learn, to change, and to *be* changed as we go.

And so our leadership odyssey begins as a gesture of faith—in the possibilities of a new age, in the callings of our organizations, and in the not-yet-fully-realized hopes and aspirations and gifts within ourselves.

We can take heart along the way from those who offer encouragement in the face of our uncertainty. From Max De Pree, who reminds us that leadership is "much more an art, a belief, a condition of the heart, than a set of things to do"

(De Pree, 1989, p. 148). From Margaret Wheatley, who describes a journey of "mutual and simultaneous exploration" where we cannot expect answers because reality is "constantly new," and says we must "muddle our way through," trusting that our odyssey will take us "deeper and deeper into a universe of inherent order" (Wheatley, 1992, pp. 150, 151). And from Peter Block, who suggests that the answers to some of our most vexing questions lie in the struggle itself (Block, 1995).

It is our hope that this book raised as many questions as it answered, and that both will serve you well as you make your way.

REFERENCES

Ackoff, R. *Creating the Corporate Future: Plan or Be Planned For.* New York: Wiley, 1981.

Argyris, C. "Good Communication That Blocks Learning." *Harvard Business Review,* July–Aug. 1994, pp. 77–85.

Asman, D. *The Wall Street Journal on Managing: Adding Value Through Synergy.* New York: Doubleday, 1990.

Autry, J. *Love and Profit: The Art of Caring Leadership.* New York: Morrow, 1991.

Barker, J. A. *Paradigms: The Business of Discovering the Future.* New York: HarperCollins, 1992.

Barry, J. F. "Adrift in Annapolis." *Washington Post,* March 31, 1996, pp. C1, C4.

Belasco, J. *Teaching the Elephant to Dance: The Manager's Guide to Empowering Change.* New York: Crown, 1990.

Bennis, W. *On Becoming a Leader.* Reading, Mass.: Addison-Wesley, 1989.

Bennis, W., and Nanus, B. *Leaders: The Strategies for Taking Charge.* New York: HarperCollins, 1985.

Blanchard, K., and Johnson, S. *The One-Minute Manager.* New York: Morrow, 1982.

Block, P. "Stewardship: A Governance Strategy for the Learning Organization." Keynote address presented at the fifth annual Systems Thinking in Action™ Conference. Boston, Massachusetts, September 1995.

Block, P. *The Empowered Manager: Positive Political Skills at Work.* San Francisco: Jossey-Bass, 1987.

Block, Z., and MacMillan, I. "Milestones for Successful Venture Planning." *Harvard Business Review,* 1985, *63,* pp. 184–196.

Bohm, D. "On Dialogue." Edited transcription of a meeting following a seminar, Ojai, Calif., Nov. 6, 1989, p. 1.

Botkin, J. W., Elmadjra, M., and Malitza, M. *No Limits to Learning: Bridging the Human Gap— a Report to the Club of Rome.* New York: Pergamon Press, 1979.

Boyer, E. L. *College: The Undergraduate Experience in America*. New York: HarperCollins, 1987.

Bridges, W. "The End of the Job." *Fortune,* Sept. 19, 1994, pp. 62–74.

Bridges, W. *Managing Transitions*. Reading, Mass.: Addison-Wesley, 1991.

Brockett, R. G., and Hiemstra, R. *Self-Direction in Adult Learning: Perspectives on Theory, Research, and Practice*. London: Routledge, 1991.

Brown, J. "Corporation As Community: A New Image for a New Era." In J. Renesch (ed.), *New Traditions in Business: Spirit and Leadership in the 21st Century*. San Francisco: Berrett-Koehler, 1992.

Brown, J. "Building Community, Building Commitment: Learning Organizations in a Democratic Society." Unpublished speech presented at the fourth annual Systems Thinking in Action™ Conference, San Francisco, 1994.

Brown, J., and Isaacs, D. "Conversation As a Core Business Process." *Systems Thinker™,* Dec. 1996–Jan. 1997, *7*(10), pp. 1–6.

Brown, J. S. "Dimensions of Dialogue." Working paper, 1993.

Burns, J. M. *Leadership*. New York: HarperCollins, 1978.

Byham, W. C. *Zapp! The Lightning of Empowerment*. New York: Harmony, 1988.

Cameron, J. *The Artist's Way: A Spiritual Path to Higher Creativity*. New York: Putnam, 1992.

Carnevale, A. P. "Learning: The Critical Technology." *American Society for Training and Development,* adapted from *America and the New Economy*. San Francisco: Jossey-Bass, 1992.

Channon, J. "Creating Esprit de Corps." In J. Renesch (ed.), *New Traditions in Business: Spirit and Leadership in the 21st Century*. San Francisco: Berrett-Koehler, 1992.

Chappell, T. *The Soul of a Business: Managing for Profit and the Common Good*. New York: Bantam Books, 1993.

Collins, J., and Porras, J. *Built to Last: Successful Habits of Visionary Companies*. New York: HarperCollins, 1994.

Conner, D. *Managing at the Speed of Change*. New York: Villard Books, 1993.

Connor, P., and Lake, L. *Managing Organizational Change*. Westport, Conn.: Praeger, 1994.

Copeland-Briggs Productions. *Valuing Diversity, Part 6: Champions of Diversity*. San Francisco: Copeland-Briggs, 1990. Videotape.

Corcoran, E. "How the Seeds of Success Spoiled Apple." *Washington Post,* Jan. 28, 1996, pp. 1, 8–9.

Covey, S. *The Seven Habits of Highly Effective People*. New York: Simon and Schuster, 1989.

De Pree, M. *Leadership Is an Art*. New York: Dell, 1989.

De Pree, M. *Leadership Jazz*. New York: Doubleday, 1992.

Dillard, A. *Teaching a Stone to Talk: Expeditions and Encounters*. New York: HarperCollins, 1988.

Drucker, P. "The New Society of Organizations." *Harvard Business Review,* Sept.–Oct. 1992, pp. 95–104.

Duncan, D. J. *The Brothers K*. New York: Doubleday, 1993.

Eisenberg, L. "Taking the Long, Sharp View." *Esquire,* Dec. 1983, p. 305.

Eliot, T. S. *Collected Poems 1909–1962*. New York: Harcourt Brace, 1970.

Etzioni, A. *The Active Society*. New York: Free Press, 1968.

Federman, I. "Can Turnaround Be This Simple?" *Journal of Management Inquiry,* March 1992, pp. 57–60.

Fisher, R., and Ury, W. *Getting to Yes: Negotiating Agreement Without Giving In*. Boston: Houghton-Mifflin, 1981.

Frankl, V. *Man's Search for Meaning*. Boston: Beacon, 1984.

Fritz, R. *The Path of Least Resistance*. New York: Random House, 1989.

Fromm, E. *Man for Himself.* New York: Holt, Rinehart, and Winston, 1947.

Garvin, D. "Building a Learning Organization." *Harvard Business Review,* July–Aug. 1993, pp. 78–91.

Gordon, J. "Rethinking Diversity." *Training,* Jan. 1992, p. 29–30.

Gore, William J. *Administrative Decision Making.* New York: Wiley, 1964.

Gozdz, K. "Building Community As a Discipline." In M. Ray and A. Rinzler (eds.), *The New Paradigm in Business.* New York: Putnam, 1993.

Greenleaf, R. *Servant Leadership.* New York: Paulist Press, 1977.

Haas, R. "The Corporation Without Boundaries." In M. Ray and A. Rinzler (eds.), *The New Paradigm in Business.* New York: Putnam, 1993.

Hamel, G. "Strategy As Revolution." *Harvard Business Review,* July–Aug. 1996, pp. 69–82.

Hamel, G., and Prahalad, C. K. "Strategy As Stretch and Leverage." *Harvard Business Review,* Mar.–Apr. 1993, pp. 75–84.

Hemphill, J. K. "Leader Behavior Description." Columbus: Ohio State University Personnel Research Board, 1950.

Hesselbein, F., Goldsmith, M., and Beckhard, R. (eds.), *The Leader of the Future.* San Francisco: Jossey-Bass, 1996.

Hock, D. W. "The Chaordic Organization: Out of Control and into Order." *World Business Academy Perspectives,* 1995, *9*(1), 5–18.

Hollander, E. P. "Conformity, Status, and Idiosyncrasy Credit." *Psychological Review,* 1958, pp. 117–127.

Howard, R. "Values Make the Company: An Interview with Robert Haas." *Harvard Business Review,* Sept.–Oct. 1990, pp. 133–144.

Huey, J. "The New Post-Heroic Leadership." *Fortune,* Feb. 21, 1994, pp. 42–50.

Isaacs, W. "Dialogue: The Power of Collective Thinking." *Systems Thinker™,* Apr. 1993, *4*(3).

Jackson, D. (producer and director). *The Empowered Manager.* Irwindale, Calif.: Barr Films, 1991. Videotape.

Kaufmann, D. L. Jr. *Systems 1: An Introduction to Systems Thinking.* Minneapolis: S. A. Carlton, 1980.

Kay, J. "Shareholders Aren't Everything." *Fortune,* Feb. 17, 1997, pp. 133–134.

Kim, D. "The Leader with the 'Beginner's Mind.'" *Healthcare Forum Journal,* July–Aug. 1993, pp. 32–37.

Kofman, F. and Senge, P. M. "Communities of Commitment: The Heart of Learning Organizations." In Sarita Chawla and John Renesch (eds.), *Learning Organizations.* Portland, Ore.: Productivity Press, 1995, pp. 15–43.

Kotter, J. *The Leadership Factor.* New York: Free Press, 1988.

Kouzes, J. M., and Posner, B. Z. *The Leadership Challenge: How to Get Extraordinary Things Done in Organizations.* San Francisco: Jossey-Bass, 1987.

Liedtka, J., and Rosenblum, J. *Making Strategy, Managing Change.* Working paper, Darden School, University of Virginia, 1996.

Long, D. G. *Learner Managed Learning.* New York: St. Martin's Press, 1990.

MacNulty, C.A.R. "Beyond Reengineering." Paper presented at the Conference of Organizational Systems Designers, Washington, D.C., June 1994.

March, J., and Simon, H. *Organizations.* New York: Wiley, 1958.

Martin, J. "Ignore Your Customer." *Fortune,* May 1, 1995, pp. 121–126.

Mauer, R. *Caught in the Middle: A Leadership Guide for Partnership in the Workplace.* Cambridge, Mass.: Productivity Press, 1992.

Maurer, R. *Feedback Toolkit: 16 Tools for Better Communication in the Workplace.* Portland, Ore.: Productivity Press, 1994.

McCall, M. W. Jr., and Lombardo, M. M. *Off the Track: Why and How Successful Executives Get Derailed.* Technical Report no. 21. Greensboro, N.C.: Center for Creative Leadership, January 1983.

McCall, M. W., Jr., and Kaplan, R. E. *Whatever It Takes: Decision Makers at Work.* New York: Simon and Schuster, 1989.

McCaskey, M. *The Executive Challenge: Managing Change and Ambiguity.* Boston: Pitman, 1982.

McGregor, D. *The Human Side of Enterprise.* New York: McGraw-Hill, 1960.

Mehal, M. (producer), and McCarey, K. (director). *Leadership and the New Science.* Carlsbad, Calif.: CRM Films, 1993. Videotape.

Miller, A. *Death of a Salesman: A Play in Two Parts.* Authorized acting edition. New York: Dramatists Play Service, 1980.

Mintzberg, H. "Planning on the Left Side and Managing on the Right." *Harvard Business Review,* July–Aug. 1976, pp. 53–56.

Mintzberg, H. "The Fall and Rise of Strategic Planning." *Harvard Business Review,* Jan.–Feb. 1994, pp. 107, 111.

Mitchell, W. *The Man Who Would Not Be Defeated.* Levittown, Penn.: Phoenix Society, 1993.

Morgan, G. *Images of Organization.* Thousand Oaks, Calif.: Sage, 1986.

Morris, L. *Managing the Evolving Corporation.* New York: Van Nostrand Reinhold, 1995.

Naisbitt, J. *Megatrends: Ten New Directions Transforming Our Lives.* New York: Warner Books, 1982.

Naisbitt, J., and Aburdene, P. *Megatrends 2000: Ten New Directions for the 1990s.* New York: Morrow, 1990.

Nonaka, I. "The Knowledge-Creating Company." *Harvard Business Review,* Nov.–Dec. 1991, pp. 96–98.

O'Reilly, B. "The New Deal: What Companies and Employees Owe One Another." *Fortune,* June 13, 1994, pp. 44–52.

Oshry, B. *Seeing Systems: Unlocking the Mysteries of Organizational Life.* San Francisco: Berrett-Koehler, 1996.

Palmer, P. J. *Leading from Within: Reflections on Spirituality and Leadership.* Indianapolis: Indiana Office for Campus Ministries, 1990.

Pritchett, P. *New Work Habits for a Radically Changing World: 13 Ground Rules for Job Success in the Information Age.* Dallas: Pritchett and Associates, 1994.

Pritchett, P. *Firing Up Commitment During Organizational Change.* (2nd ed.) Dallas, Tex.: Price Pritchett and Associates, 1996.

Pruitt, D. "Achieving Integrative Agreements." In M. H. Bazerman and R. J. Lewicki (eds.), *Negotiating in Organizations.* Thousand Oaks, Calif.: Sage, 1983.

Reilly, B. "The Secrets of America's Most Admired Corporations: New Ideas, New Products." *Fortune,* Mar. 3, 1997, pp. 60–64.

Rowan, R. *The Intuitive Manager.* Boston: Little, Brown, 1986.

Savage, D. G. "Scalia Driving Away High-Court Allies." *Los Angeles Times,* July 21, 1996.

Schein, E. "The Process of Dialogue: Creating Effective Communication." *Systems Thinker™,* June–July 1994, pp. 1–4.

Sellers, P. "So You Fail. Now Bounce Back!" *Fortune,* May 1, 1995, pp. 48–66.

Semler, R. "Managing Without Managers." *Harvard Business Review,* Sept.–Oct. 1989, pp. 76–84.

Senge, P. M. *The Fifth Discipline: The Art and Practice of the Learning Organization.* New York: Doubleday, 1990a.

Senge, P. M. "The Leader's New Work: Building Learning Organizations." *Sloan Management Review,* Fall 1990b, pp. 7–23. *32*(1).

Senge, P. M. "Building Learning Infrastructures." Keynote address at the Fourth Annual Systems Thinking in Action™ Conference, San Francisco, Nov. 1994.

Senge, P. M. "Leading Learning Organizations." In F. Hesselbein, M. Goldsmith, and R. Beckhard (eds.), *Leader of the Future: New Visions, Strategies, and Practices for the Next Era.* San Francisco: Jossey-Bass, 1996.

Senge, P. M., and others. *The Fifth Discipline Fieldbook: Strategies and Tools for Building a Learning Organization.* New York: Doubleday, 1994.

Shaw, M. E. *Group Dynamics: The Psychology of Small Group Behavior.* New York: McGraw-Hill, 1981.

Sneider, D. "Apple's CEO Switch: Effort to Remain Independent?" *Christian Science Monitor,* Feb. 5, 1996, p. 9.

Starr, N. (producer), and Cram, B. (director). *Excellence in the Public Sector.* Boston: Northern Lights Production. Videotape.

Stewart, T. "3M Fights Back." *Fortune,* Feb. 5, 1994, pp. 94–99.

Toffler, A. *Future Shock.* New York: Random House, 1970.

Tough, A. *Intentional Changes.* River Grove, Ill.: Follett, 1982.

Ury, W. *Getting Past No: Negotiating with Difficult People.* New York: Bantam Books, 1991.

Vaill, P. "Leadership Is Not Learned; It Is Learning." Keynote address presented at the National Leadership Institute Leaders and Change Conference, University of Maryland, College Park, Sept. 1996.

Wall, S. J., and Wall, S. R. *The New Strategists: Creating Leaders at All Levels.* New York: Free Press, 1995.

Watson, B. "A Town Makes History by Rising to New Heights." *Smithsonian,* June 1996, pp. 110–120.

Webber, A. M. "What's So New About the New Economy?" *Harvard Business Review,* Jan.–Feb. 1993, 24–42.

Wheatley, M. J. *Leadership and the New Science.* San Francisco: Berrett-Koehler, 1992.

Wheatley, M. J. "Understanding Organizations as Living Systems." Keynote address presented at the sixth annual Systems Thinking in Action™ Conference, San Francisco, Oct. 1996.

Wheatley, M. J., and Kellner-Rogers, M. Organizational Systems Designers workshop, Washington, D.C., June 8, 1994.

Wenger, E., and Lave, J. *Situated Learning.* Cambridge, Mass.: Cambridge University Press, 1991.

Zaleznik, A. "Letting Leaders Replace the Corporate Managers." *Washington Post,* Sept. 27, 1992, pp. 1–5.

Zaleznik, A. "Managers and Leaders: Are They Different?" *Harvard Business Review,* May–Jun. 1977, pp. 126–135.

Frontmatter

Overleaf from Brown, J. S. "Dimensions of Dialogue," working paper, 1993, p. 14. Used by permission of Judy Sorum Brown.

Chapter 1

Quotation from Hock, D. W. "The Chaordic Organization: Out of Control and Into Order." *World Business Academy Perspectives,* 1995, 9(1), 5–18.

Excerpt from Eisenberg, L. "Taking the Long, Sharp View." *Esquire Magazine,* Dec. 1983, p. 305. Reprinted courtesy of *Esquire Magazine* and the Hearst Corporation.

Excerpt from Frankl, V. *Man's Search for Meaning.* Boston: Beacon Press, 1984.

Excerpts from THE LITTLE ENGINE THAT COULD and I THINK I CAN, I THINK I CAN are trademarks of Platt & Munk, Publishers and are used by permission of the publisher.

Excerpts from Duncan, D. J. *The Brothers K.* New York: Bantam Doubleday Dell, 1993. Used by permission of Bantam Doubleday Dell Publishing Group, Inc.

bell hooks quoted in Spayde, J. "100 Visionaries Who Could Change Your Life." *Utne Reader,* January–February 1995. Used by permission.

Quotation from Edelman, M. W. *The Measure of Our Success.* Boston: Beacon Press, 1993.

Chapter 2

Excerpt from *Letters to a Young Poet* by Rainer Maria Rilke, translated by M. D. Herter Norton. Translation copyright 1934, 1954 by W. W. Norton & Company, Inc., renewed © 1962, 1982 by M. D. Herter Norton. Reprinted by permission of W. W. Norton & Company, Inc.

Excerpt from "Burnt Norton" in *Four Quartets,* copyright 1943 by T. S. Eliot and renewed 1971 by Esme Valerie Eliot, reprinted by permission of Harcourt Brace & Company.

Excerpt from *The Little Prince* by Antoine de Saint-Exupery, copyright 1943 and renewed 1971 by Harcourt Brace & Company, reprinted by permission of Harcourt Brace & Company.

Excerpt from Blanchard Training and Development, Inc., Escondido, CA. Used by permission.

Quotation from *Out of My Life and Thought* by Albert Schweitzer. Copyright 1949 by Albert Schweitzer. Reprinted by permission of Henry Holt & Co., Inc.

Overleaf from Miller, H. *The Wisdom of the Heart.* Connecticut: New Directions, 1941.

Chapter 3

Epigraph from Fulberg, Mary Vinton quoted in *A Woman's Day-to-Day Engagement Calendar.* Philadelphia: Running Press, 1993. Used by permission of the publisher.

Donald Kennedy quoted in Kouzes, J. M. and Posner, B. Z. *The Leadership Challenge: How to Get Extraordinary Things Done in Organizations.* San Francisco: Jossey-Bass, 1987. Used by permission.

Quotation from Ikujiro Nonaka, "The Knowledge-Creating Company," *Harvard Business Review* (November–December 1991). Copyright © 1991 by the President and Fellows of Harvard College; all rights reserved.

Excerpt from *The Little Prince* by Antoine de Saint-Exupery, copyright 1943 and renewed 1971 by Harcourt Brace & Company, reprinted by permission of Harcourt Brace & Company.

Quotation from Byham, W. C. *Zapp! The Lightning of Empowerment.* New York: Harmony Books, 1988. Used by permission of Crown Publishers Inc.

Chapter 4

Epigraph from Peters, T. *Thriving on Chaos: Handbook for a Management Revolution.* New York: Alfred A. Knopf, 1987. Used by permission of the publisher.

Excerpt from *Love & Profit* by James A. Autry. Copyright 1991 by James A. Autry. Reprinted by permission of William Morrow & Company, Inc.

Excerpt from Underwood, P. *Who Speaks for Wolf.* San Anselmo: A Tribe of Two Press, 1983. Used by permission.

Quotation from interview with Oscar Arias, former president of Costa Rica. NPR, *All Things Considered,* December 3, 1993.

Printed in the United States
67213LVS00006B